CITRUS,

STRATEGY,

AND CLASS

Citrus,

Strategy,

and Class

THE POLITICS OF

DEVELOPMENT IN

SOUTHERN BELIZE

BY MARK MOBERG

University of Iowa Press Iowa City

University of Iowa Press, Iowa City 52242

Printed on acid-free paper

Library of Congress Cataloging-in-Publication Data
Moberg, Mark.
    Citrus, strategy, and class: the politics of development in Southern Belize/by Mark Moberg.
        p.   cm.
    Includes bibliographical references and index.
    ISBN 0-87745-367-5
    1. Stann Creek (Belize)—Rural conditions.   2. Citrus fruit industry—Belize—Stann Creek.   I. Title.
HN129.S73M63   1992
307.72′097282′3—dc20   91-45123
                                                                        CIP

CONTENTS

MEASURES AND EQUIVALENTS

1 acre = .4047 hectare
1 task = .0506 hectare
1 manzana = .8094 hectare
1 Belizean dollar (Bze) = U.S. $.50
Unless otherwise noted, all cash values are expressed in Belizean dollars.

ACKNOWLEDGMENTS

While anthropologists report that each episode of fieldwork is a unique one, all probably experience some similar emotions in the process of ethnographic research. My initial residence in rural Belize began with a sense of profound personal isolation but culminated thirteen months later in a reluctant departure from a place and people I had grown to love. Since that first visit, each time I leave the easy-going sociability of the village I encounter a different sort of isolation—an uneasy intimacy with data that seem a pallid reflection of the people left behind. Apart from the theoretical intent of the work, I hope above all that the following ethnography recreates something of the character and lives of rural Belizeans.

Despite the isolation occasionally encountered in ethnographic research, fieldwork and writing are never undertaken alone, of course. Long before departing for the field, my ideas were influenced by many teachers and colleagues through the twin processes of emulation and critique. One of the first of these scholars was Mike Chibnik, who provided me with a detailed baseline ethnography and a role model of anthropologist as teacher. Faculty at the University of California, Los Angeles, later guided me in the development of my theoretical, research, and methodological interests. Of my teachers at UCLA, I would most like to thank Tim Earle, Nazif Shahrani, Susanna Hecht, John Friedmann, and, above all, Allen Johnson, who supervised my Ph.D. research. I believe all these individuals will recognize something of themselves in the work that follows. While gratefully acknowledging their ideas, I am solely responsible for the way in which they were modified and put to use.

The influences of such scholars on my own work could never have been realized, of course, in the absence of much support and cooperation in the field. I am grateful for the research and publication support I have received from the Fulbright Foundation, the Inter-American Foundation, the UCLA Department of Anthropology, the National Endowment for the Humanities, and the College of Arts and Sciences at the University of South Alabama. In Belize, the local sponsors of my research have always facilitated every step of fieldwork. In particular I would like to thank Joseph Palacio of the University of the West Indies, which sponsored my research, and Keith Wright of the Belize Department of Cooperatives and Credit Unions, which approved it. My first acquaintances in the Cooperatives Department in Dangriga not only offered their help in introducing me to the villages but have grown to be close friends. To Francis Lewis, Lawrence Cayetano, and Herbert Nicasio, I offer my gratitude for their assistance and for helping me learn what it is like to be a Belizean.

Within the villages, all those who assisted me in some way are too numerous to mention, but above all I would like to acknowledge the chairpersons and village councils of both communities for authorizing my research activities. I especially thank the members of the Hopkins Farmers' Cooperative, who not only tolerated my continual presence but took advantage of it by putting me to work. I also owe my gratitude to Albert Castillo, Mavis Castillo, and members of the Sandy Beach Women's Cooperative, who have looked after my housing and food needs over successive visits to Hopkins. Finally, for his friendship and gentle sense of humor, I thank the former *alcalde* of Hopkins, Victor Lewis, who has become, in local parlance, a "father" to me. The idiom of kinship here is particularly appropriate, since many residents have become like family as they extended their hospitality during my visits to the villages.

This book has undergone a prolonged gestation marked by much rethinking, repeated revision, and the assistance of many people within and outside of academe. In the earliest stages of the work, Carlos Soares, Glenn Russell, and Laurie K. Medina provided valuable technical and intellectual guidance. The final steps in the development of the manuscript owe much to the critiques and suggestions of Billie DeWalt and a second, anonymous reviewer for the University of Iowa Press. I received help in manuscript preparation from Mimi Wigington as well as Steve Thomas, Greg Waselkov, and Erich Mueller. Notwithstanding all these contributions, the most constant encouragement throughout this project has been that of my parents, who have provided unflagging moral support for my efforts in the field and in academe.

C. Wright Mills, one of the most penetrating American social scientists of this century, maintained that the mission of social inquiry should be both to enlighten and liberate. Mills felt that social research should provide people with the tools to understand and control the conditions under which they live. It is to the residents of Hopkins and Silk Grass that I dedicate this work, in the hope that with it they may better see, and affect, how the world outside their communities impinges upon their lives.

As is often the case in ethnography, the final product of my field research differed substantially from my initial expectations. One's prejudices are not long-lived in a village setting, where the everyday strategizing of rural residents acquires much greater force than the abstractions of macro-level theory. This book contrasts the perceptions of rural economic change that I gained from understanding these strategies with more conventional approaches to political economy. As such, it represents the shedding of my own prejudices on how "development" takes place, a process that began when I examined the adoption of commercial citrus farming in Hopkins, Belize.

My ethnographic research in Belize was prompted by an interest in the role of agricultural cooperatives in rural development, specifically in the expansion of export crop production. The policies of countries such as Belize, which simultaneously encourage cooperative formation and small farmer production of export crops, present an interesting paradox to the investigator. While cooperatives are generally associated with an egalitarian ethos, production of agricultural commodities for the world market often has profoundly stratifying consequences. Would cooperatives impede stratification under these circumstances, would they fall victims to it, or would they succumb to control by wealthier farmers? From my familiarity with the literature on world market incorporation and its effects, I hypothesized that the very poor would be unlikely to benefit from cooperative membership because of low incomes that preclude commercial farming for export. Yet on a 1985 survey trip to Belize intended to orient my later research, I found that the rural poor were in fact drawn to cooperatives in large numbers.

During my visits to a number of villages, I unwittingly adopted a highly normative perspective on cooperatives, since government extension agents provided my initial information and contacts with village residents. From these accommodating and often idealistic officials I first encountered the terminology of "grassroots" development. Originating with a number of development agencies in the metropolitan countries, this view envisions cooperatives, credit unions, and other voluntary associations of the poor as a means of generating equitable

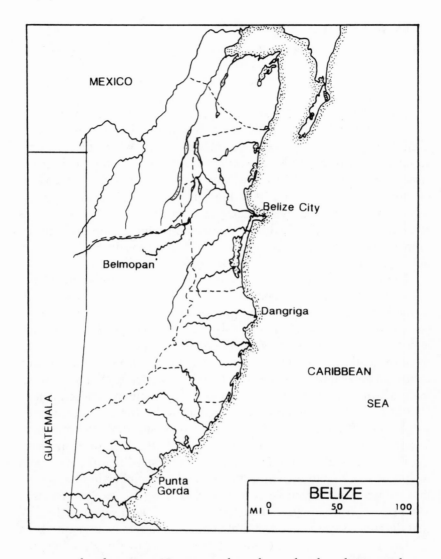

MEXICO

Belize City

Belmopan

Dangriga

CARIBBEAN

SEA

GUATEMALA

Punta
Gorda

BELIZE

MI 0   50   100

economic development. Having neglected to ask what the poor themselves derived from cooperatives, I merely assumed that the moti-
vations of those who joined co-ops mirrored the idealism of their
promoters.

After returning to Belize later in 1985, I established myself in the
village of Hopkins, where I resided over the next thirteen months.
From there, I frequently visited and stayed with residents of the com-

munity of Silk Grass, some seven miles away. In many ways, Hopkins and Silk Grass were ideal locations for the study of cooperatives in the process of agricultural development. Both communities were the sites of farming cooperatives and were undergoing an expansion of commercial citrus farming due to favorable world market prices. The selection of these villages was also fortuitous due to earlier research in the area by anthropologists (Taylor 1951; Chibnik 1975). In particular, the latter investigator's analysis of small farmer strategies provided invaluable baseline data prior to the incorporation of the villages in world citrus markets.

Over the course of a year, as I grew to know the people of both villages and to work beside them on their farms and in their homes, I steadily recognized that cooperatives could not be abstracted from other, noneconomic aspects of village life. My earlier expectations had blinded me to the way in which the poor used such organizations to advance their own political and economic goals. I was made acutely aware of the local context in which co-ops operate by the ambiguous political identity I myself acquired in the early stages of studying them. Several months passed in the village before I learned that a prominent local foe of the cooperative had reported me to the district police as a "communist alien" because of my visible association with cooperative members. Only days later a village friend confided to me that several of his fellow co-op members had initially feared I was a CIA agent sent as a spy for the national government. It was becoming apparent that the cooperative bore little resemblance to the representative, nonideological association that government officials and foreign aid agencies promoted. Instead, the Hopkins cooperative was inextricably bound in a bitter factionalism not of its own making. As I came to view faction fighting not as a quarrelsome sideshow to villagers' economic activities but as a central conflict over the distribution of resources from without the village, I realized that such disputes were critically affecting the outcome of village development. The stratification emerging in Hopkins is the result of such conscious political strategies, rather than random tendencies inherent in the production of commodities for the world market.

My field research was subsequently guided by a desire to be considered neutral in the arena of local politics. I eventually avoided identification with either faction by frequent social visiting with both parties in local conflicts and by varying my interview and work regime be-

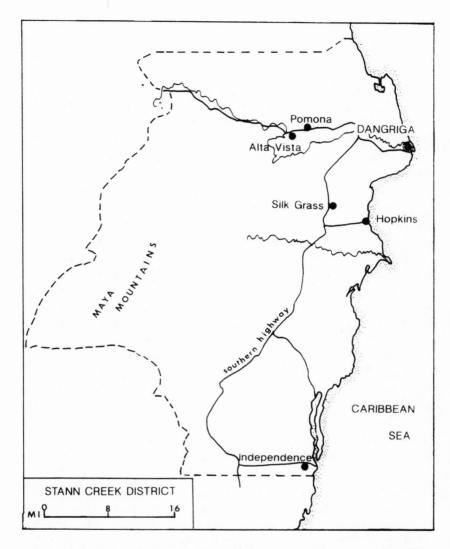

tween members and nonmembers of the cooperative. Agricultural labor became integral to my methodology, not only to acquire firsthand data on the labor process and inputs of subsistence practices but also to build rapport with informants on both sides of village factional divisions. However unwieldy (and humorous) my efforts with a machete, my contributions were welcome on local farms, where secondary growth constantly overwhelmed available supplies of household labor.

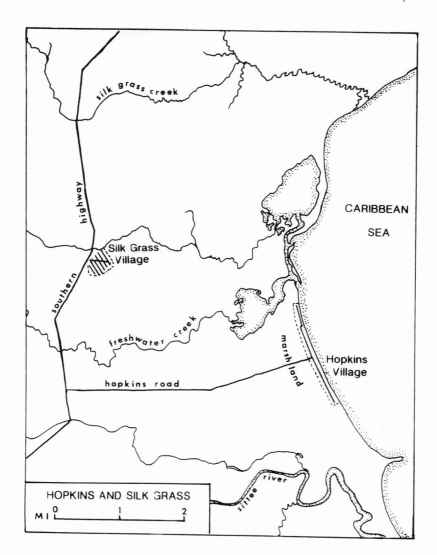

silk grass creek

highway

southern

CARIBBEAN

SEA

Silk Grass
Village

freshwater creek

marsh land

Hopkins
Village

hopkins road

river

sittee

HOPKINS AND SILK GRASS

MI   0   1   2

By the fifth month of fieldwork, I had gathered sufficient data on subsistence and cash-earning activities to design my household survey
and, perhaps more critically, I had established the neutrality necessary
to administer it. Over the remaining months, eighty-two households
were surveyed in detail in both Hopkins and Silk Grass, representing
60 percent of the combined economically active households of the villages. When compared with the ethnographic research of Chibnik

(1975), the survey data from 1986 tell of a village social order dramatically transformed by its incorporation into world markets.

The realization that agricultural development represented an essentially political process did not diminish my respect for cooperative members. Despite the fact that few had much formal education, they were remarkably sophisticated in mobilizing resources and dealing with powerful outsiders who were in a position to help them. Visiting dignitaries and the representatives of development agencies (several of whom held Ph.D.s in anthropology or economics) invariably left the village highly impressed with the earnestness of cooperative members. Returning to their agency headquarters in Washington and Ottawa, such visitors were well disposed to reward the efforts of local cooperatives. I learned that such strategies exist on a regional basis as well in the efforts of rural citrus growers and wage laborers to extract benefits from the powerful. In the decade preceding my arrival in southern Belize, mobilizations of small-scale farmers and the rural poor had yielded substantial price and wage increases for those involved in the citrus economy. Clearly, then, the rural poor were not the "victims" of this economic change, however much they may have overlooked its ultimate effects for their communities, which include stratification and dependence on volatile world markets. With gratitude to all who helped me to understand the causes and consequences of this process, I offer this account of a changing rural political economy, one which they themselves helped to transform.

CITRUS,

STRATEGY,

AND CLASS

CHAPTER 1

STRUCTURE AND AGENCY IN

A CHANGING RURAL ECONOMY

On a Sunday late in the summer of 1986, members of the farmers' cooperative of Hopkins, Belize, were called to a meeting in the village's "community center," a thatched shelter a few yards from the Caribbean shore. That afternoon a government extension agent, himself a village resident, spoke of the changes that had taken place in local agriculture since the farmers received a grant from a foreign development agency five years before. He noted that their efforts would soon be rewarded with an abundant orange harvest, representing the first citrus to be produced on local farms. With evident pride in the community's agricultural development, the official urged cooperative members to view their newly bearing citrus trees not just as a lucrative source of income for themselves but as a contribution to the village as a whole. "You can't reap 350 orange trees by yourself; you'll have to hire your brothers to do it. When you do, you'll be helping your brother, putting money back in the village, and raising up the level of Hopkins."

Since the day of that meeting, other villagers have indeed sought, and appreciated, the seasonal wage opportunities offered on their neighbors' farms. Yet the official's vision was also prophetic of divisions that have arisen between citrus producers and nonmembers of the cooperative. Wages paid under the guise of "helping your brother" are a poignant reminder that some have benefited greatly from citrus farming while others gained marginally or not at all from it. The idiom of brotherhood so often invoked between Hopkins men in the past has since become an anachronism from a time when the village was not crosscut economically. In the account that follows, it will become apparent that the roots of today's class divisions were established long before the first local planting of a citrus tree. They originated in the efforts of villagers, as they express it, "to help themselves" in the face of an uncertain and seemingly hostile economic environment.

This monograph is about two Belizean villages at different points in the process that economists conventionally term "development." By producing export crops rather than staples for local markets or subsistence needs, some farmers in the Stann Creek district of southern Belize have realized unprecedented levels of income. In citrus-growing areas, these trends are reflected in the proliferation of consumer goods once far beyond the reach of local residents. Yet citrus farming is not without its liabilities for individuals and communities alike, despite the heightened earnings and consumption levels that it has made possible. In the process of entering world commodity markets, citrus farmers have experienced increased dependence on costly inputs, diminished self-sufficiency in food production, and vulnerability to market conditions originating outside their communities. The most dramatic effects of production for export, however, are felt on the level of localities rather than households. The expansion of citrus production has set the stage for a changing local and regional political economy. This is most evident in the class divisions that have widened between commodity and subsistence producers in previously unstratified communities such as Hopkins. The integration of rural communities with export markets has also been accompanied by new forms of political conflict, for commodity producers have had to aggressively assert their interests before those who purchase their products.

This study makes use of data that I gathered in the neighboring Stann Creek district villages of Hopkins and Silk Grass between 1985 and 1989 and amplifies upon earlier ethnographic documentation of the area extending back to the 1940s (Taylor 1951; Chibnik 1975). From this longitudinal perspective, I examine the causes and consequences of the transition from milpa (shifting) cultivation of crops for domestic use to commercial citrus farming. Like other aspects in the repertoire of household subsistence activities in rural Belize, agricultural change to a significant degree is affected by factors originating outside villagers' immediate environments. By analyzing recent changes in household subsistence activities in general, and agricultural change in particular, this monograph situates rural residents' economic strategies within a global set of constraints and incentives. The general contours of village economy and social life are shaped by a world system that consumes most of the products of villagers' labor and, increasingly, that labor itself through large-scale migration to urban centers in the United States.

While adopting a political economic approach to rural class formation and underdevelopment, this account diverges from its theoretical antecedents in several significant ways. Classical Marxist views of the development of agrarian capitalism attribute class formation to differential advantages in the spheres of production and circulation. As households become integrated into commodity markets, individual economic advantage is the prelude to acquiring the land, then the labor, of those less able to compete in the market. In southern Belize, however, class formation is as much a political as economic process, for stratification arises from political affiliations that enable some households to better mobilize resources for commercial agriculture. Access to political patronage and membership in village factions determine who will obtain the resources needed to adopt citrus production and who will be barred from them. In examining the process of village class formation, then, the study moves beyond the economics of subsistence change to analyze the political processes affecting villagers' choices of economic strategies.

Second, this account challenges political economy approaches that attribute a determinant role to world markets or the logic of capital accumulation in the local outcome of Third World economic change. A common limitation of such analyses is their tendency to define rural communities in terms of the economic relations in which they are embedded. Social relations and consciousness at the local level are rendered as the epiphenomena of commodity relations, while political activity intended to define or resist such relations is "voluntarist," hence futile. In rural Stann Creek district, the political alliances that form the precursors of class are the creation of villagers themselves. They are also the primary means by which the rural poor assert their economic interests, something at which they are remarkably successful. The outcome of development, then, is defined as much by conscious activity at the local level as by external economic factors.

Although rural Belizeans are buffeted by nonlocal economic influences, they are neither unaware of such forces nor are they passively resigned to them. Villagers attempt to win some control over shifting economic forces by forming cooperatives, producers' associations, and labor unions, all of which express their interests politically. They creatively manipulate external institutions and seemingly formidable outsiders, such as patronage-dispensing politicians, to mobilize the resources needed for agricultural change. In addition, rural residents take advantage of novel opportunities to attain their goals, including the pursuit of grants from foreign development agencies. Although production for world commodity markets gives rise to regularly occurring patterns of stratification and dependence, how these features are expressed at the village level is largely determined by local courses of action. These include efforts by the rural poor to assert control over their economic well-being. By analyzing such efforts at "self-help," the monograph will offset overly determinist assumptions inherent in the conventional political economy of development. In documenting the contested claims of the rural poor over their economic destinies, this account offers a political economy that recognizes the unsung role of human agency in social change.

RURAL ECONOMIES IN TRANSITION

In its outward appearance, the agrarian transition taking place in rural Stann Creek district resembles many occurring throughout the Third World today. Since first examining the integration of the largely agrarian colonies of Europe with world markets, political economists (Marx 1977a [1867]; Luxemburg 1972 [1913]; Lenin 1975 [1917]) have long documented the eclipse of "natural" economies by those based on the production of commodities with wage labor. Nineteenth-century observers concurred that colonial societies were entering a transition to capitalism earlier charted by the industrialized nations. It soon became apparent, however, that the expansion of capitalism into the Third World was not replicating the prior experiences of the Western "developed" countries. Rather, the paradox of "underdevelopment" ensued, in which high rates of economic growth were coupled with a deepening impoverishment of the rural majority. The causes of underdevelopment in the Third World became a central issue among political economists, with two distinct orientations emerging in the post–World War II period. By the 1970s and 1980s, political economists were engaged in an acrimonious debate between adherents of world systems and neo-Marxist theories of capitalist development in the postcolonial world.

In brief, world systems perspectives emphasize the distorting effects of international trade and political relations on "satellite" or Third World economies. Theorists such as Baran (1957), Frank (1967), Wallerstein (1974), and Cardoso and Faletto (1979) worked within differing disciplines and regions but developed similar conceptualizations of capitalism and its effects upon the Third World (cf. de Janvry 1981: 1–63). World system and dependency theorists attributed the poverty of Third World hinterlands to the nature of contact between industrialized nations and the underdeveloped regions of Latin America, Asia, and Africa. The "metropolitan" or now-developed nations attained their status from centuries of colonial plunder of the Third World's human and natural resources. De facto colonial relationships have been perpetuated in the contemporary era via deteriorating terms of trade between manufactured goods and raw materials and the repatriation of profits by foreign capital. Because the prices of raw materials produced in the Third World largely benefit industrialized nations, reliance on their production involves continued transfers of wealth to the developed nations. Hence, the production of agricultural commodities and raw materials for metropolitan consumption is one way in which the interests of Third World societies are subordinated to the needs of the developed nations, resulting in the continued underdevelopment of the former. As long as growth in satellite regions is conditioned by the needs of metropolitan capital, world systems theorists argue that the Third World will be unable to recreate the consumption levels and autonomous growth of the industrialized nations.

In contrast to world systems models, other political economists have attributed underdevelopment to class and economic relations within the Third World that are responsible for the uneven growth of capitalism (Laclau 1971; Brenner 1977; Wolf 1982). While world systems theorists contend that Third World societies became thoroughly "capitalist" from their first contact with colonialism, neo-Marxist theorists discern the persistence of precapitalist modes of production in contemporary regions of underdevelopment. The difference between these models acquires more than semantic import, for with its reliance upon wage labor and marketplace competition, capitalism generates an imperative for technological development that is absent in precapitalist forms of production (Laclau 1971). Much of the work of neo-Marxist political economists examines why capitalism in the Third World has not resulted in the heightened living standards found (at least until recently) among sectors of the working class in Europe and North

America. Marx failed to anticipate improved living standards among workers in the metropolitan countries, predicting instead a deepening contradiction between capitalists' desire for low-cost labor and their need for markets among the working class (Marx 1977a [1867]: 592). Wage restraints and industrial technology ultimately lead to crises of underconsumption, as workers' depressed earnings and unemployment leave them unable to consume the collective output of industry.

Amin (1976) contends that in the metropolitan nations this contradiction has been partly resolved by a "social pact" between capital and labor that links wage increases with productivity in industry. In North America, for example, the working class forms the primary market for consumer goods produced by national industries as well as commodities produced in the "peripheral" or underdeveloped economies. In contrast, accumulation in much of the periphery is "disarticulated" in that it relies on low-cost labor combined with a modern technological base in industry. Because wages in peripheral economies are not a substantial source of demand for manufactured goods (most of which are exported), there is no countervailing need for wages to rise with productivity. Consequently, internal markets in underdeveloped nations are rudimentary, consumption standards are depressed, and the most dynamic sectors of the economy are oriented to export production.

Household production plays a critical role in satisfying the needs for low-cost labor under peripheral capitalism. Capitalist sectors are often linked to precapitalist modes of production, such as subsistence agriculture or simple commodity production utilizing unpaid family labor (Bradby 1975; Meillassoux 1981; Roseberry 1989a). Because such forms of production fulfill some of the subsistence needs of Third World wage workers and their families, wage levels in capitalist sectors are often depressed below the levels required of a fully proletarian work force. Stein's (1984) comparison of agricultural wage rates in Peru suggests the extent to which household production subsidizes capital accumulation in this manner. In areas of the highlands adjacent to smallholder farming, daily wages in commercial agriculture were found to be one-third to one-half the levels paid to full-time workers employed in areas remote from peasant farming (Stein 1984: 293). Proletarianization in rural areas of the Third World thus remains an incomplete process, as many wage workers retain some involvement in household agricultural or craft production. The resulting "functional dualism" (de Janvry 1981: 81) of combined household and capitalist sectors has become an integral component of accumulation under peripheral capitalism. For this reason household agriculture has been reinforced in many areas of Latin America by reformist policies designed to perpetuate a peasantry that provides needed low-cost labor and foodstuffs.

The need for low-cost labor in peripheral economies implies severe difficulties for rural households attempting to secure their livelihood. One direct means of restraining wage levels for the urban work force is to enact cheap food policies through price controls and agricultural importation. These measures tend to restrict the production of staple crops to "peasant" farms, since controlled prices and imports make food production a less attractive choice for commercial farmers than export crops (de Janvry 1981). Restraints on the profitability of staple crops and inability to compete with large export producers drive many households out of commodity production, agriculture becoming an activity supplemental to seasonal wages. As will be shown in chapter 4, cheap food policies of this sort significantly affect the subsistence choices of Belizean farmers, accounting in large part for the abandonment of staple crops for citrus throughout Stann Creek district.

De Janvry (1981) argues that what appears to be a symbiotic relationship between households and capitalist sectors is in actuality a parasitic one, for rural capitalism ultimately undermines noncapitalist forms of production. Cheap manufactured goods outcompete labor-intensive household production of comparable items, eliminating craft production as a household income-earning activity (Cook 1982). Depressed wage rates under peripheral capitalism diminish farmers' ability to buy inputs and to adequately fallow land or practice soil conservation (Painter 1984). Demographic growth that outstrips available land resources and ecological destruction often result from aggregate household fertility decisions, in which children are viewed as essential assets for survival (White 1975). The self-sufficiency of many rural households erodes under these conditions, and their members become precariously dependent on seasonal labor markets and "informal" sector income. The growing populations of rural landless and land poor attest to the dwindling viability of household economies throughout much of the Third World. If functional dualism encounters no countervailing policies designed to reinforce deteriorating domestic economies, it eventually eliminates many forms of household production despite their contributions to capital expansion.

This process is an accelerated variant of the social differentiation occurring in rural communities following their incorporation into commodity markets (Harrison 1977; Goodman and Redclift 1982; Reinhardt 1988; others, following Chayanov 1966, assert that differentiation is a reversible demographic process; cf. Greenhalgh 1985). The concept of social differentiation suggests that farmers become distinct classes of landowners and landless with the expansion of commodity production in agriculture. Under precapitalist conditions the potential for differentiation was limited since neither labor nor land was freely exchangeable in peasant markets. Surpluses that did arise among individual households were either expropriated as "rent" or allocated toward increased consumption or "ceremonial funds" (Wolf 1966), neither of which contributes to a change in the peasant's class position. Differentiation occurs as households increasingly rely on income from the sale of agricultural products. Competition in the market induces technological innovation as agriculturalists attempt to reduce their costs of production. Such imperatives are not encountered in "natural" economies based on the provision of use values for domestic consumption (Friedmann 1980; Chevalier 1983).

When labor and land also become saleable commodities, rural class formation follows from the ability of some households to invest profits in production and the necessity of others to sell their labor in order to survive. Interhousehold variations in production levels may occur for any reason, "e.g. fertility of soil, market conditions, labor productivity, differential control of resources, etc." (Roseberry 1976: 51). These variations ultimately determine whether household production expands from the acquisition of additional land or is undermined to the point that producers lose all or most of their land. In the former case, households become capitalist in character (producing commodities by employing wage labor), while in the latter, the members of formerly independent peasant households become part of a growing rural proletariat (Lenin 1964 [1899]: 177).

Rapid social differentiation has often been attributed to the introduction of agricultural innovations to formerly subsistence-oriented rural communities (DeWalt 1979; Cancian 1987). Since the advent of the Green Revolution in southern Asia, where new agricultural technologies induced huge disparities of wealth and landownership (Gough 1978; Griffin 1975), the anthropological literature has grown replete with examples of "development" processes that actually lowered living standards for most rural inhabitants. In rural communities throughout Latin America (cf. Taussig 1980; Gudeman 1978; Barlett 1982), class stratification arose from earlier differences in income or landownership that affected the ability of rural producers to adopt innovative crops or needed agricultural inputs. Households having sufficient incomes to employ hybrid varieties or chemical inputs often profit substantially from Green Revolution–style technologies, while those that adopt new technologies in part rather than as a complete package of innovations frequently fare worse than before (Pearse 1980). Similarly, farmers confined by limited incomes to traditional crops are entirely excluded from the benefits of technical innovations.

While neo-Marxist analyses have elucidated the extractive relationship existing between capitalist and household sectors, world systems theorists observe that rural stratification is further accelerated by the nature of export crops cultivated by many households in the Third World. Because crops such as coffee, bananas, citrus products, and sugar are consumed in metropolitan markets with highly variable levels of demand, world markets are frequently glutted with surplus commodities and producers are subject to violent price fluctuations (Lappé and Collins 1979). As will be seen in the following chapter, the "boom and bust" economic history of Belize provides a virtual archetype of such processes. At the local level, those who grow commodities that undergo volatile market swings also experience differentiation themselves. Amidst the minority of Belizean growers who persist during downward price fluctuations are many forced to abandon citrus production because of them.

THE PROBLEM OF AGENCY AND STRUCTURE

The social dislocations resulting from monocrop export agriculture (Beckford 1972; Paige 1975; Edelman 1987) lend support to the view that world market incorporation contributes to the underdevelopment of peripheral economies. World system analyses suggest that Third World societies are at the mercy of volatile markets that discriminate against their products and render them dependent upon external sources of food and technology (cf. Gross and Underwood 1971; Davis 1975). Political corollaries of these portrayals hold that the rural poor are powerless to challenge these economic conditions due to the repressive political institutions associated with "dependent capitalism" (Frank 1969; Forman 1975) or their dependence on powerful patrons for land, credit, and markets (Cotler 1970; Gilmore 1977; Handleman 1975). At their most deterministic extreme, such analyses portray Third World societies as "passive" entities whose characteristics are determined by their insertion into the world market (cf. Nash 1981: 398).

The tendency of world systems theory to derive class structures and political relations from the functional requirements of the world market has been widely criticized (cf. Clammer 1978; Mintz 1977; Sella 1977; Trimberger 1979; Orlove and Foley 1989). Yet for advocates of neo-Marxist political economy, the role of agency also remains problematic. In part this is because much political economy attributes social transformations to the "laws" or "logic" of capital rather than the actions of individuals and groups (cf. Giddens 1979). However much the logic of functional dualism constrains the strategies of peasants and rural proletarians, their consciousness and cultural activity cannot be mechanically derived from models of peripheral capitalism (Roseberry 1989b: 190–191). The long history of peasant protest against colonial rent and taxation policies (Wolf 1969; Paige 1975; Scott 1976) testifies to the willingness of the Third World poor to pursue their political and economic objectives despite oppressive class structures. Dominated groups have at times tenaciously resisted new forms of commodity production that threaten rural traditions and social relations (Bradby 1982; Ong 1987). Denying that the absence of overt rebellion indicates peasant acceptance of worsening rural livelihoods, Scott (1985) documents the surreptitious and symbolic forms that everyday resistance assumes in peasant communities. While resistance appears most often in the uncoordinated acts of individuals, Scott argues that such defiance contributes to class consciousness because it is uniformly directed against elites. Hence, class consciousness becomes apparent in the "mutuality" of peasant resistance; that is, the ethic that the poor not undercut each other in seeking benefits from elites (Scott 1985: 261).

Notwithstanding the rich documentation of peasant political strategies that Scott and other observers have provided, it is by no means apparent that individual responses to the expansion of commodity relations reinforce class consciousness. Nor can such responses invariably be characterized as resistance to "commoditization." As will be seen in chapters 5 and 6, the acts of the rural poor in Belize permit no such global generalizations. Is theft a form of class resistance when a landlord is the target but something else when the victim is poor?

Mouthing the slogan of a ruling political party might be characterized as "self-help" if it allows peasants to obtain patronage benefits, but does it contribute to elite hegemony if it results in factional fights between peasants? From Scott's assertion that individuals act in self-interested ways to secure the needs of their households (1985: 295), it is evident that class-based politics are only one means by which those needs are met. Analogously, production for the world market creates both opportunities and disincentives. An individual's strategy in the face of newly introduced forms of commodity production may be one of resistance, such as clinging to subsistence farming or invoking traditional obligations made of rural elites. Alternately, the rural poor may act in a more opportunistic manner, such as emulating those elites and striving to enter their ranks.

"Actor-oriented" or transactional social theory, which examines how social actors strategically pursue their self-interest, has not been well received by most political economists (cf. Weldes 1989). Aspects of transactionalism may nonetheless offer a solution to the problem of agency posed by political economy. The development of transactional models in anthropology constituted one reaction against functionalist theories in which individuals enact predetermined roles but do not alter or create them. Theorists such as Barth (1959, 1966) and Bailey (1969) argued that social structure was the aggregate of individual behavioral choices, much as neoclassical economists portray market economies as the sum of all production and consumption decisions. A corollary of such models is that, in Barth's words, "all relationships implying dominance are dyadic relationships of a contractual or voluntary nature" (1959: 3). As Asad (1972) argues in a critique of such assumptions, depicting social structure as the consensual outcome of individual choices denies the severe political constraints on choices made by the rural poor.

It does not follow, however, that transactional and class analyses are "fundamentally incompatible" (1972: 90), as Asad contends. While elite power obviously limits the choices available to others, the relatively powerless nevertheless decide among the limited choices available to them or continuously act as individuals and groups to expand their range (Paine 1974; Kapferer 1976). Even under extreme subordination, working people, ethnic minorities, and even servile or indentured laborers have historically influenced the conditions of their existence. Among other historians of the antebellum South, for example, Genovese (1974) has demonstrated that many of the norms governing master-slave relations were in fact negotiated responses to the implied threat of slave rebellion. In their emphasis on individual strategizing behavior, actor-oriented models accord with accounts of resistance that situate political action within individuals' calculation of self-interest (cf. Scott 1985: 289–303). Unlike them, however, transactionalism makes no presumption that such action always assumes a class character. Purged of their consensual bias, models emphasizing individual strategic behavior may elucidate why some engage in resistance, others in accommodation, and what forms of behavior these strategies assume.

It is not coincidental that actor-oriented models in anthropology developed in concert with analyses of factions, noncorporate groups organized around leaders that promote the interests of their members (cf. Boissevain 1974: 6–10). Factionalism and the related phenomenon of patronage are ubiquitous in many communities but are not easily understood apart from the strategic motives of individual participants. Transactional studies of factionalism (Boissevain 1968; Bujra 1973; Nicholas 1977) have emphasized the strategies employed within and between factions to the neglect of structural constraints on recruitment, membership, and action. Some investigators (Schneider and Schneider 1988; Silverman 1980; Vincent 1976; Schryer 1980) have analyzed the interplay of factionalism and rural development, including the monopolization of cooperative membership or development aid by local factions. Extant studies have not, however, examined how the distribution of such resources affects class formation as communities undergo agricultural change. While recognizing the instrumental uses of political affiliation in a Malayan village, for example, Scott (1985) overlooks the possibility that the village's elites, who with one exception belong to the ruling national party, may have consolidated their class position through patronage.

Since factions usually draw their members from various classes, many political economists have not considered them to be a source of social structural change (cf. Silverman and Salisbury 1977: 14). Indeed, largely because their members are recruited across class lines on an ad hoc basis, some view factions as "a device of the elite to prevent the masses from acquiring class consciousness" due to "their lack of ideology and exclusive reliance on personalism" (ibid.). When acknowledging the importance of factionalism in local politics, political economists have often described it as a residual feature of precapitalist patronage relations (Alavi 1973; Frankel and von Vorys 1972). Factional loyalties, they argue, are steadily supplanted by class consciousness as capitalist forms of production enter rural economies (cf. Gilmore 1977: 446–447). Although class-based political activity may increase following the breakdown of patron-client ties and dislocations of commercialized agriculture, there is little evidence that the intensity of factionalism has also lessened as a result (cf. Gough 1978; see also Jones 1971 for Belize).

Factionalism is not invariably neutral in its impact on social structure, especially at the village level. Because they compete to mobilize resources, those involved in factional conflict attempt "to determine, and thus to change, what is to be accepted as normal" (Boissevain 1977: 107). I would add that a faction's success in mobilizing resources or otherwise asserting its group economic interests may result in its redefinition as a locally dominant class. In villages such as Hopkins, factions have not yielded to classes as the basis of recruitment and action. Rather, factions are in time becoming distinct classes.

Factional strategies and efforts at economic assertion are neither inconsequential nor quixotic attempts to resolve the dilemmas arising from involvement in a world economy. In southern Belize, factions have an immediate bearing on how world economic factors are expressed locally. Throughout the region, local-level politics and acts of defiance have allowed the rural poor to extract genuine concessions from both foreign capital and foreign development agencies. Yet at the same time, factions have a disintegrating effect on class ideologies by creating divisions among those with otherwise similar economic interests. Analyzing these strategies elucidates how class divisions arise at the village level. In Hopkins classes developed from the strategic economic and political decisions made by local farmers. As will be seen, similar decisions, and class-based political action, are responsible for social relations defining today's citrus industry. The political economy of peripheral capitalism elucidates the broad constraints that world markets and state policy impose on local action. The account that follows will reveal the ways in which the rural poor act within these constraints and, in so doing, help shape the outcome of the region's agrarian transition.

ORGANIZATION OF THE WORK

The first part of this monograph sets forth the historical and cultural contexts of contemporary economic change in Belize. To a significant extent, the peculiar cultural and economic circumstances established during the country's prolonged period of colonial rule—its highly variegated population, sparsity of settlement, and legacy of suppressed agriculture—continue to constrain the choices that members of contemporary households face in making a living. Additional constraints, in the form of local environmental features and fluctuations of the regional economy, are discussed prior to an examination of changing economic practices within the villages themselves.

At this point the analysis presents ethnographic data illustrating the subsistence patterns in both villages, as well as the labor, cash, and technological inputs and productivity of these practices. As indicated in chapter 4, the sources of income on which villagers currently depend are heavily dependent upon an ever-shifting world economy. The most profound recent change in local subsistence practices—the gradual abandonment of subsistence-based shifting cultivation in favor of citrus farming—is a reflection of economic trends emanating from centers far removed from the villages, or the nation, in which these changes take place. This chapter concludes with a comparison of the economic costs and benefits that farmers experience in the course of agricultural change. These factors act simultaneously as major impediments and incentives for the adoption of commercial citrus farming. As the region's agrarian transition entails potentially great rewards for receptive farmers, so it also presents formidable costs for cash-poor traditional shifting cultivators.

For a group of traditional farmers in Hopkins, however, the costs of orange and grapefruit production have not impeded access to the lucrative citrus market. By applying for aid dispensed by foreign development agencies, members of the Hopkins Farmers' Cooperative have circumvented their limited incomes and begun to produce citrus on their farms. Although the cooperative has been considered a model for equitable rural development by its sponsoring agencies, this claim of "development with equity" becomes more dubious upon close examination of the cooperative's role within the village political setting. Membership in the farmers' cooperative determines which villagers will have access to the resources necessary for citrus farming but is itself closely related to an intense village factionalism predating recent economic trends. In effect, stratification is emerging not from randomly occurring advantages in production and marketing but along factional lines that divide citrus producers from traditional farmers.

The local configuration of these effects cannot be predicted from existing models of political economy. Nor do existing theories entirely account for the way in which classes emerge in a village setting. In rural Belize, the world system's political effects are manifested through human agency. Macromodels help to analyze the determinants of class formation and economic choices, but the conscious activity of individuals and groups cannot be derived from them. Consequently, the final portion of the book analyzes agency and structure as they are revealed through the working life histories of individuals and the groups in which the rural poor assert their interests. Efforts of the rural poor to control external economic forces vary in their efficacy and may have contradictory effects over the long run. However faulty and contingent, such efforts affect the impact of world economic forces on rural communities.

While the effects of village economic change are revealed by indices of household production, the ethnography of economic change is found in meetings of the cooperatives, unions, and producers' associations to which rural residents belong. From my first opportunities to attend such meetings I saw that they were not merely the forum for divergent points of view. Rather, they provided the contested arena of political conflict. In such settings the poor won and lost causes, recruited allies, and denounced enemies. The assertiveness and rhetorical performance that the rural poor exhibit in such instances betray the stereotype of hopelessly passive and mystified peasants prevailing in much of the literature on agrarian political movements. Nor do such actions always take the form of class-based resistance to capitalism, as many authors have interpreted politics among the rural poor. In Stann Creek district, political activity is overwhelmingly instrumental from the individual's point of view and is as likely to promote commoditization as to resist it.

From the co-op leader inciting other members to "fight for ourselves" to a seasonal citrus worker deriding the "big money, full belly men" that profit from his labor, these are multidimensional individuals who acutely understand and act upon their interests, even if they are frequently unable to attain their goals. What follows, then, is an account of the conditions that give rise to such efforts and of the local changes that flow from them.

CHAPTER 2

BELIZE: A PLURAL SOCIETY

IN CENTRAL AMERICA

LANDFORM AND CLIMATE

Geography has played a significant role in affecting colonization and land use in Belize and in isolating it from the remainder of Central America. Belize occupies 8,750 square miles of land on the Caribbean coast of Central America as well as 116 square miles of territory on offshore islands known as "cayes." The country extends 174 miles from the Rio Hondo river, which marks its northern border with the Mexican state of Quintana Roo, to the Sarstoon River, demarcating its southern border with Guatemala. At its broadest point, from Belize City on the Caribbean to Benque Viejo on the western border with the Guatemalan Petén, the country's mainland is 68 miles wide. These dimensions make it slightly larger than Central America's smallest republic, El Salvador, yet its population density is only one-tenth of that country's.

The extreme sparsity of settlement, so readily visible from the air in a roadless expanse of tropical forest, marsh, and savannah, is a consequence of difficult geography and the distinctive patterns of colonization that developed to exploit it. Nearly all the country's coastline is bordered by a barrier reef that rendered early navigation treacherous and isolated the mainland from more frequented routes of European exploration and settlement. Early explorers who braved the reef's few and shifting channels encountered an inhospitable shoreline of mangrove swamp and brackish lagoon. Farther inland, large open tracts of territory appear deceptively welcome to human settlement—until the coming of the wet season leaves the land inundated and plagued by stinging insects.

The central and northern regions of the country form a low-lying plateau that gradually rises from sea level to inland elevations of several hundred feet. Vegetation on this coastal plain ranges from savannah and sparse pine forest on heavily leached upland soils to dense broadleaf tropical forest in alluvial zones (Wright et al. 1959: 29 ff.). Approaching the southwestern quadrant of the country from Belize City, the traveler encounters startling, almost fanciful limestone hills projecting abruptly from the otherwise flat landscape. These eroded escarpments are outlying ranges of the Maya Mountains, a rugged, uninhabited area climbing to 3,000 feet above sea level. Belying the lush rain forest blanketing this landform, the mountain soils are actually highly erodible and have inhibited settlement since human entry into the region (ibid.).

A conspicuous feature of the Belizean geography is the country's extensive river system, which drains the marshy northern plain and the Maya Mountains into the Caribbean. From prehistory onward, rivers and lagoons constituted the major sources of inland transportation. Throughout the colonial period, the country's exports of timber were floated to sea on rivers swollen by seasonal rains. As a consequence of the monocrop forestry economy that persisted through the 1950s, the country's road network was started late and remains rudimentary, especially in the southern districts. Accordingly, the majority of settlements are located on navigable waterways, which often become their only sources of external contact when dirt roads are rendered impassable during the rainy season.

Rainfall in Belize is seasonally and locally highly variable. A dry season extends from February to May, and the height of the wet season is from June to October. During the summer, when the southern part of the country receives more than 30 inches of precipitation per month, the combined effects of humidity and the subtropical sun induce a torpor that far exceeds the actual air temperature. During the winter months from December to February, heavy rains also occur in association with severe frontal storms known as northers, which bring cool, gusty weather over the western Caribbean. The rainfall gradient increases dramatically toward the south; the northernmost town of Corozal receives an annual average of 53 inches of rain while the southern village of Barranco averages 178 inches per year (Hartshorn et al. 1984: 11). Although this gradient is fairly consistent from year to year, annual rainfall levels, monthly precipitation, and the time of the onset of rains are not. It is not uncommon for one locale to experience drought while a village twenty miles away reports "normal" rainfall.

Tropical storms and hurricanes frequently develop in the Caribbean and tropical Atlantic Ocean between May and October. Located in one of the most active tropical storm areas of the Caribbean, Belize has historically suffered severe damage from these storms at least one year of every five (Hall 1983: 150). Since 1931, hurricanes have destroyed three of the country's five largest settlements, taken well over a thousand lives, and left many more homeless (Hartshorn et al. 1984: 11). Needless to say, the economic costs of hurricane damage, in disruption of production, damage to infrastructure and natural resources, and refugee support, have been substantial for a country of this size. The common and occasionally dramatic alterations of climate in the region also have severe consequences for those who make their living on the land or at sea.

PEOPLE AND CULTURES

Among the nations of Central America, Belize is a unique political and cultural entity. As the former colony of British Honduras, it represents a vestige of imperial struggles that once netted Great Britain a string of possessions on the otherwise Hispanic mainland. Although Belize is the sole Commonwealth country on the Central American isthmus, it is not, as some have asserted, simply an enclave of West Indian culture in Central America. From proximity to its Latin neighbors as well as its history as one of Britain's Caribbean holdings, Belize has developed into a polyglot society more varied than those of either Central America or the Caribbean. The Belizeans make up an amalgam of cultures brought in contact by the machinery of empire—conquest, slavery, indenture, and exile—and bound by a tenuous national identity occasionally unable to span the differences between them. Within the small national population, seven distinct ethnic groups may be identified, each comprising at least 2 percent of the country's population (table 1). With the exception of Yucatecan Maya Indians, who occupied northern Belize prior to British settlement, none of these groups is indigenous to the country and few have settled there as a matter of choice. Once a receptacle of slave and indentured labor from various parts of the British Empire, Belize continues to experience ethnic flux as a haven for those fleeing conflicts elsewhere in Central America.

The majority of residents in northern Belize are descended not from

Table 1. 1980 Population of Belize

Ethnic Group and Preferred Language Use[a]	Population	Percent of Total
Creole	57,700	39.7
Mestizo	48,100	33.1
Garifuna	11,050	7.6
Maya	13,850	9.5
Mennonite	4,800	3.3
East Indian	3,050	2.1
Other	6,800	4.7
Total	145,350	
Creole/English	73,549	50.6
Spanish	45,932	31.6
Garifuna	8,721	6.0
Maya	9,302	6.4
German	4,797	3.3
Other	3,049	2.1

Source: Government of Belize (1983).
[a] Does not include proficiency in other languages.

the pre-Columbian Maya but from thousands of refugees who fled Mexico during the Caste War, an Indian rebellion that convulsed the Yucatán between 1847 and 1853. Both Maya and mestizos (known in Belize as "Spanish") were uprooted in the rebellion and reprisals that followed and by the 1860s already formed the bulk of population in the northern districts of Orange Walk and Corozal (Grant 1976: 17). Other Amerindian populations reside in the southern part of the country, in the Toledo and Stann Creek districts. Unlike their Yucatecan counterparts in northern Belize, the Mopan and Kekchi Maya participate little in wage labor markets and remain predominately staple crop–producing shifting cultivators. Fleeing Guatemalan economic "reforms" that alienated Indian land and labor, the Mopan and Kekchi began entering southern Belize from Alta Verapaz in the 1880s (Gregory

1984; Wilk 1987). The construction of roads in southern Belize and northward migration of many Indians from rural Toledo district have lessened the isolation of Indian settlements in the last two decades (Wilk 1984). Despite their production of staple crops for national markets, the Mopan and Kekchi are the least integrated of Belizean ethnic groups with national institutions, other than recent Mennonite immigrants.

Peoples of African descent constitute the largest portion of the Belizean population, although they are numerically dominant in only three of the country's six districts. Reports of the importation of African slaves to Belize date to the early eighteenth century, but it is probable that slaves accompanied the first British settlers, or Baymen. Other populations of African descent, including several hundred members of the British West India regiments, were settled in Belize as nominally free populations in the early nineteenth century (Bolland 1988: 81). At the beginning of the 1800s the black and "coloured" component of the population, both slave and free, was recorded as 3,675, while only 149 of the settlement's inhabitants were identified as white (Burdon 1931: 187). As late as the 1850s, after the abolition of slavery, African-Belizeans were still identified by their tribal origin, one portion of Belize City being commonly known as Eboe Town (Bolland 1986: 15). During their incorporation into a slave society, the members of these distinct tribal groups adopted a patois of their masters' tongue. Today their descendants speak an English-based Creole as their first language, as well as the standard West Indian English of primary school instruction.

Like their slave and free ancestors, Belizean Creoles were the mainstay of the country's timber industry, providing the bulk of seasonal labor in mahogany gangs and sawmill crews. While such work took place "in the bush," or remote timber camps located in the interior, most Creoles resided during the off season in town near the sites of labor recruitment. Creoles continue to predominate in Belize City in nonagricultural occupations, yet many of their settlements, particularly in rural Stann Creek district, have become increasingly involved in commercial agriculture in the wake of forestry's demise.

Members of a second African-Belizean population, the Garifuna, are physically indistinguishable from many Creoles, yet highly distinct in terms of cultural markers and history. The Garifuna originated in the eastern Caribbean in the admixture of Africans fleeing slavery and indigenous Red Carib Indians (Helms 1981). During the eighteenth century, the resulting population grew rapidly on the island of St. Vincent, augmented by a steady stream of fugitive slaves from nearby sugar-growing islands. Over time a syncretic culture emerged based on island Carib social organization and the use of Garifuna, an Arawakan language, as lingua franca. Fiercely resistant to European efforts at extending control over St. Vincent, which they equated with a return to slavery, the Garifuna waged nearly thirty years of resistance against British encroachment. By 1795, most of the Garifuna had been militarily defeated and the majority were deported to the island of Roatán off the coast of Honduras (Gonzalez 1988). From there they established a series of small settlements along the coast of Central America, entering southern Belize at the beginning of the nineteenth century. Presently Garifuna communities are found between Dangriga in Stann Creek district and central Nicaragua, with the majority being located along the coast of Honduras (Davidson 1976).

At the time the Garifuna entered Belize, the attitudes of colonial authorities to their presence ran from hostility to ambivalence. In 1802, after noting that 150 "Charibs" had settled in the southern village of Stann Creek (now Dangriga), one magistrate called for their expulsion due to "the danger of a [slave] insurrection led by these people" (Burdon 1931: 60). Initially colonial authorities considered them "a most Dangerous People" (ibid.: 146), due to their armed resistance to British control of St. Vincent. Notwithstanding the fears of the colony's white settlers, the Garifuna soon found employment in wood-cutting camps and even in the military and developed a reputation as a "good and useful laboring population" (cited in Kerns 1983: 32).

The relationship between the Garifuna and Creoles has always been a paradoxical one and is occasionally marked by antagonism. Garifuna often cultivate close relationships with Creoles in order to gain employment or obtain favors, and they identify more readily with the Caribbean and Anglophone orientation of Creoles than do the nation's substantial mestizo and Indian populations. Yet many Garifuna also complain of discrimination at the hands of Creoles and of their superior attitude, reflected in the Creole claim to have "naturally" inherited political power from the British. Prior to independence, the British cultivated Creoles as their political successors, at least partly because the Creole-dominated National Independence party was far less critical of the colonial presence than the more multiethnic People's United party (Shoman 1987: 26). Despite regular involvement in the world outside their communities and an ability to move in and out of the broader Creole language and society with ease, at home the Garifuna remain linguistically and culturally separate from Creoles and are increasingly assertive of their ethnic heritage.

Other ethnic groups coexist with African-Belizeans, Maya, and mestizos, the largest components of the country's population. In the mid-nineteenth century, around one thousand convicted mutineers from the Indian army were deported by the British to serve as agricultural labor in Belize. In succeeding decades, other indentured East Indians made their way to Belize, where they were put to work in the colony's fledgling sugar industry. Chinese indentured laborers were also brought to Belize in 1865, although a colonial official noted three years later that "great diminution . . . has taken place from death and flight" (Setzekorn 1975: 24). While East Indians assimilated linguistically and culturally to Creole norms and remain a primarily agricultural population, the Chinese have mostly retained their language and become merchants and proprietors in the towns. Much more recently, several thousand Mennonite farmers of German extraction have established rural settlements in northern Belize since the late 1950s. The Mennonites belong to a Protestant sect whose members have moved repeatedly since their arrival in North America around 1700 to maintain autonomy from national governments. While the Mennonites reject participation in politics or other national institutions, they are heavily involved in commercial farming and have come to dominate Belizean agricultural markets in a number of staple commodities.

Comparisons of 1970 and 1980 census data reveal an annual rate of growth of 1.9 percent, a low figure by Central American standards. Yet Belize had a natural population growth rate of 3.6 percent during this same period, which is among the highest in the world (Hartshorn 1984: 32). The discrepancy between natural and actual rates of growth indicates very high rates of emigration, which is occurring primarily among the country's Creole and Garifuna populations. It is estimated that one-fourth of all persons born in Belize now reside in the United States (Pastor 1985: 19). Such high rates of emigration have constituted a massive drain of skilled and semiskilled labor from the central and southern parts of the country, where African-Belizeans predominate.

While the nation's culture history demonstrates that Belize is a product of immigration, much controversy has attended the most recent immigrants to enter the country. Since the late 1970s, numerous refugees from El Salvador and Guatemala have crossed the border and settled mostly in uninhabited rural areas. The actual numbers of Central American refugees greatly exceed the 8,645 officially recorded during an immigration amnesty period (Palacio 1987: 30). Given the magnitude of these migrations and the country's tenuous ethnic balance, many African-Belizeans fear that the ethnic distribution of the country will dramatically change as a result of the refugee influx and Creole-Garifuna emigration. Whether or not the thus far peaceful cultural pluralism of Belize will survive the latest influx of immigrants remains to be seen. Ethnic cooperation depends at least as much on a willingness to avert demagogic ethnic politics as it does immigration policy. Regardless of the outcome, the ethnic mosaic of Belize in the coming years will doubtless be very different from the past.

A CROWN COLONY IN CENTRAL AMERICA

In the Papal Donation of 1493, Spain was granted a monopoly over the newly discovered lands of Central America and the Caribbean, an empire which it maintained until the nineteenth century. Notwithstanding the division of the New World into Spanish and Portuguese spheres of control, other would-be colonial powers were quick to exploit areas of weakness or unsettled backwaters within these holdings. Belize was one such area wrested by the British from the periphery of the Spanish empire. In the sixteenth century, the Spanish passed through the interior of Belize and established missions there. In 1638, most Maya under Spanish jurisdiction in Belize rebelled, burning missions, killing settlers, and forcing the Spanish to abandon the region for more than half a century (Jones 1987: 13).

The first British arrivals came not to settle the land but to seek refuge in its isolation, only later deciding to utilize its natural resources. The earliest documented English inhabitants were survivors of a 1638 shipwreck. Local sources maintain that the area was occupied as early as 1603 by the English buccaneer Wallace, whose surname, rendered as Balis by the Spanish, allegedly became the basis of the settlement's title (Burdon 1931: 3). Piracy was rampant in the western Caribbean of the seventeenth century, and the "Settlement in the Bay of Honduras," remote from other colonies and protected by its formidable barrier reef, became a sanctuary for buccaneers fleeing Spanish naval authorities. The object of piracy in the region was not the treasure of New World mines but cargo ships embarking from Campeche with logwood destined for European ports. Logwood (*Haematoxylum campechiamum* L.), found only on the Yucatán peninsula and Caribbean coast of Central America, yielded a fixing compound for clothing dyes and was in great demand by the growing textile industry of Europe.

Over the next 150 years, the settlement's growth was entirely attributable to European demand for this commodity. Often deterred in their efforts to capture heavily escorted Spanish cargo ships, English buccaneers turned to cutting the wood themselves, which they found in abundance along the Belizean coast. When Britain agreed to suppress piracy in the late seventeenth century, it tacitly encouraged the growth of settlements by former buccaneers to avert extortionate Spanish trading practices. The Spanish repeatedly tried to dislodge these settlers to preserve their logwood monopoly and assert political control over Central America. After periodic expulsions, persistently followed by the reestablishment of British settlements, Britain agreed in 1763 to recognize Spanish sovereignty in exchange for permission to continue cutting logwood.

By the late eighteenth century, however, the logwood market had declined greatly from oversupply and was finally eliminated altogether by the introduction of synthetic dyes. In its place, the Baymen turned to harvesting mahogany (*Swietenia macrophylla*), then much in favor among English furniture makers. Although the settlers had surreptitiously cut mahogany for many years, they received the legal right to do so by treaty between England and Spain in 1786. While expanding the territory permitted for logging operations, the treaty restated Spanish sovereignty and prohibited the construction of forts, establishment of local government, or development of commercial agriculture by the settlers (ibid.: 172).

After war broke out between the two powers, the Spanish attempted to capture the settlement militarily in 1798. Their defeat at the Battle of St. George's Caye marked the final attempt by Spain to seize the territory and the beginning of official English recognition of the settlement, at least to the extent of defending it against rival powers. In the early nineteenth century, Britain appointed superintendents to oversee local affairs, finally imposing its own form of local government and declaring British Honduras a formal colony in 1862. Partly because of the British delay in establishing sovereignty and because it claims to have inherited the rights of Spain, Guatemala never recognized English control of the territory. Even as Belize became an independent nation in 1981, Guatemala reasserted the claim, prominently posted at its frontier with Belize, that "Belice es nuestro."

COLONIAL LAND, LABOR, AND CLASS

Because the Baymen were unable to control the elusive and often rebellious Maya as a labor force (Bolland 1988: 92), they looked elsewhere for labor supplies to exploit the settlement's timber resources. For the most part, this labor was provided by African slaves and small numbers of indentured workers imported following abolition. Slavery in Belize differed substantially in organization from the plantation slavery practiced in the Caribbean. Woodcutting slaves were put to work in small groups in isolated, seasonally occupied timber camps, where they made daily use of axes and machetes. During the off season many were encouraged to cultivate subsistence crops by their owners, whose maintenance costs were lowered as a result (Bolland and Shoman 1977; Bolland 1988). The fact that slaves worked without whip-wielding drivers, had access to potential weapons, and retained some control of subsistence resources has led some colonial-era historians to claim, following the slaveowners themselves, that slavery in Belize was "much less oppressive than elsewhere" (Waddell 1961: 14).

Notwithstanding organizational differences between slavery in Belizean timber camps and Caribbean plantations, there is evidence that slaves were systematically subjected to "extreme inhumanity," in the words of an early colonial superintendent (Burdon 1931: 235). After capture, rebellious slaves were usually tortured to death as a deterrent to others, and any slave could be hanged for causing injury to a slaveowner (Bolland 1988: 57). Nonetheless, slaves occasionally accepted such risks for the possibility of freedom. An examination of early legislative minutes indicates that slaveowners were continually obsessed with the prospect of insurrections and frequently diverted ships carrying slaves implicated in rebellions elsewhere. Colonial documents record four revolts between 1765 and 1820, the last of which was occasioned by an owner's "very unnecessary harshness," according to contemporary accounts (Burdon 1931: 228). More commonly, slave-owners experienced large-scale defections of their laborers. Facing improbable escape through the region's difficult terrain, hundreds of slaves fled to settlements in the Yucatán and Guatemala, where they received guarantees of asylum by the Spanish. Other escaped slaves established maroon colonies in the interior that attracted a continual drain of fugitives from slave camps. The exodus of servile labor was so great that by the early nineteenth century timber interests actively recruited other populations, such as the Garifuna, to replace them (Bolland 1988).

Slavery was abolished throughout the British Empire in 1838, but the essential patterns of labor organization changed little in Belize. Several factors conspired to extend the servitude of timber workers long past the demise of formal slavery and to inhibit the growth of a free-holding peasantry. The first of these was the method of abolition itself, for a system of "apprenticeship" was instituted prior to the end of slavery. During the five years of apprenticeship that preceded 1838, former slaves had to continue working without pay for their masters, even while the latter received compensation for their loss of property. In the absence of savings or land, few slaves had any choice upon emancipation but to continue working in the mahogany camps of the interior.

In the nineteenth century, a system of labor contracting developed that insured a continued flow of labor into forestry camps and strengthened the dependence of former slaves upon their employers. Each year that workers were recruited they received a wage advance to purchase some of the supplies needed for the following season in the timber camps. By itself the advance seldom sufficed to meet the worker's food requirements. The balance of his supplies then had to be purchased on credit from the employer's camp store at prices exceeding the worker's seasonal wages. Under this combined "advance-truck" system of recruitment and contract, workers were rarely able to pay off their debts at the end of each season, thereby remaining "virtually enslaved for life," according to a colonial official of the time (Ashcraft 1973: 36). By mid-century, the colony's laws prescribed imprisonment with hard labor for an employee's failure to uphold his contract, a sentence that was "easily enforced within the Settlement because the population was so small" (Bolland and Shoman 1977: 64).

Debt servitude was not the sole factor compelling an annual exodus of labor to inland forestry camps, as workers were also tied to the timber industry for sheer want of alternatives. In a country with abundant and largely unoccupied land, the obvious alternative to wood cutting was smallholder agriculture. Throughout the period of slavery, forest workers had been encouraged to "cut plantations," or small subsistence farms, in the off season to spare their owners some of the cost of their maintenance. Yet after emancipation, a series of measures insured that the former slaves did not leave the labor market to become a full-time peasantry. Despite the unoccupied and unutilized appearance of the colony's arable land, its ownership was concentrated in the hands of a timber oligarchy that denied access to land in the form of smallholdings.

This powerful "forestocracy" originated when British settlers allocated forest lands among themselves prior to colonial administration. Although the Spanish nominally retained all sovereignty over the land, settlers passed a series of resolutions known as "location laws" by which they simply claimed land as freehold property. The concentration of land and wealth into an ever smaller portion of the settler population coincided with the shift from logwood to mahogany as the colony's economic mainstay. Whereas logwood was found in dense clusters near the coast and could be harvested by a settler having few or no slaves and little capital, mahogany trees were scattered in inland forests, necessitating cattle trains and up to fifty men to remove them (Bolland 1986: 16). By 1787, twelve settler families already controlled four-fifths of the land allocated to the woodcutters by treaty the previous year (ibid.: 19). These families also controlled the settlement's several import mercantile firms. Because import houses benefited from the labor contractors' advance system, timber oligarchs and merchants were closely allied by an identity of interest.

This alliance of dominant classes imposed a virtual prohibition on smallholder farming in the settlement. Timber interests and merchants acquired extensive landholdings not for use but to deny land to others. With the advent of British administration, the Crown asserted control over all lands not previously claimed by private individuals, leaving intact the vast tracts earlier seized by mahogany firms. Crown land was distributed gratuitously to the timber cutters until 1838, when land grants were made available only for a fee "high enough to be out of the reach of the average freedman" (cited in Bolland and Shoman 1977: 59). It was no coincidence that a fee system was introduced just as the former slaves became eligible for land. At the time, the secretary

of state for the colonies maintained that free land grants "create indo-
lent habits [and] discourage labour for wages" (ibid.: 60). The potential
of smallholder farming as a source of income for the newly freed population was further diminished in the same year when Sunday markets
were abolished, apparently to discourage production that would compete with imported foods (ibid.: 64).

In southern Belize, where mahogany trees were generally inaccessible, timber interests nonetheless restricted access to land in an effort
to control resident labor. The Garifuna had cultivated land for staple
crops near their settlements since the beginning of the nineteenth century, but were denied freehold property when the colonial government
awarded legal titles to all residents of the colony occupying land prior
to 1840 (*History of Belize* 1983: 38). In 1857 the Garifuna were warned
to apply for annual Crown leases lest their land be sold to others, although they themselves were prohibited from purchasing land (ibid.:
38). The Crown Lands Ordinance of 1872 established Carib Reserves
of land available for communal use by Garifuna villagers, again denying
them the right to apply for title. The intent of such denials, according
to the Crown surveyor, was to "attract near Belize [City] a valuable
body of labourers" (Bolland and Shoman 1977: 99).

The consolidation of land in large unutilized tracts accelerated after
the mid-nineteenth century, when depression struck the colony's mahogany industry. Production costs rose rapidly after easily accessible
trees were harvested, yet after 1870 metropolitan prices for the colony's
mahogany exports declined. The land and assets of many of the colony's less successful woodcutters, as well as the mercantile firms that
serviced them, were liquidated by metropolitan banks or acquired by
their competitors within the colony (Ashcraft 1973: 39). One British-
based firm that emerged from the depression of the late nineteenth
century, the Belize Estate and Produce Company, possessed half the
private land in the colony and became the single most important actor
in its political economy until the late 1940s. Due to the disproportionate political influence of Belize Estate and other absentee landowners,
the British Colonial Office ignored proposals to diversify the colony's
economy with agriculture even as the mahogany industry slumped into
prolonged crisis.

With the help of an expanding American market the colony's trade
in forest products improved after the beginning of the twentieth century. Chicle, a chewing gum base extracted from the sapodilla tree,

became the colony's second largest export. The introduction of tractors and other mechanized means of extracting and processing mahogany logs also opened previously remote or uneconomic stands of mahogany. In the late 1920s, record volumes of timber were exported at substantial profit, while merchants enjoyed a lucrative trade in smuggling whiskey to the United States during Prohibition. Yet the improved earnings of timber companies were not shared by their woodcutting employees, for mechanization reduced the traditional nine- to eleven-month working year to six months for most workers (Ashcraft 1973: 53). The bulk of the working population was left destitute during the 1930s, when the timber industry virtually suspended operations due to the Depression in the developed countries (Ashdown 1978: 62). After prolonged labor unrest, authorities finally abolished the advance-truck system of labor recruitment and legalized membership in labor unions, although most of the colony's woodcutters remained unemployed until the 1940s (ibid.).

Conditions in the colony's economy improved during the Second World War, when several thousand men volunteered for work in Britain, the United States, and the Panama Canal Zone. Production also increased as the colony's forest resources were channelled into the war effort. With the conclusion of the war and the return of men from abroad, however, the colony's economy relapsed into a deep recession. By the late 1940s, it was chronically dependent on British financial assistance to overcome balance of trade deficits. Facing an aggressively anticolonial and unionized work force for the first time, as well as the prospect of a continued financial drain on the central treasury, colonial authorities in the postwar period finally began to promote economic diversification. The dramatic demise of forestry and growth of commercial agriculture in the 1950s were not simply the result of policy changes, however. The timber companies that once ruled Belize by fiat no longer operated profitably in a changing world economy, due in part to their overexploitation of the country's valuable hardwood resources. By the 1960s, Belize Estate and Produce had become the minor subsidiary of a transnational corporation willing to relinquish much of its land to the Belizean government in lieu of taxes (Bolland 1986: 77).

Even as many of the political impediments to agricultural growth were cleared away in the postwar period, remnants of the colonial attitude toward agriculture persist to this day. In many areas roads have improved little over the crude forest tracks in use during the heyday of mahogany. Markets for most staple crops are notoriously unpredictable, with the result that relatively little produce actually makes its way from rural villages to town dwellers. Even more striking in a country of rich potential and chronic shortfalls in domestic food production is the cultural legacy of suppressed agriculture. The corollary of efforts to prevent cultivation of the soil was a general disparagement of all it produced, an attitude that persists today in the unfavorable comparisons many Belizeans make between food they themselves grow and foodstuffs imported from abroad (cf. Lewis 1969: 293). For these reasons, as well as the political economic factors that will be analyzed in chapter 4, the postwar expansion of export agriculture has not been coupled with corresponding growth in the production of staple crops.

EMERGENCE AND CRISIS IN THE MODERN ECONOMY

Since the mid-1800s, sporadic but persistent efforts had been made to develop an agricultural export sector in Belize. Refugees from the Caste Wars brought sugar cultivation to the colony in the 1850s, ex-Confederates established sugar estates in southern Belize after the U.S. Civil War, and cocoa was cultivated in various localities in the late nineteenth century. In Stann Creek district, where citrus is widely cultivated today, the United Fruit Company shipped bananas through the 1920s. All these efforts collapsed after a short period or remained small-scale, largely unprofitable enterprises due to the timber industry's juggernaut over labor and land and the lack of infrastructure provided to agriculture (Ashcraft 1973: 58). The sugar industry of the north and citrus industry of Stann Creek district originated under similarly adverse conditions. Since the demise of forestry in the 1950s, however, these industries have grown rapidly to become the country's primary sources of export earnings.

Both industries owe their recent growth to development concessions from the British and Belizean governments. Processing factories in sugar and citrus have received government loans, tax relief, and permission to import equipment free of duty. Belizean sugar and citrus products are predominately sold in Commonwealth markets offering sugar quotas and tariff barriers against products of non-Commonwealth origin. Belizean sugar is also marketed in the United States via a quota established in the 1960s, while provisions of the Caribbean Basin Initiative recently eliminated tariffs against Belizean citrus products. Commonwealth market preferences and development concessions have also been extended to the banana industry in Stann Creek district since the late 1960s. Despite producers' reliance on them, market preferences have not insulated growers from the effects of downward world market trends. Since preferences and tariffs are subject to political exigencies, they contribute to the vagaries of pricing that confront Belizean producers.

Production in both the sugar and citrus industries takes place on large factory-owned estates as well as independent smallholdings often no larger than a few acres. The processing plants for these crops are largely controlled by foreign capital, but small-scale sugar and citrus producers have had some success in negotiating price increases in years of favorable world prices. Yet the processors wield ultimate power in export agriculture, as was demonstrated by the British transnational Tate and Lyle's decision to shut one of its two sugar-processing factories in 1985 after several years of losses. The closure affected thousands of cane farmers, farmworkers, and factory employees, heightening the considerable distress experienced by sugar producers since export prices began falling several years earlier. These difficulties were compounded by a reduction in the U.S. quota for Belizean sugar, forcing the country to sell much of its crop at lower world market prices (Central Bank of Belize 1985: 8). Because sugar has been the country's largest export earner since 1959, the industry's crisis has had profound effects throughout Belize. The crisis also highlights the fact that after four decades of "diversification," the economy remains narrowly based on a few commodities subject to volatile world prices.

As Belize moved toward formal independence in 1981, its trade deficit reached unprecedented levels, largely due to rising oil prices and the inability of the agricultural sector to satisfy domestic food needs (Government of Belize 1985: 3). When the cost of the manufactured goods that Belize imports are taken into account, it is apparent that the country operates at a growing disadvantage in the world market. Terms of trade, calculated as the prices a country receives for its exports relative to the price it pays for imports (figure 1), have turned against Belize since the mid-1970s (Central Bank of Belize 1985: 31). This in turn severely limits the government's capacity to promote investment in agricultural and industrial self-sufficiency. The country's fortunes

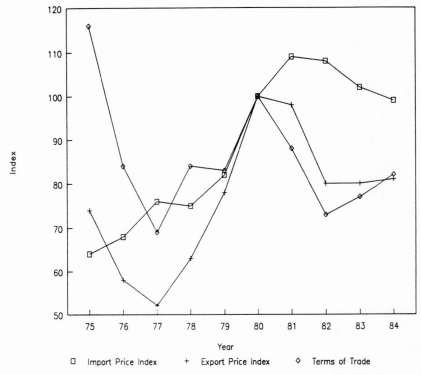

Figure 1. Belize terms of trade: 1975–1984 (1980 = 100). Source: Central Bank of Belize (1985).

remain closely tied to those of a handful of commodities for foreign consumption, making the many plans for diversification ever more remote from reality.

THE VIEW FROM STANN CREEK DISTRICT

Different ethnic groups, geographical features, and climatic conditions predominate in each of the country's districts, so no region of Belize can be said to reflect the character of the country as a whole. This applies above all to the two southern districts of Stann Creek and Toledo, whose geography insulated the region from some of the consequences of the timber economy that prevailed elsewhere. Due to the narrow, unnavigable rivers flowing from the Maya Mountains, inland timber resources were inaccessible to mahogany cutters, who concentrated their efforts instead on the more readily extracted stands of timber in the northern and central regions of the country. Meanwhile, southern Belize, evocatively (if somewhat uncharitably) characterized elsewhere as the "back of beyond" (Kerns 1983: 42), became even more sparsely settled and undeveloped than the rest of the colony. Many residents of the more populous areas of the country continue to disparage the region as one of remoteness and sleepy isolation.

In a country of considerable ethnic variety, Stann Creek district stands out as perhaps the most diverse region. In 1980 the district was inhabited by 14,181 people, the majority of whom (7,520) are identified in the census as rural residents (Government of Belize 1984). The balance reside in the coastal town of Dangriga (formerly Stann Creek Town), by far the district's largest settlement and the center of its administration and commerce. Since its founding around 1800, Dangriga has been primarily associated with the Garifuna, who were its original settlers and continue to make up about 70 percent of its population. The next largest segment of town residents, Creoles, comprise only 22 percent of its population. In general the town's Creoles are wealthier than Dangriga's Garifuna residents and until recently they exercised a near-monopoly of political power in the community. The remainder of the town's population is composed of "Spanish," East Indians, and whites, as well as a very small but prominent group of Chinese and Middle Eastern (generally Palestinian) residents who own many of the local businesses.

In contrast to town, rural settlements are more ethnically homogeneous, although the region as a whole retains great diversity. A thirty-minute trip by motor vehicle is likely to take one from a Garifuna village through a Creole settlement and finally to a Maya-speaking community. Creoles, who are a minority in town, form the largest single portion (43 percent) of the rural population, followed by the Garifuna (24 percent) and Spanish (18 percent). The latter mostly reside in scattered homesteads in the mountainous western portion of the district, where they practice shifting cultivation and pursue seasonal labor in the citrus industry. South of town and away from the Stann Creek valley, more established villages are either entirely Creole or Garifuna. Since the mid-1970s, Mopan Maya settlers have migrated to the region from Toledo district in search of new farmlands. Creating the new villages of Santa Rosa, Maya Centre, Red Bank, and San Roman, Maya now make up about 10 percent of the people of rural Stann Creek.

The district's approximately 840 square miles can be divided into three general environmental zones. The largest of these is a low coastal plain extending the length of the district between the Caribbean and the foothills of the Maya Mountains. The coastal zone is covered with savanna grasses interspersed with occasional pine trees (generally *Pinus caribaea*), an impoverished combination that Belizeans refer to as pine ridge. The use of the term *ridge* in Creole refers to plant-soil associations rather than a specific type of topography. The pine ridge savanna is formed of heavily leached topsoil and an acid subsoil incapable of supporting most agriculture (Wright et al. 1959: 149). This sparsely covered and largely uninhabited strip extends ten to fifteen miles inland from the coast until abruptly meeting forested foothills and steep granite outcroppings. Some "broken ridge" soils associated with the foothill region are capable of supporting tree crops, but the area as a whole has been uninhabited since prehistory due to its unsuitability for shifting cultivation (ibid.: 162).

Only in the district's smallest environmental zone, comprising about 17 percent of its land area, is agriculture actually feasible. Dissecting the infertile pine ridge region at several-mile intervals, creeks and rivers drain the Maya Mountain watershed into the sea, bringing with them alluvial deposits that allow the growing of many crops (ibid.: 150). These zones are comprised of cohune ridge lands, marked by dense broadleaf forests and cohune palms (*Orbiguya cohune*). With the exception of a narrow sandy shoreline that supports some coconut farming, all the district's agriculture occurs in these circumscribed but fertile zones. Much arable land remains uncultivated, although a good deal of it is inaccessible to existing villages and roads, particularly where commercial citrus cultivation has placed a premium on fertile land.

The timber industry that long dominated the rest of the country's economy here exerted much less influence. Not coincidentally, it was here that many early, albeit unsuccessful, ventures in commercial agriculture began. Forestry activities in the Stann Creek district have been confined to the production of cheap, crudely finished pine lumber for the domestic market. While pine production was limited by the small size of that market, as well as low capitalization and reliance on natural regeneration, it was also immune to the violent boom-and-bust cycles that devastated the mahogany industry. After many of the private timber lands passed into government control in the postwar period, the few forestry jobs that remained were full-time, public sector employment, leaving timber workers scant opportunity for farming. The demise of forestry as a seasonal employer and its overall contraction have contributed to increased reliance on farming by rural residents since 1950.

The timber industry in Stann Creek district was centered on the infertile pine ridge and did not entirely monopolize land and labor, allowing the development of some commercial agriculture in the region. On a visit to rural Stann Creek in 1882, Morris observed the remnants of a cohune oil factory and two active sugar and banana plantations near the Sittee River (1883: 30). Residents of the area were also employed at the nearby German-owned Kramer estates, where coffee and cocoa were produced for export until the early twentieth century (Wright et al. 1959: 118–119). Banana production for export rapidly expanded in the region in the late 1800s, the United Fruit Company at first marketing the crops of local producers and then establishing a 12,500-acre estate at Middlesex in the Stann Creek valley (Ashcraft 1973: 58). What appeared at the time to be a promising export industry collapsed after 1913, when Panama disease, a soil-based virus, destroyed United Fruit's banana plantation (ibid.). Although many small-scale producers were unscathed by the disease, United Fruit's cessation of marketing arrangements in 1927 left them with no nonlocal outlets for their crops. Coconut exports from the district, most of which originated on smallholder farms, also underwent cyclical swings due to changing levels of metropolitan consumption (Wright et al. 1959: 119). During each contraction of the export market, small-scale producers returned to seasonal employment in forestry or subsistence production on their farms.

A wealthy expatriate merchant cultivated citrus in the Stann Creek valley as early as 1913, making the first shipment of fresh grapefruit to Britain ten years later (Furley 1972: 110). In 1936 processing of citrus began when the Citrus Company of British Honduras opened a juice-canning plant at Pomona, later expanding its operations to include the canning of grapefruit sections. Production and income levels remained very low until the negotiation of market guarantees and development incentives with Britain in the 1950s. In 1962, Salada Ltd., a subsidiary of Nestlé, purchased a citrus-processing plant at Alta Vista to produce frozen concentrate for the Canadian market (Government of Belize 1966: 15). Within a decade, 96 percent of Stann Creek's citrus crop was being processed for export, either as concentrate or canned fruit (Furley 1972: 110).

Throughout this period the residents of Stann Creek district have grown increasingly involved in the region's citrus economy as producers, suppliers of labor, or both. Prior to the 1950s, citrus cultivation was confined to the large estates of the district's wealthiest families, who quickly consolidated their landholdings in the most fertile and accessible areas of the Stann Creek valley (ibid.: 112). By 1970 the remaining more marginal lands in the valley had been subdivided among small-scale citrus growers. Today much of the Hummingbird Highway, a steep, tortuously winding road that provides the district's only surface connection with the northern half of the country, is lined with citrus groves ranging from a few acres in size to over a thousand. Along this route, shanty towns of single-room barracks have sprung up at Pomona, Alta Vista, and Middlesex to accommodate seasonal workers in the valley's processing plants and corporate estates.

The district's only land route to the south, the unpaved and seasonally impassable Southern Highway, connects the Stann Creek valley with a number of widely dispersed villages and hamlets. For the most part, the Southern Highway crosses barren and uninhabited pine ridge terraces, but river valley and creekside farmland up to thirty miles south of the Stann Creek valley attest to the growing influence of the citrus industry along the route. Until recently considered marginal to the country's citrus economy (cf. Chibnik 1975: 43), southern Stann Creek district in the 1980s became the major site of its expansion. As villages near the Southern Highway such as Silk Grass and Hopkins are swept up into the rapidly spreading effects of these economic changes, they are tied more closely not only to the center of the industry some twenty miles away, but also to a world market from which they had been relatively isolated in recent decades.

CHAPTER 3

"TO HELP YOURSELF":

AN OVERVIEW OF VILLAGE ECONOMY

AND SOCIAL RELATIONS

V illage economies in Belize bear the imprint of many factors. People pursue subsistence activities that make use of the particular natural resources and technical means at their disposal. Yet village livelihoods are not simply the product of ecological and technical factors, for rural residents act in an environment that has been shaped by political forces not of their making. Until recent years, for example, arable land was abundant throughout Belize but was denied to would-be agriculturalists. In addition, the economic activities of rural Belizeans are organized by the cultural setting and local traditions in which they occur. Within close proximity to each other, Creoles, Garifuna, and Maya have reached substantially different solutions to the problem of making a living.

This chapter examines the livelihoods of people who reside in Hopkins and Silk Grass, nearby villages in central Stann Creek district. The villages contrast sharply in local history, settlement patterns, demography, and resource endowments. In some respects, such as the pronounced ethnic distinctions existing between the communities, the differences between Hopkins and Silk Grass belie the scant seven miles that separate the villages. Such cultural traditions continue to structure residents' choices of subsistence activities in a variety of ways. For all their differences, however, Hopkins and Silk Grass have both become heavily integrated with world markets for citrus crops in recent years.

With this involvement has come a growing convergence of residents' livelihoods and the class structures of their communities.

HOPKINS: A COASTAL GARIFUNA ENCLAVE

The placid appearance that Hopkins presents to outsiders affords little evidence of the economic changes taking place among its residents or of the turmoil of the community's founding and recent history. The village stretches for almost two miles along a sandy ridge of coastline that separates the Caribbean from a brackish marsh lying to the west. Characteristic of coastal Garifuna settlement patterns (cf. Davidson 1976), the village's houses are aligned in three or four rows within a hundred yards of the shore. Although varied in their materials and construction, villagers' houses are uniformly bleached by the salt air and frequent storms from the sea. In contrast to the marshy grassland behind it, Hopkins luxuriates in the shade of coconut palms, cashew trees, and four species of mango. With its lush vegetation, moderating trade winds, and unbroken sand beach, Hopkins is not only a refuge from the heat and humidity of the interior but suggests to the temperate zone imagination the archetypal Caribbean village.

With the exception of a handful of intermarrying Creoles, the village's 749 residents retain their indigenous Garifuna language in most local interaction. Prior to the 1941 hurricane that struck the coast of Stann Creek district, the area that is presently Hopkins was occupied by only four families. Most of the land was leased to an Englishman who cultivated a coconut walk at the present site of the village (in Creole, the term *walk* refers to a farm planted in permanent crops). The operation employed both the resident Garifuna families and a number of men from Newtown, a Garifuna settlement about two miles to the north. The 1941 hurricane not only destroyed all the houses in Newtown but swept away so much of its shoreline that reconstruction at the same site was impossible. The coconut walk at Hopkins was also leveled and, after the Englishman left the country rather than rebuild, the colonial government made his land available to the displaced residents of Newtown. To this day, villagers continue to pay annual rent to the government for the house lots they occupy, although population growth has led many residents to double up on single lots.

The people who moved to Hopkins in 1941 were of diverse origins, notwithstanding their common ethnicity. According to elderly informants, Newtown was founded in the 1890s by residents of Stann Creek Town, so some villagers were probably descended from the earliest Garifuna arrivals in Belize. A steady stream of migrants from Garifuna settlements in Honduras and Guatemala continued through the early twentieth century, with their number greatly increasing after the onset of systematic Garifuna persecutions by the Honduran government in 1937. When some Honduras Garifuna became involved in an opposition political movement, the military retaliated against villages believed to be harboring opponents of the regime. At least one village was annihilated during these operations, and Garifuna who once resided in Honduras tell of widespread atrocities committed by the army. Older residents recount in graphic terms the arrival of dugout dories overloaded with refugees from Honduras. Many refugees settled in Newtown and accompanied residents of that village to Hopkins in the 1940s. Despite painful recollections of the flight into exile, some older people in Hopkins retain contact with family members in Honduras and remain curious about life in Garifuna villages there.

The movement of villagers from Newtown to Hopkins after the 1941 hurricane did not spare them the devastation of later storms. Four hurricanes have struck since then, as well as uncounted tropical storms and depressions. Only two structures in Hopkins survived Hurricane Hattie in 1961, which claimed three lives and destroyed all the boats, fishing equipment, and farms from which villagers made a living. Some Hopkins residents left for safer inland destinations following Hattie, but most returned to the reconstructed village within three years. Despite the perils of Hopkins' coastal location, villagers consider themselves fortunate to live away from the heat and swarming insects of inland villages. As one elderly man explained it, "Even with the storms, our people need to be by the sea. Most of us would rather die than live to the back [inland]."

Residents express this preference for village life in a variety of ways. All adult villagers visit town on occasion to work, shop, or resolve some matter with government officials. Most residents also have kin ties to other Garifuna villages. For those villagers born in Hopkins, life in these other places is found wanting in some significant respect. Among townsmen, villagers assert sadly, the Garifuna language and "old ways" are fast dying out, while the residents of other villages are firmly believed to be untrustworthy or lazy. A corollary of this village insularity is that those born in Hopkins will forever "belong" to it, even if they spend the bulk of their adult lives elsewhere. Many of those who "be-

Hopkins.

long" to Hopkins are now scattered as far afield as Chicago or New York, yet even emigrants periodically visit the village and express their wish to permanently go "home" someday. Those born elsewhere who move to Hopkins as adults usually find acceptance in the community but never become full members of it. One man who moved to the village from Dangriga in 1955 explained over thirty years later that he doesn't vote in village council elections because he doesn't really "belong" to Hopkins.

Yet for most people, the exigency of making a living requires occasional periods of residence elsewhere, for local sources of cash have historically been limited despite ready access to fishing areas and farmland. The village's demographic structure (figure 2) reflects both a high rate of population growth and patterns of labor migration that periodically remove large numbers of adults from the village population. Of the 376 residents recorded in household surveys, 48 percent are twelve years of age or less. Only thirty-six female and twenty male residents are between the ages of twenty-two and forty-two, accounting for 14.8 percent of the sample. This constriction in the village's age-sex distribution during early to middle adulthood reflects the exodus of young adults

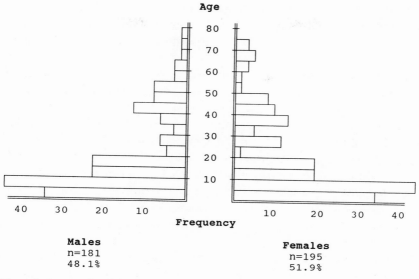

Figure 2. Age-sex distribution: Hopkins (n = 376).

in pursuit of earnings elsewhere. Many of these individuals will return to the village in their forties to begin farming or fishing with equipment purchased from savings. A growing number, however, will leave to pursue jobs in the United States, where an estimated three hundred people from Hopkins already reside. Although most foreign-bound migrants state their intention to reside only temporarily in the United States, in actuality few will ever return to the village to live. The impression that even the casual observer gains of the village's population is substantiated by household data: To a large extent Hopkins is a place that young people leave and older people return to.

Labor migration from the village is not a recent development, but the foreign destination and largely nonrecurrent nature of that migration is. Conducting ethnographic research in the same locale over forty years ago, Taylor wrote that "most of the men and nearly half the women between the ages of eighteen and fifty are away for five or six months of the year" (1951: 55). This seasonal absence from the village is no longer characteristic of most Hopkins residents, either male or female. As can be seen from figure 2, sex ratios in the village are nearly equal, contrary to older accounts that stress a preponderance of females in Garifuna villages. Further, only 24 percent of all resident men report that they reside outside the village for two or more months of the year. Gonzalez (1969, 1988) has attributed many characteristic features of Garifuna social organization to this tradition of male labor migration. As skilled sailors in a region of difficult overland travel, Garifuna men have always enjoyed the advantage of mobility in entering nonlocal labor markets. The earliest references to the Garifuna in Central America note their ubiquity in almost all wage occupations while documenting a scarcity of men in their natal communities (cf. Kerns 1983: 33). Gonzalez contends that the lack of a permanent male presence at home resulted in a pattern of matrifocality, by which domestic units were organized around co-residential kinswomen (1969: 35 ff.). While men engaged in nonlocal labor or fishing, women became self-sufficient subsistence producers and predominated in farming with seasonal help from men (ibid.).

In the past, male mobility and female independence were compatible with the community's coastal location remote from overland routes. Until the construction of a road linking the village to the Southern Highway in 1971, the only access to Hopkins was by sea. Like their forebears in Newtown, a generation of Hopkins residents sailed dugout dories from the village in search of jobs and returned by sea when their work was finished. Hopkins Road not only changed this pattern of access but has also opened the possibility of commercialization of the village's agricultural economy. In so doing, the road exposed them anew to the effects of an all-encompassing world market.

SILK GRASS:
A RELOCATION PROJECT IN DECLINE

The village of Silk Grass is situated on the Southern Highway seven miles northeast of Hopkins. Unlike most settlements in rural Stann Creek, the village is neither on the coast nor in immediate proximity to alluvial areas. Its location on the otherwise uninhabited pine ridge savanna differs from the settlement pattern of nearby villages, but its history and population are closely tied to theirs.

Silk Grass originated as a resettlement project after Hurricane Hattie devastated a number of coastal communities in 1961. The village was established in the following year by the colonial government in order

Silk Grass.

to relocate people from vulnerable coastal areas and to promote agricultural development. The government encouraged settlement at Silk Grass by offering services to people displaced by storm damage elsewhere. Among these were free homes and electricity, free transportation to town, allocation of free farmland, and provision of marketing services for staple crops. Because Hattie destroyed local farms and disrupted most sources of wage labor, the government provided food rations for new settlers at Silk Grass and allotted each head of household 75 cents per day for expenses until new farms came into production. Such benefits were undoubtedly attractive for residents of coastal villages, who faced major reconstruction costs and had never enjoyed electricity in their homes (a service that remains unavailable in Hopkins to this day). Within months, the government's inducements had lured hundreds of settlers from the coast to Silk Grass. By the end of 1962, 117 local households had been established containing almost seven hundred people.

The site selected for Silk Grass was intended to control construction costs, but over the years the project's expedient location has proven less than fortuitous. Planners located the village on a barren pine ridge terrace, rather than the arable but densely forested cohune ridge lands several miles away, to reduce the costs of land clearing. Most of the new houses were already occupied when planners learned that the intended water supply for the community, a small creek to the north, was unfit for drinking. The government hastily drilled wells and established a potable water system, but local water tables are so low that the system runs dry in the last two months before the rainy season. Residents attempt to store rainwater in barrels and cisterns against this seasonal scarcity, but for most the months of April and May require trips of four miles to retrieve drinking water from Freshwater Creek to the south.

In its first years, the image that Silk Grass offered to newcomers must have seemed a bleak contrast to its planners' optimistic projections. Early photographs depict the village as a closely packed collection of identical two-room wooden houses, all painted the same bluish-green hue. The houses stood in uniform rows in the midst of a savanna, the only vegetation being knee-high burrs and sedges. Farmland set aside for villagers was three to four miles from the settlement, often more distant than the farms settlers had cultivated in their previous homes. For new arrivals, these unpromising conditions, combined with the stifling afternoon heat and stinging "botlass" flies of the interior, must have compared unfavorably to the coastal villages they had just left.

Unlike most other villages in Stann Creek district, Silk Grass has always had an ethnically heterogeneous population, reflecting the diverse origins of its settlers. At the time of its establishment, approximately one-third of its residents were displaced Garifuna from Hopkins, with the balance of villagers from Sittee River, a Creole settlement to the south. By the mid-1960s, most of the settlers from Hopkins had returned there, and presently no more than 10 percent of the village's population is Garifuna. A second population movement into Silk Grass occurred in 1974 and 1975, when Mopan and Kekchi Maya from Toledo district entered the area in pursuit of new farmlands. In the last half of the 1970s, most of these arrivals also moved on, many of them settling in the new Maya villages of Red Bank, Maya Centre, and San Roman to the south. From 1975 to 1986, Silk Grass's Maya population diminished by two-thirds, to about 8 percent of the village's current residents.

Although Creoles remain the largest segment of the village population, their numbers have decreased as well. Virtually from the moment of its completion, Silk Grass steadily lost population to other areas, a

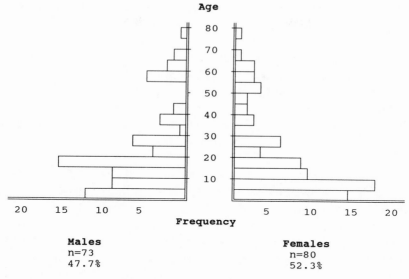

Figure 3. *Age-sex distribution: Silk Grass (n = 153).*

problem that has afflicted other resettlement projects in Belize (Palacio 1982). This outflow of people reflects the high rates of United States migration characterizing Creole and Garifuna settlements countrywide, as well as several fundamentally flawed aspects of the relocation project. Within two years of the village's inception, government officials reneged on most of their promised amenities. Villagers were required to make monthly installments to purchase houses formerly described as "free." Electricity service was cut back, then settlers were billed for their consumption, and finally the village generator was left in disrepair when it broke down. Weekly transportation to town, which had been provided at government expense, also ceased. Angered by what appeared to be a series of broken promises by the government, many settlers abandoned the site in the mid-1960s for their previous villages. Others simply found the location too inhospitable to live there permanently. By 1986, the village's population had dwindled to 250 people in fifty-two households, considerably less than half its size at inception. Of these households, six are Garifuna, five Maya, two "Spanish," one East Indian, and the remaining thirty-eight are Creole.

The village's demography reflects this outflow of people (figure 3). As in Hopkins, children under twelve are the largest segment of the population, making up 40 percent of all those recorded in household surveys. Unlike Hopkins, however, migration from Silk Grass is almost entirely unidirectional and nonrecurrent. Few, if any, residents who leave the village in their twenties or thirties choose to return. Despite continued outmigration, the village's population is beginning to stabilize as young men inherit citrus farms established by their fathers and no longer seek wages outside the community. Some village residents in their twenties are already second-generation citrus growers. These men are not about to leave their substantial investments in tree crops behind for employment elsewhere.

Ironically, as Silk Grass has lost population, it has become less barren and regimented in appearance. Until recently the village consisted of more boarded-up houses than occupied ones. Today the community appears less desolate as outsiders buy up abandoned houses and move them to other locations. Remaining villagers have constructed additions to the original standardized house designs or erected entirely new houses. This diversity is complemented by coconut and mango trees planted in the early years of the village that now provide some shade over its dusty streets. More significant than any of these external attributes, however, is the distinct sense of community that has developed among its diverse residents, despite the fact that ordinarily little interaction would take place between Creoles, Garifuna, and Maya. As the remaining residents form extensive ties of interethnic marriage and friendship, it could be said that a natural community has supplanted a planned one. This evolution has also been accompanied by agricultural changes that have divided the community economically. A few farmers have acquired the lands of the many residents who left the village, increasing local disparities in landownership. Hence, the flawed features of the original relocation project have contributed to the stratifying trends of agricultural change.

OVERVIEW OF THE VILLAGE ECONOMY

In the past, Hopkins and Silk Grass were economically dissimilar in most respects. Reflecting the village's coastal location and Garifuna traditions, male Hopkins residents primarily fished and pursued migratory labor to earn income, supplementing these activities with subsistence agriculture on inland milpas, or swidden farms. Traditionally, men practiced agriculture on a seasonal basis or between cash-earning excursions from the village, often limiting their labor contribution to the heavy work of clearing and burning new farms during the dry season. In the remainder of the year, farm labor was usually performed by women or men too elderly to engage in wage work (Taylor 1951: 56).

While most village households maintained farms and depended upon local produce for subsistence, the cash-earning potential of traditional agriculture remained limited. Prior to the construction of Hopkins Road in 1971, visiting a local farm required a dory trip of two to four miles up a narrow creek from the lagoon north of the village. Once the dory could proceed no farther upstream, the farmer trekked through several miles of dense forest to reach his or her farm. Since all produce had to be backed (carried by hand or tumpline around the forehead) and then returned by dory to the village, farmers rarely produced a significant agricultural surplus above their household needs. As no overland route existed to town markets, the difficulties in marketing crops were also enormous. Virtually all crop sales occurred among village households, and due to its small size this informal market was rarely able to absorb much surplus. Many Hopkins residents continued to rely on fishing and migratory wage labor even after the construction of Hopkins Road. The road greatly improved access to farmland and enabled farmers to increase the size of their farms, but market conditions for traditional crops remained poor. While it had little immediate effect on the incidence of cash cropping, the completion of the road allowed some villagers to respond to improved opportunities for commercial agriculture a decade later.

Silk Grass was established in part to promote commercial farming among rural residents, a policy that entailed considerable subsistence change for some of its early settlers. Rural Creoles are associated with a somewhat stronger agricultural tradition than the Garifuna, for whom mobility and coastal settlement patterns long inhibited involvement in commercial agriculture. Until recently, however, exclusive reliance on farming as an income source has been as rare in Creole communities as among the Garifuna. In both populations men viewed wage labor as more remunerative and far more prestigious than farming. An earlier commentator (Lewis 1969) astutely observed that traditional attitudes toward agriculture among African-Belizeans reflected an ethnic and occupational hierarchy established during colonialism. Because agriculture was historically relegated to mestizos and Maya, "occupational prejudice was compounded by racial disdain; to be a farmer, thus, was not only socially inferior, it was also racially degrading" (Lewis 1969: 293). Only in recent decades have the increased incomes made possible by export crops lessened such long-held aversions to commercial farming as an occupation.

The government's incentives for commercial agriculture did for a time encourage some staple crop production for the market among Silk Grass residents. In the early years after the establishment of Silk Grass, many villagers produced paddy rice for sale to the local outlet of the government's marketing board. Commercial rice cultivation ended by the late 1970s due to a relative decline in crop prices and increasingly unreliable marketing arrangements. Reflecting their traditional occupational preferences, many early settlers came to the village not to establish farms but to gain more convenient access to nearby sources of wage labor. Although these villagers, like all original residents, were allotted ten-acre blocs of land by the government, most full-time wage laborers subsequently sold their lease rights to farming households seeking additional land. Others have retained their land to practice part-time cultivation on a few acres to supplement their wages with staple crops. Thus, for many Silk Grass residents, reliance on commercial farming as a livelihood has diminished since the village's founding.

Some Silk Grass farmers planted citrus trees as early as 1969, primarily to establish permanent title to their land or as a source of retirement income. Citrus was viewed in the past as a reliable but not particularly profitable source of income. Processing factories in the Stann Creek valley purchased as much fruit as farmers could produce but rarely paid prices much above the producer's break-even point. Nonetheless, planting citrus at the time was one means of satisfying the government's requirement that lands be developed in permanent crops before the assignment of private titles. Citrus was also held to be a better source of cash income for one's old age than milpa crops, which require very heavy labor in annually cutting new farms from dense secondary forest.

The residents of Silk Grass have always engaged in a variety of occupations, each household depending to a greater or lesser extent on wage labor, agriculture, or some combination of the two. At the time of his research in the area in the early 1970s, Chibnik noted that despite the variety of occupations among villagers, little income or class stratification could be detected (1975: 143). Villagers' choices of cash-earning and subsistence strategies were related to the developmental cycle of domestic groups, individual and cultural preferences, and aversion to environmental and marketing risk (ibid.: 247). By residents' own accounts, this situation remained unchanged through the late 1970s. Whatever advantages certain economic strategies had in satisfying the needs of particular households, subsistence practices in the past did not enable villagers to accumulate a surplus for investment. Village stratification was to arise later, as the citrus trees planted by some residents in anticipation of meager returns instead yielded unexpectedly great profits.

HOUSEHOLD CONSUMPTION AND PRODUCTION

No household in either village is entirely self-sufficient in producing its food requirements. Indeed, there is probably not a single family in Hopkins or Silk Grass that does not consume some purchased food each day. Apart from a common need to buy those foods that households themselves do not produce, dietary preferences differ substantially between Creoles and Garifuna. In addition to the distinct occupational traditions of villagers, food preferences influence households' choices of subsistence activities.

The staple of Garifuna diets in rural Belize remains what is locally known as groundfood, or root crops. A wide range of edible tubers are cultivated by all Hopkins farming families, most of whom consume sweet cassava, yams, coco yam, sweet potatoes, and other groundfood more often than rice, the primary staple of Creole and urban diets. Five distinct varieties of yam are grown locally, each having a specific dietary application, albeit no exact English equivalent by name. Second only to groundfood as a Garifuna staple, plantains are also consumed in versatile ways. Residents often boil or fry green unripened plantains as an accompaniment to groundfood. Meals are frequently based on a large serving of "boil up," a platter of plantains and groundfood boiled in coconut milk. Women pound green plantains with a large mahogany mortar and pestle to prepare *hudut*, a thick paste consumed in place of groundfood. Many households also cultivate a somewhat squat plantain (*blogo*) to prepare *durasa*, which resembles a tamale made with grated plantain in place of corn.

Cassava bread (*areba*) remains a widely consumed food in Hopkins, although its contribution to the diet is secondary to its symbolic importance as a marker of Garifuna ethnic identity. Cassava is made from the tubers of bitter manioc (*Manihot esculenta*), which requires lengthy preparation to remove the toxic hydrocyanic acid found in the plant. After harvesting, manioc tubers are peeled, grated, leached in a *ruguma* (a six-foot woven strainer known in Creole as a *woula*, or boa), sifted, and finally baked in circular sheets on an iron griddle. The preparation of several weeks' of cassava bread for an average family requires two full days of labor from harvest to baking, a fact that accounts for its demise as other, more remunerative uses have developed for the labor of rural women.

The primary protein component in Hopkins diets is fish, consumed either when fresh or corned (salted and dried). Every afternoon Hopkins women line the beach and scan the horizon for returning fishermen in the hope of purchasing fresh fish for dinner. Many will be unsuccessful, since adverse weather often keeps this staple in short supply. Better than average catches also cause local shortages if men decide to market their fish in Dangriga. Many households maintain chickens for sale or home use, but chicken is consumed infrequently and usually as an accompaniment to large servings of groundfood, rice, or rice and beans. Some households also maintain pigs, which are butchered for local sale or, very rarely, for a ceremonial occasion. Small amounts of pork are consumed by most households in the form of cured pigtail or snouts, which are sold by local shops and used as seasoning.

While traditional staples persist to various degrees in Hopkins households, many Creole elements, such as flour, rice, and beans, have also been added to the diet. Older villagers assert that current diets incorporate many more Creole features than in the past, a claim that is not entirely corroborated by earlier ethnographic work. Taylor noted that purchased white flour was already more prominent than cassava in the diet of Hopkins residents by the late 1940s (1951: 52). Today, cassava's contribution to the diet has been eclipsed by white bread and other home-baked flour products bearing such Creole names as fry jack, johnny cake, and tortilla. Rice and RK (red kidney) beans were not cultivated at the time of Taylor's research but are now grown by many village households and consumed by all with some frequency. Many farming households also cultivate corn, and even nonfarming families consume it seasonally in the form of tamales, corn cakes, or roasted green corn. In addition to white flour, most households regularly purchase imported processed foods from local shops, ranging from instant coffee and powdered milk to Spam. After the addition of import duties, transportation costs, and markups by village shops, such products are more expensive than in the United States yet remain major elements of local diet.

In Silk Grass, as in all of Belize, rice and beans is considered synonomous with Creole cooking and is prepared several times per week by most Creole households. Commonly this dish is complemented by a small portion of chicken or cured pig tail. Rice is by far the major staple of Silk Grass diets, but some groundfood is occasionally consumed in place of it, usually in the form of boil up. Plantain is more frequently eaten than groundfood and is usually served as a fried or boiled accompaniment to rice. Corn is roasted after harvest or consumed as *dukanu* (green corn tamales) or corn cake, but Creoles do not dry it to make tortillas, as do Maya and "Spanish" rural residents.

As a historically semiagricultural population, Creoles have relied heavily on processed foods purchased with wages. Even for agriculturalists in Silk Grass, dietary preferences tend to be more independent of agriculture than those of Hopkins residents. No farming households in Silk Grass, for example, grow the rice and RK beans that they consume, although many farming residents of Hopkins satisfy some of their own needs in these staples. As will be shown later, the absence of rice cultivation today is attributable to scheduling conflicts between commercial citrus farming and subsistence production rather than cultural preferences. One result of this allocation of household labor to commercial agriculture is that household cash needs are demonstrably higher in Silk Grass than in Hopkins. Annual household food expenses in Silk Grass average Bze $3,178, compared to Bze $2,288 in Hopkins.

In 1986, the livelihoods of village residents continued to reflect local subsistence traditions and resource endowments. The differences in local economies were apparent in composite data reflecting the contribution of various subsistence activities to household incomes (table 2). In that year, fishing and wage labor continued to provide the monetary basis of most Hopkins households, while citrus farming and wages were the mainstay of Silk Grass livelihoods. 1986 also marked the last year before Hopkins farmers began to sell citrus to the processing companies, a shift that is rapidly blurring these longstanding cultural and historical distinctions in the village economies.

Table 2. Average Household Income by Source, 1986 ($Bze)

Source	Hopkins (n = 56)		Silk Grass (n = 25)	
Milpa crops	280	8.2%	231	3.2%
Wages[a]	1,554	45.6%	2,468	34.8%
Citrus	12	0.3%	3,679	51.8%
Coconuts	50	1.4%	2	0.0%
Fishing	1,104	32.4%	2	0.0%
Entrepreneurial[b]	26	0.8%	524	7.4%
Remittances	201	5.9%	72	1.0%
Processing[c]	99	2.9%	75	1.0%
Livestock/fowl	49	1.4%	0	0.0%
Artisan[d]	22	0.6%	0	0.0%
Total	3,411	99.9%[e]	7,103	100.0%

[a]Wages include earnings from local and nonlocal employment.
[b]Entrepreneurial activities include income derived from a village shop, operating a transport, or renting equipment.
[c]Processing includes sales of baked goods or coconut oil.
[d]Artisan activities include the manufacture of household implements and crafts.
[e]Due to rounding, the column total for Hopkins does not add to 100 percent.

LAND, LABOR, AND TECHNOLOGY
IN HOUSEHOLD ECONOMIES

Despite the central role of farming in domestic economies, both settlements are located some distance from arable land. Most Hopkins and Silk Grass farmers complete a four- to eight-mile round trip between home and farm each day. In Hopkins, much land is not cultivated, but residents note that all is either privately claimed or held in reserve. Established by the colonial government in the nineteenth century, the reserve system allotted common lands to Maya and Garifuna settlements but did not permit individuals to receive title to such allotments. While an official Carib Reserve was not designated for Hopkins as it was for older Garifuna communities, villagers informally defined approximately 150 acres of land as common property following the settlement of their community. By tradition reserve lands are not planted in permanent crops and are used for the cultivation of groundfood and other staples. In Hopkins, only 26 percent of all reserve land is under cultivation or fallow. The fact that much reserve land remains out of cultivation and is ostensibly under communal control does not imply that land allocation is free of disputes. Because the reserve does not enjoy legal status, conflicts have arisen in recent years when local farmers applied for, and received, government permission to privately lease land that had traditionally been under communal control. As land comes under increasing pressure from village residents, such conflicts between private and community jurisdiction will no doubt increase.

Most of the private land farmed by Hopkins residents is located between three and five miles west of the village. The growing local interest in commercial farming has resulted in land scarcity for the first time in the community's history. Because all blocs are presently claimed, whether fully cultivated or not, land is scarce for younger residents who want to establish farms of their own, unless they have inherited land from a parent. Some younger men cut one- or two-acre milpas on uncultivated portions of land belonging to relatives. Under this practice, they provide the labor for establishing the first-year milpa and retain all its produce. In the second year they abandon the cleared land to its owner, who cultivates it in plantains, as they repeat the milpa cycle on another uncultivated section of the farm. While this arrangement allows some men to satisfy some subsistence needs, it obviously does not permit them any long-term investments in farming, such as tree crops.

Silk Grass farmers as a whole control more land but face even more scarcity than Hopkins residents. Despite repeated assignments of lands to villagers, the acts of government and villagers alike have perpetuated this scarcity. When the village was inaugurated in 1962, residents were given access to two hundred acres of land at Silk Grass Creek, approximately three miles north of the village. The land is divided into twenty ten-acre blocs, although some farmers hold more than one bloc each due to their purchase of titles and use rights from other villagers. The government ceded a second two hundred–acre bloc of land to the Silk Grass Farmers' Cooperative in 1978. The allocation of this highly fertile alluvial land fueled considerable strife, some farmers contending that the co-op officers deceived them while consolidating their landholdings there. According to several former cooperative members, the officers announced that land had been assigned for collective use and that no individual titles would be issued. Subsequently it was learned that the co-op leaders had applied for private leases to the land. Eight farmers now control all two hundred acres while other co-op members received none. The latter are confined to single blocs along Silk Grass Creek and lack any further land for expansion. The ensuing land dispute was a primary factor in the dissolution of the cooperative. As one farmer noted bitterly, "The co-op [leaders] them say they raise-up the village, but in truth and in fact they lone help themselves."

In 1980, the government allotted another seven hundred acres of land two miles west of the village for use by its residents. In the following years, villagers opened trails into the once inaccesible area, cut milpas on the land, and, in several cases, planted citrus trees. Then, to the shock of those who had begun to cultivate the area, the government cancelled existing leases and sold the land to an expatriate Jamaican. Now one of the largest landowners in the country, the Jamaican controls over twenty thousand acres of land in Stann Creek district, most of which is planted in citrus. His operations have become a major source of employment for Silk Grass residents who own no land of their own. Some residents who once farmed the land allotted in 1980 now confront the painful irony of working on the same land for scanty wages.

There is no longer any unclaimed land available for Silk Grass farmers. Residents who settled in the village since 1980 have been blocked from farming due to this scarcity. For already established farmers, the completion of citrus walks on their land has signalled an end to cultivation of milpa crops such as rice, maize, and groundfood. These crops, which were formerly an important contribution to household subsistence, were annually grown prior to the planting of citrus on cleared land. For farmers unable to expand their holdings, the transition from subsistence to commodity production has been abruptly completed.

Farmers in either community do not clear more than two acres of land per year for new farms unless they have access to outside labor. Most open even less than this amount, demarcating the area to be cleared by tasks (an area measuring twenty-five by twenty-five yards, or one-eighth of an acre). Farmers usually measure the areas to be cut because measurement provides a good indication of the quantity of crops to be produced in a given year, the number of citrus trees that may be planted on a farm, or the amount to pay someone if labor is hired for clearing. In March, farmers begin the work of underbrushing, or cutting the undergrowth by machete. In the dense secondary forest covering local lands underbrushing is hot, laborious, and occasionally dangerous work. Uncleared bush provides a sanctuary for venomous snakes, scorpions, stinging insects, and thorny plants known as burr burrs and tiger claws. The final steps in establishing a new milpa involve felling trees by machete and axe and cutting branches of the larger trees into smaller portions to facilitate burning. Very large trees, or those whose dense wood cannot be easily cut, such as the cohune palm, will be left standing in the midst of the otherwise leveled jungle. Depending on the density of secondary growth, a farmer working with axe and machete will spend ten to twelve days underbrushing and felling an acre of forest.

After a new farm is cleared, the cut foliage quickly withers and dies in the heat of the dry season. Felled trees are dry enough to burn completely within several weeks of cutting, but farmers wait as long as possible before burning them since weeds quickly establish themselves after farms are burned. To successfully compete with weeds, crops must be planted shortly after the farm is burned when the rainy season is imminent. If the farmer waits until the rains have started the cleared area will not burn thoroughly, resulting in an incomplete nutrient flush. Consequently, the onset of the rainy season is the most critical climatic factor affecting the outcome of traditional agriculture. The extreme variability of rainfall in the region is perhaps the major agronomic risk facing local farmers.

Planting practices for milpa crops differ little according to ethnic group, Creoles and Garifuna adopting planting methods that originated with Maya shifting cultivators. What does differ, however, are the quantities of the various crops grown under shifting cultivation. In Hopkins, 41 percent of farming households grow rice and 69 percent cultivate corn. The average amount of rice cultivated is just .52 acre, and the average amount of corn only .58 acre. Although Silk Grass residents produced rice for the market until the late 1970s, all rice production ended locally by the mid-1980s. The majority of farming households (73 percent) continue to grow corn, with the average amount much greater (1.5 acres) than in Hopkins. The difference in acreage between villages is due to the presence of Maya farmers in Silk Grass, who rely much more heavily on corn in their diet than do Garifuna or Creoles.

Burning a new milpa.

In the past, Hopkins farmers cultivated milpas for three years before fallowing them. During its first year, a farm would be planted in rice and corn intercropped with plantains. Following the harvest of rice and corn, kidney beans were often planted on the cleared fields in December. After these were harvested, the land was turned over to other milpa crops, such as plantains and groundfood, while a new parcel was cut to secure that year's rice and corn crops. By the third year of cultivation, farm labor inputs increased and yields declined due to weed competition. In the past, the farmer would usually fallow the land at this point for at least five to ten years.

The transition to citrus farming occurring on area farms develops out of the traditional milpa system. When initiating an orange or grapefruit farm, farmers clear a parcel of land and plant staple crops on it, as in the first year of the shifting cultivation cycle. Thereafter, they intercrop young citrus trees with plantains and groundfood. To grow to bearing maturity, the trees require applications of fertilizer and other inputs not associated with traditional agriculture. After the farm has been in cultivation for three years, the farmer begins clearing secondary growth with agrochemicals and machinery. As the trees ap-

Cooperative labor in roof thatching—Hopkins.

proach maturity and compete with staple crops, the latter are removed. If a full complement of inputs is employed in this process, citrus trees may bear a commercial crop within five years of planting. As will be seen in the next chapter, the cost of these inputs far exceeds the investable income of milpa farming households, constituting the major obstacle to tree cropping among shifting cultivators.

Although young citrus trees demand specialized skills and inputs, the labor involved in planting them does not initially conflict with the scheduling of milpa crops. Preparing seedbeds, budding young trees, transferring them to the farm, and fertilizing them are completed in the months after new milpas have been planted. Young citrus trees in the farm are kept clean of weed growth by machete and the use of herbicides (usually paraquat) throughout the year. As trees approach maturity and milpa crops are removed, farmers rent a tractor and bushhog to clear the groves of secondary growth. Severe scheduling conflicts between staples and citrus develop once the trees begin producing fruit. Grapefruit and orange harvests begin in October and continue through February. During harvest season in Silk Grass, family members who otherwise do not work on the farm are called on to help harvest the fruit. Households possessing more than eight acres of bearing citrus always hire labor to assist in harvesting, as do many small households having fewer acres. Because the citrus harvest coincides with the ripening of milpa rice, households with mature citrus trees find it virtually impossible to cultivate both crops. Many Silk Grass citrus growers have continued to produce some corn by planting fast-growing hybrids. Nonetheless, the transition to citrus farming has sacrificed household self-sufficiency in rice, the most important local staple, due to its irreconcilable labor demands with citrus.

NONFARMING LIVELIHOODS

Important as agriculture is in household subsistence, it is not the sole or even primary livelihood for most rural residents. In Hopkins, fishing remains an important subsistence activity for most families. Of all Hopkins households, 62 percent contain at least one member who fishes, but the frequency with which individuals fish and the extent to which households rely on fishing as an income source vary greatly. About 28 percent of all male heads of household fish exclusively for subsistence, doing so no more than once or twice per week. Despite their skill as sailors, subsistence fishermen employ shallow dugout dories that are not sufficiently seaworthy to reach commercial fishing areas ten or more miles from the coast. A part-time fisherman's average catch of five pounds of mackerel or mullet per fishing trip might feed his family for two days. Any surplus above the family's immediate needs is salted and dried, given to kin in other households, or sold to neighbors. As a part-time subsistence activity, fishing is easily combined with agricultural and wage labor.

Commercial fishing demands much more time and larger cash outlays than subsistence fishing and preempts many other economic activities. Only 9 percent of male heads of household in Hopkins own dories adequate for fishing at the cayes or deep water beyond the barrier reef. Because each of these men works with one or two partners, however, many villagers with little capital of their own depend on commercial fishing. Fishermen acknowledge that partnerships are often uneasy alliances, and many would prefer to work by themselves if they could own equipment and safely manage it by themselves. Men are at the mercy of their boat-owning partners as to the timing and duration of the trip and the choice of markets. The boat owner also withholds an equal share of the catch "for the boat" to defray its operating expenses. Men often complain that boat owners exaggerate the amount of fuel used to shift the burden of operating expenses onto them. Lacking any recourse if boat owners take advantage of them, fishermen without equipment of their own tolerate such aspects of the partnership, albeit with scarcely concealed resentment.

Fishermen rarely go to sea every day, preferring instead to make trips of three to fourteen days' duration, during which they remain at camps on the cayes. Fresh fish need not be sold immediately, since most fishermen keep their catch alive in smacks or offshore pens until the volume of fish warrants a trip to market. Fishermen remain at sea for even longer periods during the spawning seasons of several species that account for most of their annual incomes. The most intensive labor inputs in fishing correspond to Lent season, grouper season (late November to early January), and snapper season (May to July). During these periods, fishermen often stay at the cayes for months at a time, returning infrequently to the mainland to replenish their supplies, market their catch, and briefly rest before their next journey. The ease of marketing fish through cooperatives, which control export outlets in Belize, has made certain types of fishing profitable by local standards. Part-time fishermen who are partners of boat owners report incomes of over Bze $1,000 for the five- to six-week grouper season, a sum that far exceeds the earnings generated by most sources of day labor available in the district.

While some farmers and fishermen realize considerable earnings, wage labor in general holds no such promise. Some 84 percent of Hopkins households and 68 percent in Silk Grass contain wage-earning members, yet only a handful of these individuals hold full-time employment. For most villagers, wage employment is seasonal, low-paying piecework known in Creole as catch and kill or jack and bolt. Village residents often describe the pursuit of wages as hustling to piece together a living from various kinds of formal employment and infrequent odd jobs for other villagers. Wage returns from the employment available to village residents vary considerably. The lowest-paying casual labor available—day labor for other residents—averages Bze $12 per day for farm work paid on a piece rate basis. Unlike Hopkins residents, men in Silk Grass have access to two sources of full-time nonmigratory labor. The Jamaican investor who usurped the lands once used by Silk Grass farmers hires ten local men for agricultural labor at Bze $13 per day, a level that is low by district standards and much resented by employees. The other nearby source of full-time employment, a government-run sawmill, pays Bze $20 or more per day but offers relatively few jobs.

Many rural residents are seasonally employed in citrus harvest labor on farms throughout the district. Harvesting citrus on company estates is migratory labor, the workers residing for up to five months in shanty-like camps at Alta Vista, Pomona, and Middlesex in the Stann Creek valley. Both processors pay Bze $.50 per ninety-pound bag of harvested fruit, which averages Bze $100 per six-day week. The much smaller citrus farmers of Silk Grass and Hopkins also employ their neighbors or family members during reaping (harvest) season. Although the quantity and duration of work available on small farms are much less than those on corporate estates, local citrus growers pay higher wages than the companies. Since 1983 some Hopkins women have also periodically worked at South Stann Creek, some seventeen miles south of Hopkins, in packing bananas for export. For their labor women are paid Bze $1.40 per hour, a rate 35 percent lower than comparable employment held by men.

The only exception to these forms of low wage employment is periodic waterfront work by fourteen members of the United General Workers' Union in Hopkins. These residents work together on the Dangriga waterfront to load drums of frozen citrus concentrate on ships bound for foreign markets. The waterfront workers in Hopkins form part of a roster of six work gangs that await job assignments when shipments of concentrate are to be made. During the processing season between November and June, each gang receives up to four work assignments of twelve hours each. Because payment for this work varies according to the performance of the entire gang, workers have a strong incentive to load as many drums as possible. Although they work only three to four shifts per year, waterfront workers may earn more than Bze $300 per shift. As will be seen in chapter 5, these high wages are the result of the union's assertive negotiations with the citrus companies and have made waterfront work one of the most eagerly sought forms of employment in the district.

For most younger rural residents, the most promising livelihoods are not to be found in the village itself. Since the 1940s, when several men from Hopkins and Silk Grass volunteered for war-related work abroad, hundreds of villagers have sought job opportunities in the United

States. Despite stricter immigration laws, diminished prospects for employment in the United States, and the disillusionment of returning or deported migrants, the United States exerts a powerful pull on rural residents, particularly young men. The rate of outmigration from Belize, already one of the highest in the Caribbean, has accelerated in recent years. Some Belizeans attribute this to the influence of television, which only became available in 1982. Belizean television consists for the most part of intercepted United States programming, which portrays an array of consumer goods not remotely attainable in Belize. In the brief period since its introduction, at least one study already associates exposure to television with greater aspirations to migrate (Chaffee 1986).

As expatriate communities formed in New York, Chicago, and Los Angeles in the 1960s, communities of origin in Belize started to receive earnings from abroad. By the mid-1970s, according to the U.S. State Department, the number of Belizean migrants in the United States was approximately equal to the remaining working population in Belize (Pastor 1985: 19). By 1986, close to one-fourth of all adults born in Hopkins resided in Chicago alone. Some of these migrants periodically remit cash or consumer goods to family members in the village. Most recipients are elderly parents who lack other sources of income, but occasionally earnings are sent back as contributions to the village school or health center.

Generally, remittances in rural Belize are expended on consumer goods rather than directly productive investments, similar to patterns noted elsewhere in the Caribbean and Latin America (cf. Massey et al. 1987: 216). Among a few Hopkins and Silk Grass residents, income from remittances can attain quite substantial levels, but such earnings have little direct effect on village subsistence activities since their recipients are well past their productive years. Several returning migrants in Hopkins used their savings to purchase outboard motors for commercial fishing, but no comparable purchases were noted among remittance recipients. Residents of both villages contend that remittance levels in general have declined and become more sporadic since the early 1980s. If remittances have had little effect on villagers' subsistence activities, they have nonetheless had a striking visual impact upon the village. Approximately two-thirds of the cement houses in the village have been constructed with remittances, mainly for migrants who intend to return one day to retire.

While outmigration has made little direct contribution to the village

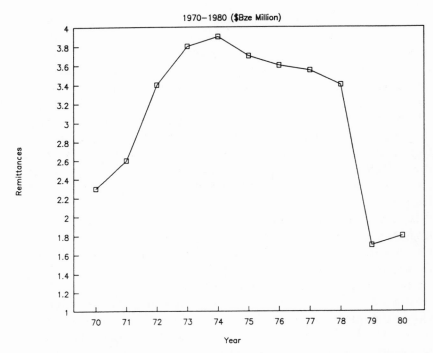

Figure 4. Foreign remittances: 1970–1980 ($Bze million). Source: Government of Belize (1970–1980).

economy, through the loss of much of the young population it has had a significant effect on village economy and social relations. Villagers attribute increased theft and diminished cooperation to outmigration, since young men easily avoid community sanctions by leaving the community. Older villagers complain that the desire to emigrate instills little incentive among the young to learn trades or invest time in local livelihoods. Paradoxically, as emigration attracts ever more rural Belizeans, the conditions faced by migrants in the United States have deteriorated. Like most of the African-American population, with whom they compete for jobs, Belizean immigrants experienced a decline in their standard of living during the 1980s. Between 1970 and 1980, the value of remittances from the United States fell over 40 percent, a trend apparent from figure 4. The decline in remittances sent to Belize from its migrants abroad was attributed "to a shortage of job opportunities for Belizeans in the U.S.A." (Government of Belize 1980: 19).

SOCIAL RELATIONS OF PRODUCTION

In both Silk Grass and Hopkins, the household is the primary unit of production and consumption, although it is variously defined and its boundaries are often fluid. Regardless of ethnicity, most Silk Grass households consist of male-headed nuclear or extended families in which the primary adults are married or joined in a common-law relationship. Relationships between men and women in their twenties are often transitory and noncoresidential due to the great mobility of younger men. As older adults form coresidential unions, their households usually include the woman's children from previous relationships. Legally, men are considered responsible for supporting their outside children (those resulting from previous or current liaisons and residing with their mothers in other households). In actuality, males have a good deal of freedom from these obligations. Women and their parents frequently provide complete support for such offspring. Young mothers reside with their parents, as do most young men, until they establish independent households in their late twenties or thirties. A number of Silk Grass households defy categorization as conjugal families or their variants. Three female-headed consanguineal families exist in the village, including one consisting of several kinswomen, their mates, and children (table 3).

Greater variability exists among Hopkins households, although their most common form remains that of male-headed nuclear or extended families. The next most frequent variant, making up 22 percent of all, consists of female-headed consanguineal households. These are composed of an adult woman, her children, and frequently her mother and one or more sisters. One consanguineal household within the village constitutes a compound of several residences on a single houselot, each house occupied by a different kinswoman and her children. Households of this sort retain common funds (cf. Wolf 1966) from which their members ensure their subsistence and deploy labor cooperatively. Finally, in both villages a few households consist of single individuals, most of whom are elderly and dependent on remittances or family members elsewhere for support.

In Hopkins, and to a lesser extent in Silk Grass, interhousehold exchanges, both of goods and personnel, make household boundaries highly permeable. As individuals mature and enter into and leave conjugal relationships, they move through successive households. Occa-

Table 3. Household Composition in Both Villages

Form	Mean Size	Frequency	Percent of Total
Hopkins (n = 57)			
Male-headed nuclear	6.1	28	50
Male-headed extended	8.1	12	21
Female-headed nuclear	6.5	11	19
Female-headed extended	10.5	2	3
Female-headed compounds	12	1	1
Single individuals	1	2	3
Silk Grass (n = 25)			
Male-headed nuclear	6.2	14	56
Male-headed extended	5.5	8	32
Female-headed nuclear	5	1	4
Female-headed extended	8	1	4
Female-headed compounds	9	1	4
Single individuals	—	0	0

sionally individuals contribute simultaneously to different households according to their varying functions within those units. In Silk Grass, for example, one man jointly cultivates inherited land with his brother, provides labor on the farm of his common-law mate, and supports children in yet another household. In Hopkins the delimitation of household boundaries is even more complex, as some children and elderly individuals take meals in households other than those in which they sleep. The cycling of individuals between Hopkins residences is part of a larger ethic of reciprocity that links families in continuing exchanges of goods and labor. Despite the instances of cooperation that bind them to each other in response to adversity, villagers cling to an ideal of autonomy unfettered by obligations. Residents assert that "you have to help yourself" to achieve economic well-being, since obligations to others only diffuse a chance windfall or profit. It is indicative of the poverty of Hopkins residents that few households can afford the comparative luxury of such individualism.

The nonmonetary exchanges that occur between Hopkins households generally take place along lines of kinship. Except for fishermen, who prefer partnerships with nonkin, most local cooperation in production occurs between siblings in different households. This usually takes the form of labor contributions by men and women on the farms of their siblings or other relatives. Because those who contribute work may farm little or no land of their own, their labor contributions may be repaid with some farm produce. Hiring labor for wages occurs in Hopkins, but generally among unrelated individuals, while relatives either receive labor or produce in exchange for previous work. Where no labor is directly exchanged between close kinsmen in Hopkins, food items are often exchanged in nonmonetary transactions (cf. Palacio 1981). Food exchanges often integrate households emphasizing different forms of production. A fisherman, for example, will give his siblings a portion of his catch with the future expectation of farm produce in return. Alternately, food is exchanged in times of individual hardship or when similar foods are produced at different times. Men who raise pigs will sell most of their pork at the time of slaughter but will also offer meat to other pig keepers in exchange for some of their pork at a later date.

In contrast, nonmonetary exchanges between related households in Silk Grass almost never occur. Farmers prefer to employ the labor of relatives rather than nonkin, but this labor is hired at prevailing wage rates and is rarely reciprocated. The lack of reciprocity in labor exchange is due to citrus growers employing their nonfarming or small farming relatives. Small farmers rarely require nonhousehold labor but are hired by wealthier relatives on citrus farms where seasonal labor absorption is high. When villagers exchange produce it is also usually sold, even to close relatives in other households. There are no apparent differences in nonmonetary labor exchange among members of the different ethnic groups which comprise Silk Grass. Maya and Garifuna residents, whose forebears reciprocated labor and produce in nonmonetary exchanges, are as likely as Creoles to hire their relatives for wages when they require additional labor.

Contrary to Taylor's claim that formal work groups ceased to exist in Belizean Garifuna villages by the 1940s (1951: 56), a few Hopkins men continue to contribute to a form of village cooperative labor known as *fajina*. In addition, much informal labor sharing takes place when houses are erected or when women prepare food for ceremonial occasions. According to older residents, villagewide *fajina* predated the settlement of Hopkins, the displaced residents of Newtown having brought the practice with them. Through the 1950s work parties of eighty or more people met weekly to clear village common areas of undergrowth and to maintain the school, public latrines, and beaches. Older residents note that *fajina* contributions were required of men between the ages of eighteen and sixty. The village headman, or *alcalde*, imposed small fines each time men failed to participate. The *alcalde* was an elected leader who served as the main governing authority of Garifuna villages in Belize until the village council system found throughout British colonies was introduced in the late 1940s. The village council suspended penalties for noninvolvement in *fajina* around 1960, and labor contributions to village work groups steadily declined after that. As will be seen in chapter 5, large-scale cooperative labor later succumbed to a government work program that provided patronage awards for supporters of the ruling political party. *Fajina* nominally exists today, but its participants are drawn exclusively from one of two political factions and rarely number more than ten men.

Creole villages do not have a tradition of organized cooperative labor, and past efforts to introduce *fajina* in Silk Grass have been notably unsuccessful. In the early 1970s, the village chairman, a Garifuna man originally from Hopkins, tried to organize work parties among village residents. He eventually enlisted thirteen men, most of whom were recent Maya settlers, to clean the village sports field, footpaths, and school buildings. Florentino Bol, a Maya resident who participated in such efforts, recounted an instance in which he helped the group clean the school's pit latrine. As they were in the midst of this particularly noisome task, Bol noticed several Creole residents standing at a distance and laughing about their predicament. Bol returned home in fury and never rejoined later *fajina* groups. All further efforts to organize work parties in Silk Grass were suspended after the mid-1970s for lack of volunteers.

In comparison to Hopkins, where the remaining *fajina* participants clean undergrowth from common areas, much of the village has an unkempt, slightly overgrown appearance. While Maya residents expressed the most interest in village cooperative labor in the past, there is no longer any labor exchange among the remaining Maya households in Silk Grass. As Florentino expressed it, "We've gotten to be like these other nations here. Now we go our own way; nobody works together, no matter they race."

Former alcalde *of Hopkins, holding ceremonial staff of office.*

MEN AND WOMEN IN THE DOMESTIC ECONOMY

Unlike their Maya and Creole counterparts, Garifuna women have an ongoing direct role in agricultural production. In Hopkins, nearly half of all households maintain at least two farms, one devoted to marketable crops, such as grains, plantains, and citrus, and another devoted entirely to groundfood. Women assume primary responsibility for maintaining and harvesting the latter, although they also work on their men's farms during periods of peak labor demand, such as planting and harvesting. Hopkins residents make a distinction between plantations or bush (*icari* or *arab*) and cassava or groundfood farms (*gaiage*). Further, they often state that men work on the former while women work on the latter. In reality, neither type of farm is entirely segregated by sex. In addition to women's work on men's farms, men are responsible for clearing new sections of their women's farms, as well as a certain amount of labor in weeding and harvesting.

From earlier ethnographic data from Hopkins (Taylor 1951: 56 ff.), it is evident that the sexual division of labor in village agriculture has changed radically in recent years. Hopkins men themselves note that their agricultural roles were far more limited in the past than at present. In the late 1940s Taylor reported that men confined their involvement in agriculture to clearing farms that were then cultivated by women for the remainder of the year (ibid.). Local men maintain that this pattern characterized farming practices among most village households well into the 1970s, after which many men came to view agriculture as a year-round albeit still part-time occupation.

In accounting for the shift in male and female agricultural roles it is useful to analyze the economic activities of conjugal households in terms of their subsistence and cash-earning dimensions. Female and male domains in Garifuna households were traditionally demarcated along such lines, men satisfying the bulk of the household's income requirements with fishing and migratory wage labor and women procuring domestic staples. The growth of the cash-earning potential of farming since the early 1970s has been accompanied by a concomitant expansion of the role of men in agriculture. Nearly all crop sales occur in produce grown on "men's" farms, men almost always conduct the transactions in such crops, and they generally control their proceeds.

When an agricultural cooperative was organized in Hopkins to develop commercial citrus farming in 1982, women, the village's traditional agriculturalists, were conspicuously absent from the membership roll. While the matrifocal character of Garifuna households has been previously widely noted (Gonzalez 1969, 1988; Kerns 1983), it remains to be seen whether this attribute will persist with increased village involvement in agricultural markets. Garifuna women traditionally derived much of their domestic authority from their role in subsistence and the transient nature of male involvement in the household. As men increasingly enter commercial agriculture, their presence in the household and community has become more permanent than in the past, undoubtedly augmenting their domestic authority. In the process of market incorporation in Hopkins, it is likely that women may be marginalized in a manner akin to development processes elsewhere (Beneria and Sen 1981).

The range of productive activities of Creole women in Silk Grass is somewhat narrower than that of Hopkins residents. Some Creole women assist their men in agricultural work, but only when male household labor is insufficient for seasonal tasks, such as planting or harvesting. As a rule they do not maintain separate farms nor do they concentrate on the production of particular crops. Silk Grass women also do not engage in wage labor, with the exception of two village women employed as schoolteachers. In the village's more entrepreneurial families, such as those operating shops or "clubs," women take a more active part than their men in managing the family business, since the men are engaged in full-time farming. With this exception, women in Creole households predominate in domestic rather than productive labor and take a leading role in production only if the male head of household departs, becomes incapacitated, or dies. Despite their traditionally greater emphasis on agriculture, Maya households in Silk Grass conform to a similar sexual division of labor. In the village's Garifuna households, the division of labor more closely approximates that of Hopkins, women spending more time in agricultural labor than their Creole or Maya neighbors. No female Garifuna residents of Silk Grass maintain farms separate from those of their men, however, nor do any work for wages.

The contribution of children to domestic production is limited by their attendance at school, which is compulsory through standard six, the equivalent of eighth grade. Young children in both villages are nonetheless expected to complete certain tasks before and after school and during weekends and holidays. By the time they enter school at the age of five, boys and girls are already assisting their mothers in simple domestic tasks. As soon as they are able to carry a ten-gallon pail of water, children are given much of the responsibility for drawing water for household use. Because wells are located some distance from most residences, this represents a substantial expenditure of time and energy for small children. By the age of eight or nine, children accompany their parents to the farm in the predawn hours to collect firewood or bring food crops back to the village. Children haul bundles of wood or crops with a tumpline around the forehead, often carrying loads in excess of twenty pounds for two to three miles. Upon finishing these chores, children wash, "drink tea," and leave in time for school at eight o'clock.

As children grow older, they are assigned more sex-specific tasks. Girls from ten through adolescence continue to collect water and firewood but spend more time in tasks at home, especially child care and meal preparation. By age twelve, most males cease to make direct domestic contributions, except for carrying firewood when returning from the farm. When a boy finishes school he generally accompanies his father or other male household head to the farm or on fishing trips. If he is the oldest male in the household, most of his time is spent assisting his mother on her farm until he eventually establishes one of his own.

Often, however, the farm labor contributions of adolescent and young adult males after finishing school are slight and made grudgingly. Many Creole and Garifuna males leave their natal villages at this point to pursue the allure of wage labor elsewhere, which they consider more rewarding than village opportunities. Even if the pursuit of work takes them permanently away from the village, as is usually the case when young men migrate to the United States, parents recognize the value of their children as old age support. When referring to the gifts and remittances they receive from their grown children, older men and women occasionally cite the Creole proverb that "Pikni da po' people's riches" (Children are the assets of the poor).

THE CONVERGENCE OF SUBSISTENCE TRADITIONS

Notwithstanding their close proximity, Hopkins and Silk Grass represent cultural microcosms. It is not uncommon to encounter residents of one village who have never visited the other, and misconceptions abound in each village concerning its neighbor. Some Creoles in Silk Grass, for example, describe the rarely performed ancestral rites in Hopkins as "devil worship," a slur apparently as old as some of the earliest published accounts of the Garifuna (cf. Kerns 1983: 74). Given the scant contact existing between the communities and the varying culture histories of Creoles and Garifuna, it is not surprising that village economies have been so dissimilar for so long.

The foregoing description adopts the perspective of an idealized ethnographic present, for existing points of contrast are rapidly vanishing under the impact of an expanding world economy. To a moderately attentive observer, it is facile to discern differences between the villages today and to find echoes of earlier ethnologists' descriptions in contemporary practices. Male labor migration and female participation in agriculture, both of which are readily encountered in Hopkins today, may suggest direct continuities with practices documented in earlier ethnographic studies (cf. Conzemius 1928; Taylor 1951; Gonzalez 1969). Yet analysis of a changing rural political economy cannot be informed by the search for cultural "survivals," most of them ceremonial, that animates many studies of the Garifuna in Central America. If change, rather than stasis, orients observation and analysis, a rather different view of local economies emerges; one of a convergence between villages, rather than persisting divergent traditions.

Convergence is apparent in the roles of men and women in the domestic economy, where male contributions to agriculture in Hopkins now approach levels found in Creole settlements. It is found as well in the variety of crops that men have chosen to cultivate in both villages, which represents a willful rejection of the unprofitable production of staples for domestic markets. Finally, convergence is becoming evident in the structural consequences of these individual decisions for local communities, where class divisions are arising on the basis of export agriculture. Such changes may seem inconspicuous in the face of exotic "survivals," but they are not easily reconciled with earlier cultural traditions. New subsistence patterns and social relations threaten to supplant older ones entirely. It is the cause of these irreversible, if still nascent, changes that will be the subject of the following chapter.

CHAPTER 4

HOUSEHOLD ECONOMIES WITHIN

A CHANGING WORLD SYSTEM

The changes taking place in household economies throughout Stann Creek district today ultimately stem from nonlocal factors that make some alternatives more attractive than others. Food policies established by the state for political expediency have unintended and contradictory consequences for staple crop producers at the village level. Increased demand for certain commodities in metropolitan markets creates powerful albeit short-lived incentives for agricultural change. Although many have suffered the vicissitudes of past booms and busts, villagers are not positioned to fully apprehend the causes of volatile commodity cycles. This chapter examines the policy and market factors influencing rural households to elucidate local economic change within a global context. As is demonstrated at the end of the chapter, changing economic strategies do not simply alter the subsistence base of rural households. As some villagers enter lucrative export production while others are confined to less profitable alternatives, a newly stratified rural social order also emerges, one characterized by increasingly inequitable income distribution and growing consolidation of land by citrus producers.

THE POLITICAL ECONOMY OF STAPLE CROP PRODUCTION

Several investigators (Ashcraft 1973; Bolland and Shoman 1977) have attributed contemporary deficits in staple crop production to the legacy of a colonial economy dominated by the forest products industry.

As noted in chapter 2, the forestry-mercantile class alliance that controlled colonial institutions also neglected the roads and marketing infrastructure necessary to support domestic agriculture. In the postforestry period, as official antagonism to staple crop production waned, a major impediment remained in the form of a small population that generates little demand for most staples. This itself is an artifact of the country's colonial history, stemming largely from Britain's uncertain sovereignty and consequent discouragement of settlement in the colonial era (cf. Grant 1976; Wright et al. 1959). If selling produce directly to town consumers, farmers usually lack any prior knowledge of market conditions and often find markets glutted with unsaleable crops when they arrive in town. The problems resulting from limited demand in local and national markets are magnified during the harvest seasons of staple crops when, as one Silk Grass farmer expressed it, "ten pound of plantain bring profit, but one hundred pound de bring loss."

In addition to the colonial legacy of rudimentary roads and markets and preferences for imported foods, shortfalls in Belizean staple crop production have been attributed to the country's unpredictable rainfall and destructive tropical storms. Hall (1983) notes that variable climatic conditions adversely affect individual farmers, who are rarely able to maximize crop output as a result. Environmental hazards lead to an aversion to input-intensive farming, for producers fear that the cost of inputs would not be recouped in the event of bad weather and a meager harvest. While climatic risk complicates agricultural decision making for individual farmers, in the aggregate its effects are more difficult to determine. Deviations in precipitation from long-term averages are mostly evident between locales, rather than over the nation as a whole. Nor do climatic fluctuations by themselves account for long-term trends in agricultural production. Belize attained record harvests of staple crops between 1978 and 1982, yet this period did not correspond to particularly favorable climatic conditions.

With the exception of Hall's work, analyses of Belizean agricultural deficits attribute contemporary conditions in staple crop agriculture to factors originating in the past. Wright et al. (1959), Ashcraft (1973), and Bolland and Shoman (1977) all identify critical impediments to food production during the colonial era. Yet no extant analysis of Belizean agriculture is wholly adequate in the present. All previous observers have attempted to explain contemporary production trends (which are in fact highly variable) in terms of constants. Explanations such as the following presuppose stagnation in production levels of domestic crops and imply that cultural-historical factors will override market considerations in determining farmers' production strategies:

> The quantity produced by small-scale farmers . . . does not vary according to price patterns set at the market, but instead according to extra-market factors. Productive decisions reflect commitments to traditional crops, traditional agricultural methods, transportation problems, the presence of estate agriculture, availability of wage-work, and the limitations imposed by . . . a burdensome exchange system. (Ashcraft 1973: 147)

Neither the effects of colonial labor control and land use practices nor agroclimatic risk can entirely account for contemporary agriculturalists' production decisions. Contrary to the common characterization of Belizean agriculture as one of unrelieved stagnation, production data suggest that farmers do respond to market factors. These data also imply that, theoretically, self-sufficiency in staple crop production is not precluded by past factors.

Primary among the factors directly affecting Belizean farmers' decisions about commercial food production is the institution responsible for national food policy. Since 1948, most transactions in staple crops have been handled by the Belize Marketing Board, a government agency that purchases rice, corn, and RK beans from farmers, processes them, and then wholesales them to retail outlets nationwide. Until 1985 the marketing board also exclusively controlled the importation of staple foods, but it has since partly delegated that role to private retailers by issuing import licenses. By its effective monopoly on the processing of rice and regulation of staple imports, the marketing board has become the primary means of implementing state policy toward food and agriculture. The board was established to encourage national self-sufficiency in staple crop production, which remains its stated goal to this day. In actuality, the marketing board's objectives have shifted repeatedly since its creation. These changes have caused severely fluctuating levels of service and prices to rural producers. The result has been that many farmers have altogether ceased to sell staple crops to the marketing board. Because the board is the only local purchaser of paddy rice in most areas, however, commercial rice producers cannot select other markets if they find its prices and services to be unsatisfactory.

When farmers decide to sell their produce to the government, they arrange for the transportion of their harvest to a marketing board buying depot. There the produce is analyzed for moisture and foreign matter levels. If these measures fall within the board's allowable levels, the farmer is paid according to a sliding scale based on the crop's foreign matter and moisture content. Producers of minimally acceptable paddy rice, for example, are paid approximately 40 percent less than the maximum price. Because the procedure is repeated for every bag of rice, corn, or beans that the farmer wishes to sell, he must bring his entire harvest to the buying depot without any assurance that it will be purchased. It is not uncommon for the board to reject the harvests of milpa rice farmers for excessive moisture, forcing them to find alternative buyers on the spot or return home to further dry their paddy.

In addition to the uncertainty of transactions with the marketing board, residents of Silk Grass and Hopkins who had formerly sold crops to the board remain highly distrustful of its operations. Several farmers allege that the board's buying agents in Silk Grass paid them for minimally acceptable produce and then pocketed the difference between the purchase price and the crop's actual value. In the 1970s, when the marketing board maintained several buying depots in each district (including one in Silk Grass), transportation costs were minor for most farmers. If crop sales to the government were risky and suspect, then, they were at least convenient. By the mid-1980s, however, the board had closed half its previous outlets, including its Silk Grass buying center. Presently, residents of Hopkins and Silk Grass would have to travel seventy miles to the nation's capital, Belmopan, to sell their rice to the marketing board. The government's decision to close many buying depots is related less to budgetary constraints than to a secular decline in crop sales to the board. Because many buying centers were conducting so little business after 1983 the board found no point in keeping them open.

By formal mandate, the marketing board is obliged to calculate producer prices that cover production costs and afford the farmer a "reasonable" monetary return to his labor. In actuality, the upper limit of producer prices is not governed by farmers' costs but by a complex system of retail controls and consumer price ceilings. Since 1963, retail staple prices have been controlled by the government's Price Control Advisory Board, which fixes maximum consumer prices for domestically grown staples and regulates retailers' profit margins for imported foods. In reviewing retail price ceilings, a past government committee acknowledged "the need to encourage local production as much as possible, but we also see the need to protect the interests of the consumer . . . And the majority who make up the state must therefore be protected" (Government of Belize 1971: 28). Insofar as producer prices are constrained by consumer price controls, the board's implicit objective has been to "keep prices of staple foods to the urban consumers in Belize City relatively low" (Robinson 1983: 94).

Price controls are reflected in a widening gap between staple food prices and other consumer goods. While overall consumer prices in Belize recorded an approximately 240 percent increase between 1971 and 1986, consumer prices of most staples were permitted only a 40 percent increase during the same period (World Bank 1984: 22; Government of Belize 1986). For two of the three primary staples, rice and corn, retail prices in 1989 remained at the level established eight years earlier. Fixed consumer prices have been attained by suppressing the price that producers receive for their crops. With the exception of the period between 1978 and 1982, marketing board producer prices since 1971 increased at only one-third the rate of the overall cost of living. It is apparent, then, that government policies have favored town residents at the expense of rural producers, despite the marketing board's stated goal of promoting staple production. This fact is not lost among farmers, many of whom "feel that they subsidize urban nonproducers, while they are themselves forced to live at subsistence level with insufficient returns to encourage increased production" (MacInnes 1983: 106).

The government's attempt to deliver low-cost food to urban populations via price controls has strongly discouraged staple crop production in rural areas. Rice production in the mid-1980s was no greater than levels attained fifteen years earlier, despite a 25 percent growth in national population in the interim (Government of Belize 1971–1988). Pricing policies discourage the use of mechanization or chemical inputs promoted by the government as a means of increasing agricultural output. According to government agronomists, mechanized rice production utilizing rented equipment requires an investment of Bze $174 per acre, but net returns were only Bze $58 more than an acre of milpa rice, which requires no cash inputs of any kind (Aldana and Lee 1982). Under prevailing market conditions for paddy rice, in which a milpa farmer would realize a gross income of Bze $390 per acre under ideal conditions, it is doubtful that the rural poor would invest so substantially in staple production merely to increase their cash returns by about 15 percent. When one takes into account such slight potential profits, as well as the riskiness and transportation costs inherent in sales to the marketing board, it is understandable why farmers are reluctant to expand the scale of staple crop production or to rely upon it as an exclusive income source. The same disincentives account for the fact that almost all staple crop farming in Belize is practiced under low-intensity milpa agriculture.

In the mid-1970s policymakers attempted to address the growing contradiction between pricing policies that favored urban consumers and self-sufficiency in crop production. Beginning in 1975 the marketing board steadily increased producer prices to stimulate cultivation of rice, corn, and beans, whose importation had become a major contributor to the country's balance of payments deficits. Revised producer prices had a dramatic effect on staple crop production, as rural residents delivered record volumes of crops to marketing board outlets. Between 1978 and 1983, production nearly doubled for the three primary staples, moving the country from a staple crop importer to a net food exporter. Yet in the same period that it increased producer prices between 30 percent (for rice and corn) and 100 percent (in the case of RK beans), the government also retained consumer price controls. This decision entailed government subsidization of marketing board operations. By 1983, the board's purchasing activities had sustained Bze $2.4 million in losses, which coincided with a period of sharply falling revenues from taxes, duties, and exports due to contraction in the world economy (see chapter 1).

In its worsening economic situation, the government adopted an austerity budget in 1983 and applied for standby credits from the International Monetary Fund (IMF) in the following year (Economist 1985: 23). These credits were obtained only when the Belizean government surrendered effective control over its revenue and budgetary policies to the IMF. Among the IMF's conditions for standby credits were an end to government subsidies for several insolvent state agencies and utilities, including the marketing board. At this point the government faced two mutually exclusive options: either modify its system of retail price controls or remove the incentives it had earlier introduced for farmers. Rather than lifting price ceilings that benefited urban consumers, the government returned the marketing board to solvency by lowering producer prices during the 1983 growing season. Relative to the previous year, 1983 crop prices were slashed 12 percent in the case of rice and 32 percent for beans.

These reductions had a devastating effect on staple crop production nationwide. Although the board has operated free of subsidy since the 1983 revision of its pricing policies, it has also greatly curtailed its purchases of domestic crops. When interviewed in 1986, the board's director acknowledged that it had become a market of "last resort" for most staple crop producers. Since small-scale rice producers lack any alternative market, however, the board's drop in prices has caused many simply to withdraw from commercial rice production. This can be inferred from the fact that Belizean rice production by 1984 had fallen to just half the level attained two years earlier.

The deficits that have accrued in domestic crop production since 1983 have been made up by importation of surplus grain from the United States and neighboring countries. Since the devaluation of the Guatemalan and Mexican currencies in 1982 and 1983, unauthorized importers have sold grains to retail outlets at prices far below those of the marketing board. As domestic rice production fell in the wake of price reductions, the marketing board itself began to make up deficits through increased importation from the United States and issuance of import licenses to private wholesalers. In allowing producer prices to settle to free market levels, the board has discovered that many Belizean farmers will not commercially produce staple crops for as little as the crops can be imported from other countries.

The indexed relationship between producer prices, staple production, and food importation is indicated in figure 5 (actual values for prices, domestic purchases, and importation between 1978 and 1983 are provided in table 4). Steadily increasing producer prices after 1978 were reflected in increased deliveries of crops to marketing board facilities and in diminished reliance on imported foods. By 1982, a year of peak producer prices, the marketing board processed record volumes of domestically produced staples, eliminating all reliance on imported rice and reducing importation of corn and RK beans to a fraction of their 1979 levels. Following drastic reductions in producer prices in 1983 and 1984, farmers' deliveries to the marketing board also declined, while legal staple imports began once again to rise. Given the proliferation of contraband importing since 1983, official figures probably suggest only a portion of the staples imported into Belize since that year.

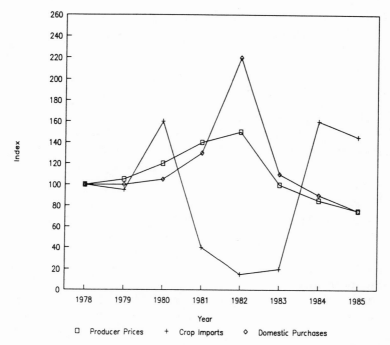

Figure 5. Crop prices, purchases, and imports: Marketing Board (1978 = 100). Sources: Belize Marketing Board; Government of Belize (1971–1985).

In its decision to import low-cost staples rather than stimulate do-mestic production with higher producer prices, the national govern-ment has strengthened a longstanding "cheap food" policy favoring urban and town consumers. Pricing policies that discriminate against rural producers are prevalent in Latin America and other areas of the Third World and have been implicated by economists in the agricul-tural deficits experienced by such regions. For neoclassical economists (Johnson 1967; Schultz 1968), such policies represent "market distor-tions" that undermine economic growth. From this perspective, food price controls are viewed as expedient measures to control inflation resulting from overvalued currency exchange rates that cheapen im-ported goods for domestic consumption. Overvalued exchange rates and domestic price controls are ultimately self-defeating in that they discourage agricultural production and make exported commodities uncompetitive in world markets. Yet exchange and price control poli-

Table 4. Staple Crop Prices, Domestic Purchases, and Imports:
Belize Marketing Board, 1979–1985

Year	Rice	Corn	RK Beans
1979			
Producer price $Bze/lb.[a]	.18	.13	.45
Purchases (millions lbs.)	4.8	.40	.29
Imports (millions lbs.)	.91	.69	1.1
1980			
Producer price	.21	.15	.60
Purchases	4.5	.75	.18
Imports	.53	3.6	1.4
1981			
Producer price	.21	.22	.80
Purchases	4.7	2.0	.30
Imports	0.0	.45	.50
1982			
Producer price	.26	.22	1.0
Purchases	6.3	5.3	.55
Imports	0.0	.06	.30

cies are politically difficult to resist, since they subsidize the consumption of urban dwellers and provide the illusion of economic development. The recognition that agricultural price policies discriminate against rural residents is also expressed in "populist" interpretations of underdevelopment (cf. Lipton 1977; Chambers 1983), which attribute much responsibility for rural poverty to the purportedly disproportionate political influence of urban masses. Both neoclassical and populist analyses concur that agricultural self-sufficiency requires a rise in producer prices to competitive levels. Only then will farmers deliver crops to urban markets and invest in technological change.

From both the neoclassical and populist perspectives, discriminatory producer prices are interpreted as errors in economic planning that can be rectified through policy changes. While these views cor-

Table 4.
(continued)

Year	Rice	Corn	RK Beans
1983			
Producer price	.23	.16	.68
Purchases	4.0	1.4	.49
Imports[b]	.06	.14	.18
1984			
Producer price	.24	.16	.58
Purchases	3.1	1.8	.06
Imports	.15	4.0	.42
1985			
Producer price	.24	.16	.58
Purchases	3.4	.6	.10
Imports	.17	3.3	.43

Sources: Belize Marketing Board; Government of Belize (1971–1985).
[a] These are maximum marketing board producer prices; actual prices depend on crop foreign matter and moisture levels.
[b] 1983 to 1985 crop import figures indicate only legal imports in these years and are probably low estimates.

rectly implicate price controls in agricultural stagnation, they do not situate such policies within the political economy of underdeveloped nations. Given the ubiquity of food price controls in much of the Third World, as well as the related problems of production and investment in staple crop agriculture, pricing policy merits systematic analysis. Individual errors of policy making cannot logically account for features of underdevelopment that occur consistently throughout the Third World. Further, neoclassical and populist approaches imply that the solution to such problems is politically facile. As the experience of Belize between 1978 and 1982 illustrates, the state is clearly constrained in its ability to revise agricultural pricing policy. Faced with a fiscal crisis resulting from its deteriorating position within the world economy, the Belizean government was forced to select between the alternatives of prourban or prorural food policies. It is no coincidence that it adopted the same policies as states sharing similar positions in the world economy and patterns of capital accumulation.

As noted in chapter 1, the tendency of Third World governments to enact food price controls reflects patterns of capital accumulation based on the employment of low-cost labor. Unlike the sectorally articulated economies of the metropolitan countries, wages in peripheral capitalist economies are not a major source of demand for manufactured items, most of which are exported or consumed by elites. Because accumulation under peripheral capitalism does not entail significant consumer demand among wage earners, wages tend to be suppressed to the minimal levels required to sustain the labor force. This pattern of "disarticulated accumulation" in turn implies a need for low-cost subsistence. Third World governments such as Belize frequently attempt to satisfy this imperative through cheap food policies such as retail price controls or importation of foodstuffs. Where exceptions to this pattern exist, as in the cases of Green Revolution wheat in Mexico and rice in Colombia and the Dominican Republic, high levels of production and investment generally result from massive government subsidies directed toward the commercial farmers who produce such staples. On the other hand, other widely consumed wage foods, such as maize and beans, have not been the objects of research and development or subsidies for production and are increasingly confined to capital-starved farms that comprise the "peasant" sector of Latin America (cf. de Janvry 1981: 124–126).

Empirical support for this pattern of disarticulated accumulation is seen in the worsening income distribution in almost all the countries of Latin America since 1965 despite overall high rates of industrial growth and capital formation (ibid.: 35). The most dynamic sectors of Latin American economies have been those producing export and luxury goods, while industrial sectors that provide wage goods for domestic markets are relatively slow growing (ibid.: 47). In contrast to the United States, where wage rates kept pace with labor productivity in the period 1960 through 1980, real wages have declined throughout Latin America despite levels of industrial labor productivity that compare favorably with the United States (ibid.: 35). In Belize capital investment and manufacturing growth have grown at slower rates than in other nations of Central America, due partly to the small size of the domestic urban work force. Yet an essentially "disarticulated" relationship can be discerned between overall urban incomes and labor productivity in wage sectors. While the former declined in relative terms between 1975 and 1985, labor productivity increased at an annual average of 8 percent over this period (Government of Belize 1970–1980, 1986a, 1986b).

In the Belizean countryside, the consequences of food-pricing policy are apparent from the diminishing contribution of agriculture to rural incomes and farmers' decisions regarding land allocation. Data from Silk Grass suggest a significant deterioration in the contribution of staple crop agriculture to household incomes between 1971 and 1986. In 1971, Silk Grass households on average derived 31 percent of their cash income from staples (Chibnik 1975: 160) but received just 3 percent of their income from these sources in 1986. Formerly most agricultural income had been earned through rice production for the marketing board, with an average of 1.5 acres of rice under cultivation by each household in 1971 (ibid.: 161). By 1986, Silk Grass farmers had abandoned rice production, while the staple crops that remained on their farms were grown mostly for household consumption. The diminishing role of staple crop agriculture in Silk Grass household incomes is illustrated in table 5, which compares aggregate survey data from 1971 and 1986.

Present household production and income-earning decisions are fairly direct reflections of the costs and benefits of alternative economic strategies. At 1986 producer prices, an acre planted in rice, corn, or beans generates between Bze $390 and Bze $590 of net income. The same land planted in orange trees, however, provides over Bze $1,500 of income after the deduction of input costs and other expenses. Evidence from Silk Grass and other Stann Creek district villages indicates that farmers who are able to invest in agricultural inputs readily decide to shift from the production of staple foods to agroexports, which are not price-controlled. Because of the incompatible labor demands mentioned earlier, if a farmer decides to grow citrus as a cash crop he must also abandon rice cultivation on a subsistence basis. Conversely, low-income villagers who produced rice for sale in the early 1970s have since resorted to other sources of income, primarily wages, that offer a higher return for labor. Wage workers, too, have abandoned rice production for subsistence. By 1986, the opportunity costs of rice cultivation (i.e., the income forgone if households allocate labor to rice rather than citrus or wage work) were such that even poorer villagers

Table 5. Silk Grass: Annual Income by Source ($Bze)

Source	1971 Mean Income	Percent of Total	Source	1986 Mean Income	Percent of Total
Staple			Staple		
crops	$253	31	crops	$231	3.2
Wages	439	54	Wages	2,468	34.8
Tree					
crops[a]	93	11	Citrus	3,679	51.8
Fowl and			Fowl and		
other	31	4	livestock	0	0.0
Total	$816	100%	Entrepreneurial[b]	524	7.4
			Remittances	72	1.0
			Processing[c]	75	1.0
			Total	$7,103	100%

Sources: Chibnik (1975); author's survey data.
[a] Includes citrus and coconut sales.
[b] Includes income derived from keeping a village shop, operating a transport service, or renting equipment.
[c] Includes sales of baked goods or coconut oil.

considered it more rational to purchase rice with their earnings than to cultivate it themselves.

THE POLITICAL ECONOMY OF CITRUS FARMING

According to the Citrus Growers' Association of Belize (CGA 1985, 1989), nearly all the grapefruit and oranges grown in Stann Creek district are processed as frozen juice concentrate and exported. Two processing companies, both of which are located in the Stann Creek river valley, control the production and export of citrus products. Belize Food Products (BFP) is a subsidiary of the Nestlé Corporation, and the Citrus Company of Belize (CCB) is controlled by a consortium of Belizean and Trinidadian investors. Most of the country's concentrate production is destined for markets in the English-speaking Caribbean, Canada, and the United Kingdom, where Belizean produce is protected by duties on concentrate of non-Commonwealth origin (Government of Belize 1966). Despite these market guarantees, the Belizean industry was plagued for many years by inefficiencies that raised the costs of production and restricted the profitability of citrus for processors and growers alike. Prices fluctuated on the world market but in general remained so low as to induce little modernization on the part of processors or expansion among growers.

For most small-scale farmers prior to 1975, citrus conferred few income benefits over staple crops grown under milpa conditions and entailed relatively high costs for inputs, budded trees, and maintenance. Even when no more profitable than other crops, however, citrus offered distinct advantages to some small farmers. Under the country's land tenure laws, applications for land title are denied unless at least half the land applied for is "developed" (i.e., cleared or under permanent cultivation). The planting of tree crops, such as citrus or coconuts, thus provides a means for small-scale farmers to formalize their claim to land. Citrus is also attractive to farmers as a source of old-age income because once established it requires much less strenuous labor than milpa farming.

More formidable incentives for citrus production developed in the mid- to late 1970s as world prices for citrus increased. Initially, price increases resulted from heightened consumption of orange juice in metropolitan countries, but several factors combined to send producer prices spiralling upward in the early 1980s. In 1983 and 1985 severe freezes struck northern and central Florida, killing 204,000 acres of citrus trees and causing a loss of U.S. $3 billion in property and revenue. Other setbacks befell the Florida citrus industry in 1984, when citrus canker was discovered in several nurseries, leading agricultural officials to destroy 20 million young trees in an attempt to control the disease. The outbreak of canker did not by itself reduce crop output but greatly impaired the ability of Florida growers to replace trees earlier killed by cold weather. Following these developments international prices for both fresh citrus and concentrate soared, while citrus producers in other nations scrambled to meet the unfulfilled demand in world markets.

Belizean concentrate did not initially compete in the United States market due to the U.S. $.33 per pound duty imposed on foreign concentrate entering the country. Nonetheless, its export price increased 57 percent between 1982 and 1984 solely in response to depleted world market supplies of concentrate (Central Bank of Belize 1985). Concentrate prices continued upward in 1985 as a result of the ratification of the Caribbean Basin Initiative by the United States Congress, which repealed tariffs against citrus products of Caribbean origin (Belize Chamber of Commerce and Industry 1985). For the first time, the expanding American market was opened to Belizean citrus producers.

While the citrus processors realized large profits from world price trends, it was by no means assured that these benefits would be passed on to citrus farmers. Citrus producer prices in Belize were relatively stable prior to 1976 in part because the processors paid no more than necessary to insure continued shipment of fruit to their factories. The companies closely collaborated in setting their annual producer prices in defiance of the country's Citrus Ordinance of 1967, which required that producer prices reflect processors' assets and revenues. Neither the government nor the Citrus Growers' Association (CGA), which ostensibly represented the interests of growers, challenged such price setting. Small farmers had long resented the prices paid for their crops, but most were unaware that processors were in collusion or that dramatic price increases prevailed on world markets. For its part, the CGA leadership was unwilling to challenge pricing practices because the association's managing committee was dominated by large growers with investments in the processing companies.

By the mid-1970s, a younger generation of citrus growers—one with no ties to either processor—had amassed substantial acreage in Stann Creek district. Some of these growers maintained contact with the citrus industry in Florida and knew of the disparity between producer prices in Belize and world prices that reflected strong demand in export markets. Proclaiming themselves allies of the "small man" who would seek more favorable pricing agreements with the processors, these growers urged small-scale farmers to support their candidacies for leadership positions in the CGA. Partly as a result of these candidates' campaign efforts, small farmers became increasingly aware of the unfair pricing practices to which they were subjected. Farmers who had formerly accepted returns that barely covered their costs now demanded prices that reflected the value of their crops on world markets. In 1975, the entire slate of reform-minded growers was swept into the CGA managing committee in a deluge of small farmer support.

The new leaders acted quickly to curtail the processors' traditional domination of the CGA. The association prohibited membership on its managing committee of any grower who served as a citrus company director or held a managerial position for a processor. The CGA also demanded that the processing companies abide by the Citrus Ordinance regulations on pricing for the next crop year. While the companies' directors were startled by the ouster of their allies from the CGA leadership, they underestimated the vehemence of grower sentiment on the pricing issue. Despite the CGA's insistence on improved prices, the companies announced 1976 crop prices that were little higher than the previous year. The CGA leaders responded with a call for a growers' strike, urging all citrus producers to refuse to sell fruit to the factories. The processors again failed to realize the severity of the situation. Their refusal to negotiate with the CGA apparently stemmed from the belief that traditionally passive and poorly organized small farmers would not participate in the strike.

As the 1975–76 harvest season began, company directors were startled to learn that small growers throughout the district were withholding their fruit from the factories. Most preferred to let their oranges and grapefruit fall from the trees and rot than accept the processors' price offer. Initially, the processors continued operating with production from company estates and the farms of their directors. Before long, however, both factories were forced to close for lack of deliveries from the independent farm sector. The government had initially taken no position in the dispute, but several cabinet ministers now expressed alarm at the factories' closure and growing unrest among laid-off industry workers. Eventually government mediators intervened to insure that the citrus industry, the country's second largest source of export earnings, continued to operate.

The compromise pricing formula adopted in that year fell somewhat short of growers' demands but was widely regarded as a defeat for the processors. Through a complicated pricing mechanism, the formula insured that increases in world market prices would be transmitted to small farmers. More critical for the balance of power between growers and processors, the formula split the processors' ranks so that future price fixing would be impossible. Since price formulas take processor revenues into account, different producer prices are calculated for CCB and BFP each year. In recent years, this situation has triggered a pricing war in which each processor pledged to match or exceed the

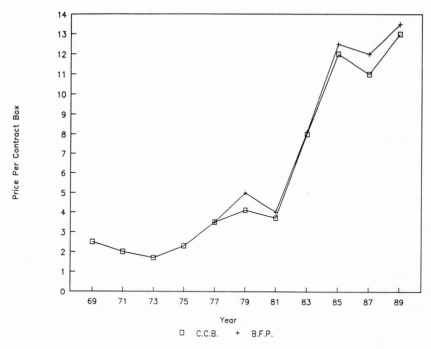

Figure 6. Orange producer price trends: 1969–1989 ($Bze/90 lbs.). Source: Belize Citrus Growers' Association.

other's price in order to garner for itself the greater part of smallholder production. The dramatic price increases that orange and grapefruit farmers achieved from both processors in the 1980s are reflected in figures 6 and 7, which illustrate long-term citrus producer price trends.

Price trends on the world market and the CGA's success in asserting its members' interests have led to a rapid expansion of citrus acreage and production. Older, neglected orchards have been returned to production through renewed maintenance and the application of chemical inputs, and land clearing has rapidly brought once uncultivated land into production. From the 11,000 acres of Stann Creek district under citrus cultivation in 1980, the CGA recorded a near-doubling to 20,000 acres by 1990 (CGA 1990). As new lands were brought into production and older farms rehabilitated, orange production in Belize increased 63 percent from 36,090 tons in 1976 to 56,925 tons in 1985.

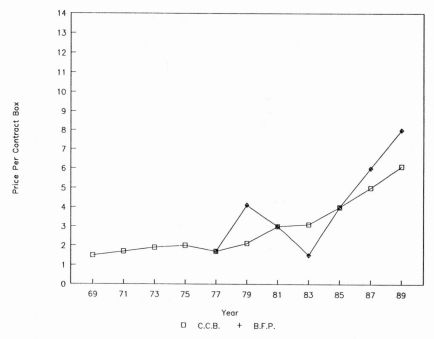

Figure 7. Grapefruit producer price trends: 1969–1989 ($Bze/80 lbs.). Source: Belize Citrus Growers' Association.

A major portion of this increase has occurred in the company groves of CCB and BFP, which respectively controlled 17 and 14 percent of all land under citrus cultivation in 1985. In the mid-1980s, both companies sought to expand their citrus holdings. CGA members charged that this strategy was designed to lessen dependence on the independent farm sector and to become less susceptible to its newfound political strength.

Much as Belizean producers responded to new incentives from the world market, other nations underwent a rapid expansion of citrus production during the early 1980s. Brazil is the world's largest citrus producer and can significantly affect world prices by virtue of its volume of production. As of 1986, Brazil was expanding its citrus acreage by 10 million trees per year and processing 224 million boxes of citrus. Belize, whose 1987 crop was of record size at 2 million boxes, obviously exerts little world market influence in comparison. Although the market is dominated by this single producer, the demand for citrus concentrate originates in metropolitan countries, where tastes change in ways that seem bewildering and capricious to Belizean producers. World prices for orange juice concentrate fell slightly between 1985 and 1987, due in part to the massive scale of production in Brazil. Meanwhile, demand for a less sweet alternative—grapefruit juice— accelerated in the metropolitan countries, triggering a rapid increase in world market and local prices for that commodity. Unfortunately this increase occurred too late for Stann Creek citrus producers, most of whom refrained from planting grapefruit or even bulldozed grapefruit trees and replaced them with orange groves during a prolonged period of depressed prices in the 1970s.

INPUTS AND OUTPUTS IN AGRICULTURAL CHANGE

For farming households, milpa crops such as rice, corn, beans, and plantains have the advantage of satisfying subsistence needs at virtually no cost in purchased inputs. In Hopkins, 65 percent of all farming households make no expenditure on inputs except hand implements, such as machetes, an axe, and a hoe or spade. Further, households fulfill their needs for staple crops with relatively little land under cultivation. In a year of few climatic extremes, an acre of rice will yield sixteen to eighteen hundred pounds of paddy. This would satisfy the needs of even the largest households for more than a year. Similarly, an acre of land would produce sixteen hundred pounds of shelled (dried) corn, far exceeding any Creole or Garifuna household's annual consumption. At a yield of eighty pounds per task (.125 acre), RK beans could theoretically be grown to satisfy villagers' subsistence needs. Because of the crop's poor storage qualities, however, no household cultivates more than three tasks of beans, or what it is able to consume in several months.

Due to an infestation of the air-borne Sigatoka virus (*Mycosphaerella musicola*) on local farms, plantain yields have diminished and become more unpredictable in recent years. A healthy plantain tree produces an average of twenty fruit per year, but even households maintaining two to three acres of plantains occasionally purchase fruit due to the low yield of plants affected by Sigatoka. The importance of plantain in Hopkins diets and scarcity of supply have led to a practice that deeply disturbs many residents: crop theft by other villagers. Because farms are usually unoccupied in the late afternoon, thieves can remove plantains with little risk of detection. The problem has become so severe that one farmer stated he was propagating two acres of plantains in 1986, "one for myself, one for the thief." Largely because of crop theft, however, most farmers are reluctant to expand their acreage to accommodate the heightened local demand for fruit.

In contrast to all these milpa crops, citrus entails substantial input expenses and a long delay in recouping investments through crop sales. Table 6 summarizes input expenses per acre of citrus from planting until first harvest, usually a period of five years. Although most trees bear fruit before this time, some groves do not have marketable crops until six or seven years after planting. Input costs in citrus vary between the times of planting and maturity but are a major if not insurmountable expense for most rural households. First-year start-up costs are higher than the annual maintenance costs of mature groves, but annual expenses for fertilizer and insecticide increase with maturity due to the greater nutrient demands of mature trees and the larger pest populations that they harbor. None of the calculations in table 6 include labor costs, other than bushhogging, due to the variable nature of wage labor inputs. These depend on the amount of family labor that can be deployed in citrus walks, the amount of involvement in outside employment by the farmer, and the size of the citrus farm. Although one person would be able to harvest an acre of oranges in four days (three days for grapefruit), harvesting must be completed within a short time to ensure that ripe fruit does not drop from the tree and spoil. Unless the household has an unusually large amount of labor at its disposal, farms as small as four acres often require hired labor to ensure that harvesting is done quickly.

Notwithstanding the high costs of inputs and maintenance, net earnings from citrus far exceed those of any other crop cultivated by local farmers. Table 7 summarizes the potential net income from each acre of milpa crops as well as the net earnings provided by citrus. In the late 1980s, income from each acre of orange trees was two to five times that of traditional crop choices, even when a full complement of citrus inputs was employed. In addition to its much greater profitability, citrus exhibits other advantages over alternative crops. Unlike staples such as rice, corn, or plantains, Belizean citrus enjoys a virtually guaranteed market due to continued growth in metropolitan demand for

Table 6. Citrus Input Costs: Planting to Maturity ($Bze)

1st Year		2nd Year	
300	budded trees (100 @ $3.00)	45	fertilizer
45	fertilizer (100 lbs.)	38	herbicide
38	herbicide	24	insecticide
24	insecticide	8	lime
8	lime	$115	
$415			

3rd Year		4th Year	
90	fertilizer (200 lbs.)	157	fertilizer (350 lbs.)
38	herbicide	38	herbicide
40	insecticide	50	insecticide
8	lime	12	lime
$176		$257	

5th Year
75	bushhogging ($25/acre, 3 ×/yr)
270	fertilizer (600 lbs.)
38	herbicide
62	insecticide
24	lime
$469	

Total cost of establishment: $1,432[a]

---

[a]This does not include the cost of agricultural implements (machetes and knapsack sprayers). Annual maintenance costs per acre for mature groves are the same as establishment costs during the fifth year, with the addition of labor costs for reaping (averaging Bze $100/acre).

concentrate, as well as export market preferences. Although seedlings and young trees are vulnerable to a variety of diseases and pests, once established, mature citrus is far less risky than other potentially profitable crops such as RK beans. Citrus also requires far fewer labor inputs and is much easier to market than peanuts, the only other crop that rivals it in potential profits. The severity of agronomic and mar-

Table 7. Potential Cash Income per Acre of Selected Crops (1985 Prices, $Bze)

Milpa Crops
Rice: 1,800 lbs. × $.22 = $396
Corn: 1,600 lbs. × $.30 = $480
RK beans: 640 lbs. × $1.00 = $640 (gross)
                          −   48 (seedstock)
                                 ―――――
                                 $592 (net)
Plantains: variable, up to $300
Groundfood: negligible
Peanuts: 1,600 lbs. × $.75 = $1,200 (gross)
                          −   120 (inputs)
                              ―――――――
                              $1,080 (net)

Citrus
Oranges: 224 boxes × $10 = $2,240 (gross)
                        −   469 (inputs/expenses)
                        −   134 (transportation @ $.60/box)
                        −   89 (dues to CGA @ $.40/box)
                            ―――――――
                            $1,548 (net)
Grapefruit: 300 boxes × $5.05 = $1,505 (gross)
                             −   469 (inputs/expenses)
                             −   150 (transportation @ $.50/box)
                             −   45 (dues to CGA @ $.15/box)
                                 ―――――――
                             $ 821 (net)

---

keting problems associated with RK beans and peanuts means that the actual incomes they generate are invariably far lower than the potential returns indicated in table 7. In contrast, citrus farmers can reliably expect good harvests with adequate input use and, unlike producers of other crops, encounter no difficulty in marketing their harvests, regardless of their size.

Despite cyclical world prices, many citrus producers sustain high net earnings during years of low prices by temporarily cutting back on input use. CGA agronomists concluded in field tests that citrus trees can tolerate three years of no fertilizer application with only a 17 per-

Hopkins fishermen process fish for shipment to Belize City.

cent drop in yield, a strategy that saves the farmer Bze $810 per acre in cash inputs. As small-scale producers have discovered, however, this practice severely impairs yields if continued indefinitely. A major distinction between small- and large-scale citrus producers is the latter's ability to consistently apply a full complement of inputs in years of adverse as well as favorable prices. Small farmers unable to fully employ inputs on their farms in years of low prices realize fewer benefits from years of high prices than do large farmers. This is because the cost of inputs may not be recouped in higher yields during the year of their initial application, so small farmers refrain from input use until crop prices have already reached high levels. Several years of adequate input use are required to raise yields on formerly neglected farms. Small farmers therefore remain "out of synch" with price fluctuations, since they may not attain higher yields from input applications until several years after citrus prices have reached a peak.

Large farmers who can afford annual input use to sustain high production levels are poised to benefit from upward fluctuations in prices. Averaging 325 ninety-pound contract boxes of oranges per acre, the company groves of BFP and CCB obviously attained much higher unit profits during the mid-1980s than did Silk Grass farms, which produced an average of only 150 boxes per acre. Historically, disparities in production between large- and small-scale farmers have acquired greater significance in periods of deeply depressed prices, when many small farmers scarcely generate a profit above their operating expenses. Naris Thompson, a Silk Grass resident with just four acres of orange trees, summarized the dilemma of growers such as himself in times of falling prices: "When razor fall, de small man bleed de mos'."

CITRUS INPUTS AND DIFFERENTIATION

Despite the attractive income potential of citrus in the early 1980s, most farming residents of Stann Creek district have been unable to adopt it because of its high establishment and maintenance costs. Neither milpa crops nor most wage labor sources generate sufficient income above subsistence requirements for most village households to adopt citrus cultivation. On the other hand, farmers who planted oranges or grapefruit in the early 1970s, before citrus conferred any advantage in income over other subsistence activities, experienced substantially lower start-up costs than farmers in the mid-1980s. According to earlier data collected in the area (cf. Chibnik 1975: 76–77, 207–210), an acre of citrus could be established for as little as Bze $75 in 1971. Annual maintenance costs following establishment were also much lower than current maintenance costs, totalling about Bze $70 per acre (ibid.: 77, 208). In comparison, the establishment costs for citrus in 1986 were Bze $1,430 per acre, and annual maintenance costs amounted to Bze $470 per acre. While citrus input expenses in 1971 were major investments in real earnings of the time, they were nonetheless within the range of many rural households. In Hopkins, the establishment costs for one acre of citrus amounted to about 9 percent of the average total income of households in Chibnik's sample (ibid.: 125) but had climbed to 42 percent of the average household income by 1986. At present, 55 percent of the households in Hopkins earn less disposable income each year (that is, income above the household's subsistence requirements) than the annual cost of maintaining an acre of citrus. (For a discussion of how disposable household income was calculated, see appendix 2.)

Citrus input prices rose more quickly than household earnings between 1971 and 1986 due to the heavy reliance of citrus farming on petrochemicals. Price trends for petrochemicals and manufactured inputs have sent the cost of tractor rental from Bze $4.50 to Bze $30 per hour and fertilizer from Bze $8 to Bze $40 per 100 pounds. In addition, as the profitability of citrus grew, agricultural suppliers have reacted to stronger demand for their products by raising prices. In 1971, nurseries sold budded trees for $.50 each, but by 1986 they were able to sell them for six to seven times that amount due to the many farmers requiring trees for expansion. While a comparatively large number of households were able to adopt citrus in the early 1970s, then, most milpa farmers and wage laborers a decade later could not due to the escalating price of inputs.

As citrus prices rose and the cost of inputs was driven beyond the reach of milpa farmers and wage laborers, a rift of earnings and land-holdings widened between citrus producers and other rural residents. Growing disparities of income are among the most apparent consequences of the expansion of citrus farming in the area during the 1970s and 1980s. The relative absence of stratification among Silk Grass households prior to this expansion is reflected in Chibnik's 1971 survey data on cumulative household incomes, which are plotted as a Lorenz curve in figure 8. This distribution reveals that the poorest 50

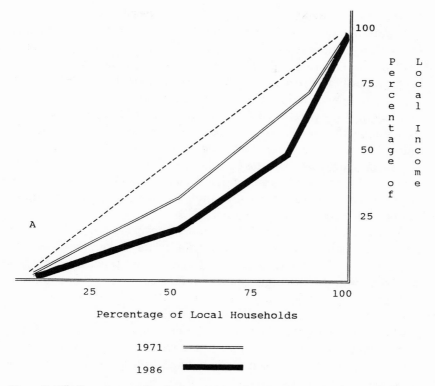

Figure 8. Silk Grass income distribution: 1971 and 1986. Income distribution in Silk Grass is plotted as a Lorenz curve, indicating the cumulative percentage of households that control a given percentage of total village income. An egalitarian income distribution, here represented hypothetically by the broken line (A), would suggest that 50 percent of village households earn 50 percent of all local income. As wealthier households control a greater percentage of local earnings, the Lorenz curve deflects inward from line A. Sources: Chibnik's household survey data; author's survey data.

percent of all households in that year commanded 38 percent of the village's total income. By 1986 disparities between the returns of citrus farming and other subsistence strategies were reflected in an increasingly skewed distribution of income and landownership. The plot of cumulative household income in figure 8 indicates that by 1986 the share of earnings received by the poorest 50 percent of villagers fell to 24 percent of the total.

The concentration of much of the village's agricultural income among relatively few households corresponds to their consolidation of farmland as well. In 1971, virtually all Silk Grass residents cultivated fewer than eight acres of land, and much land reportedly remained available for expansion. By 1986 citrus growers, who accounted for a slight minority (46 percent) of the village's households, earned 77 percent of its income and controlled 87 percent of its land. Five farmers had emerged by 1986 as the community's major landowners, controlling among themselves 48 percent of all locally cultivated land. All arable land near the village had been claimed prior to that year, foreclosing any further expansion by other local farmers. As shifting cultivators and wage laborers surrendered their lands to expanding citrus farms, they surrendered as well any future possibility of regaining parity with their citrus-growing neighbors.

A comparison of household economies between 1971 and 1986 denotes more than community stratification in the wake of commercialized agriculture. It attests as well to the divergent trajectories of villagers' lives and the disparate opportunities that are passed to the next generation. In the Silk Grass of 1971, Dembigh Williams and Sebastian Blackmon shared similar occupational and demographic profiles and might have reasonably expected similar economic destinies. Both men were Creole residents in their mid-forties who had moved to the village upon its founding, and both made a living from full-time wage labor at a nearby sawmill. Each maintained a few acres of land under weekend and off-work cultivation, Blackmon growing rice, plantains, and corn to supplement his wages, while Williams planted several dozen orange trees to anticipate his retirement. To judge from his slightly higher earnings and the probable contribution of subsistence crops to his family's diet, the household of Sebastian Blackmon probably enjoyed a somewhat higher standard of living in 1971 than did Dembigh Williams' family.

By 1986 these families had long ceased to resemble each other economically, and the youngest generation in each household could look forward to widely differing life prospects as a result. In the late 1970s Williams quit his job at the sawmill in favor of full-time work on his citrus farm, which was already yielding a modest income above his expenses. In 1986 Blackmon continued to work at the sawmill but no longer cultivated staple crops. Years earlier, he sold his use rights to land when the district land officer informed him, among other farmers, that his bloc was not sufficiently "developed" for him to renew his lease. Having reinvested his initial citrus income, Williams by 1986

Silk Grass citrus farmer and family.

had expanded his holdings to forty acres, much of it obtained from residents in a position similar to Sebastian Blackmon. Of Williams' four children, three had finished or were attending high school, two of these were working in the United States, and his eldest son, the farm's eventual heir, worked as a full partner with his father. In contrast, Blackmon could not afford to enroll any of his surviving five children in secondary school, while his coresident eldest son pieced together a livelihood from a variety of seasonal jobs. Among these were harvest labor on Dembigh Williams' citrus farm. In 1986 the Williams household generated over Bze $32,000 in net income from the sale of citrus, earnings which were reflected in the family's remodeled and expanded house, its diesel electrical generator, and numerous appliances. On the other hand, the combined wages of Sebastian Blackmon and his eldest son just surpassed Bze $4,000, from which a family of five precariously satisfied their food and material needs. From the quantitative indices of the 1971 and 1986 household surveys there emerges a portrait of individuals and communities in transition, one whose changing nuances are told in the shorthand of income, consumption, and demography.

Having sold their rights to land, village residents such as Sebastian

Blackmon are never likely to close the gap that has widened between themselves and farmers such as Dembigh Williams. Even for those residents who have retained their land or obtained formal title to it, the barriers to agricultural investment remain formidable. Milpa farmers and wage laborers lack access to alternate sources of financing to adopt citrus, while established citrus farmers easily expand their holdings through profits generated by existing acreage or loans from commercial and state sources. One such loan program, initiated by the Commonwealth Development Corporation and the government's Development Finance Corporation, provides low-interest credits for citrus farm expansion and rehabilitation of neglected farms. While the terms of the loan (12 percent interest with a five-year deferment) are more generous than loans issued by private banks, repayment by farmers with little or no established citrus remains difficult.

In the early 1980s, Henry Castillo, a resident of Silk Grass, succeeded after some years of sacrifice in establishing an acre of mature orange trees. Castillo then found himself eligible for citrus development credits and applied for a Bze $4,555 loan to plant and maintain three acres of citrus until maturity by using his single acre as collateral. Castillo soon found that his annual interest payments alone amounted to Bze $546, consuming most of the earnings from his established acre. Despite his efforts to make payments, he fell behind on his obligations within three years, establishing a record as a bad credit risk and unlikely prospect for any future loans. An unintended consequence of this loan program may be to widen the gap between those farmers who have some citrus and those who have none at all, since the former are eligible for expansion credits while the latter are excluded from the program. While credit programs such as these are one means by which rural residents attempt to take advantage of favorable market opportunities, they are not the sole avenue to agricultural change. Some farmers in Hopkins have entered citrus production despite adversities of high establishment costs and limitations of income. In doing so, they have mobilized a novel resource not governed by the collateral and repayment obligations of bank loans; that is, development aid administered by foreign agencies.

THE TRANSITION TO CITRUS IN HOPKINS

At the beginning of the 1980s, very few Hopkins residents enjoyed incomes high enough to invest in lucrative but costly citrus production. In 1982, twenty-one village residents organized an agricultural cooperative primarily to gain outside financial support for the adoption of such export crops. With contributions from two North American grassroots development agencies active at that time in Belize, members of the cooperative set up a revolving credit fund to assist them in the transition to citrus. In the ensuing years, members obtained seedlings and inputs for their farms on credit from the co-op with the promise to repay their debts from the proceeds of future crop sales. The credits that the Hopkins Farmers' Cooperative provides to its members are designed specifically to promote citrus farming among individuals with no established citrus and little collateral. The cooperative's program has allowed its members, regardless of income, the opportunity to shift from milpa farming to citrus. Social differentiation has developed in Hopkins in the wake of this transition, but unlike communities such as Silk Grass differentiation is based on cooperative membership rather than the prior ability to purchase inputs.

Economic activities in Silk Grass and Hopkins continue to reflect the villages' differing endowments of resources and distinct culture histories. Due to the continued reliance of many village residents on fishing, Hopkins' subsistence base will never entirely converge with that of Silk Grass. Nonetheless, the Hopkins Farmers' Cooperative has been responsible for an agricultural transformation of the village that replicates many of the features of stratified communities such as Silk Grass. Ten Hopkins farmers made commercial sales of citrus to the processing companies in 1988, each earning at least twice the average village agricultural income in that year. As co-op members grow more heavily involved in the regional and world citrus economies, they will not merely emulate the profitable income-earning strategies of their Silk Grass counterparts. Today's divergence between the economic choices of Hopkins residents signifies future divisions as well in living standards, opportunities, and, no doubt, political and economic power.

Class boundaries as sharply defined as those of Silk Grass remained latent as citrus trees in Hopkins began to bear their first commercial crops toward the end of the decade. But by 1989 villagers themselves were aware of the imminent divisions in their midst. Some residents referred in tones both joking and derisive to the "rich men" who were beginning to ship citrus to the processing plants. These changes are not easily reconciled with a village milieu in which relations between men were traditionally represented in the idiom of kinship. Yet this village symbolic order, one summarized to the casual visitor in the statement "we are all brothers here," was breached long ago by other divisions that made today's economic disparities a reality. These earlier divisions, and their transformation into boundaries of class, are the subject of the following chapter.

CHAPTER 5

FROM FACTIONS TO CLASSES:

VILLAGE POLITICS AND

SUBSISTENCE CHANGE

Villagers praise the hard work of some and disparage the idleness of others, but few among the rural poor recognize labor by itself as a means of attaining well-being. Regardless of ethnic group, most rural residents believe that material success is achieved through luck or the assistance of others. Hard work is recognized as essential to survival, but only their good fortune or connections set the comparatively wealthy apart from the poor. Within the context of the village economy, there exists little to contradict this belief. Livelihoods that permit accumulation above subsistence, such as citrus or commercial fishing, require starting investments far beyond the earnings of the poorest members of rural communities. Novel cash-earning possibilities, such as hybrid crops or peanut production, are initially profitable but encounter unforeseen risks or fall upon deep market slumps. The few sources of wealth occasionally accessible to the village poor invariably originate from outside, from the earnings of migrants or the whims of government officials.

This chapter examines how the rural poor pursue their economic objectives in the arena of local politics, which for many appears to offer more promising opportunities than the realm of production. Because nonresident politicians may dispense significant favors, proximity to well-being is often measured by one's connections to powerful outsiders or their clients within the community. Cultivating these political relationships forms a major component of the survival strategies of the rural poor. While political strategy is often instrumental and individualistic, it nonetheless contributes to changing group relations by affecting how material resources from without the village are distributed within it. As will be illustrated in this chapter, individuals' pursuit of political patronage in Hopkins has resulted in local class divisions between staple crop cultivators and growers of citrus. In the arena of local factionalism, some villagers have gained access to resources permitting investment in agriculture, while others have not been so favored.

ORIGINS OF VILLAGE FACTIONALISM

Patronage rewards for political loyalty are a major means by which politicians have tried to win control over the electorate in rural Belize. "Spoils" such as employment in work projects, government loans, and land title assignments are regularly made available to party workers on the local level. Far more substantial benefits, such as road construction, health posts, or new schools, are provided to communities that have repeatedly demonstrated their loyalty to the ruling party. Opportunities for political patronage have set off intense factionalism in some communities, as well as strategizing within factions to maximize individual access to those distributing patronage.

Like rural communities elsewhere, Belizean villages are marked by sporadic personal conflicts, but not all are polarized into opposing camps professing loyalty to political parties. Such is the case for Hopkins and Silk Grass, for factions based on party membership comprise the basis of social affiliations in Hopkins, while class is far more significant in Silk Grass. Factionalism under the guise of party loyalty is most acute in those areas that represent major, yet contested, sources of electoral support for elected officials and would-be officeholders. As the largest village in the region, Hopkins is pivotal to political parties that hope to control the rural assembly district in which it is located. For all its political importance, Hopkins has become a site of intense political activity in recent years. Because of its dwindling population, on the other hand, Silk Grass attracts few visits by nonlocal politicians and party activists. The different levels of external political involvement in the communities largely account for their differences in the incidence of factionalism.

In light of its multiethnic composition, Silk Grass is surprisingly devoid of exclusivist sentiments that would suggest interethnic conflict. Proportional to their numbers, non-Creole villagers are equally represented in the village council and farmers' cooperative. Social class, as represented in the divisions between citrus growers and other residents, is instead the primary basis of group identity in Silk Grass. This does not imply that overt conflict is a continuous feature of interclass relations in the village, although many poor residents are openly resentful of the wealth exhibited by kin and neighbors who cultivate citrus farms. Citrus growers belong to each party in approximately equal numbers, yet work together in the local farmers' cooperative and Citrus Growers' Association when requesting services or land from the state. The community's wage earners and staple crop farmers describe the differences between themselves and local citrus growers in terms of the readily apparent disparities in living standards and economic well-being. Yet poorer members of the community are also far more politically atomistic than the comparatively wealthy citrus producers. There are, for example, no voluntary associations, producers' groups, or unions that claim the membership of traditional farmers or wage laborers in Silk Grass.

The absence of class-based organizations among the village poor is probably attributable to the diversity of interests and workplaces represented among those who are not citrus producers. A majority (73 percent) of the wage earners in Silk Grass are employed either at the government's nearby sawmill or seasonally on local citrus farms. The remaining wage earners work in migratory labor on the corporate estates in the Stann Creek valley or even in the remote sugar industry in northern Belize. Most wage laborers thus have little or no contact with other villagers at their places of employment and, as a result, perceive little common interest.

In contrast, residents of Hopkins primarily interact with other members of the same faction and frequently cite someone's political affiliation when explaining why they distrust or avoid that person. The population of Hopkins is almost evenly divided between supports of the two major national parties, the United Democratic party (UDP) and the Peoples' United party (PUP). The differences in factional intensity are reflected in rates of political participation in the two villages. While many Silk Grass residents express a preference for one national party or another, their preferences do not structure interaction, nor do the adherents of the parties act as cohesive blocs. In contrast, Hopkins heads of household are twice as likely as their Silk Grass counterparts to identify themselves as consistent UDPs or PUPs when voting in national and local elections. For most residents, such loyalties are strong enough to preclude interaction with members of other factions.

In Hopkins, factional conflict under the guise of party politics does not express underlying divisions between kinship, religious, or ethnic identities. Most Hopkins residents are nominal Roman Catholics, although North American Mennonite missionaries have made minor inroads into the community in recent years. Unlike villages in southern Belize, where the Mennonites' Maya converts have been major participants in factionalism, their followers in Hopkins are teenagers or young adults with little interest in village politics. Nor can ethnicity account for factional alignments in the entirely Garifuna community. This is not to say that ethnicity and party politics are unrelated at either the national or local level. While overt interethnic conflict has not been widespread in Belize, in part due to the spatial segregation of the various ethnic groups (Young 1978), Garifuna often express resentment at the discrimination they have experienced at the hands of Creoles. A former Hopkins man who is active in party politics was denied a national leadership position in the United Democratic party, a rejection he attributed to anti-Garifuna sentiment. He eventually defected to the People's United party to protest the "Creole racism" that he discerned in the UDP. Interestingly, his former followers in Hopkins disputed his view of the UDP and denounced him as a traitor to their cause. Despite the predominately Creole composition of the UDP at the national leadership level, few UDP supporters in Hopkins perceive the party as overtly racist.

In Hopkins there is no consistent relationship between kinship and factional membership. Sons and daughters usually adopt their parents' party affiliations, and most individuals have the same political affiliation as their siblings. Some exceptions to this pattern do occur, however. One of the village's most acrimonious political conflicts exists between two brothers whose relationship deteriorated when one was excluded for political reasons from the farmers' cooperative, which the other had helped to organize. There are also a few instances in which siblings with opposing affiliations maintain polite, albeit occasionally strained, relations. In general, however, local political conflict is so divisive that switching to an affiliation different from that of one's family runs the risk of alienation from them. That this strategy is occasionally adopted, as is illustrated below, attests to the potential rewards of factional membership. Although individuals ally themselves with factions for instrumental and not ideological reasons, the intense competition between factions for control of resources stands in the way of civil relations between individuals belonging to opposing groups.

While not based on kinship or ethnicity, Hopkins's factions are acquiring some of the features of corporate groups over time. There is a widely recognized association between place of residence and factional membership, with PUP supporters more likely to reside in the southern half of the village ("False Sittee Point") and UDPs in the northern half (known as "Baila"). In local parlance, pejorative references to a certain area of the village (for example, "False Sittee is a dirty place and the people there are no bloody good") serve as thinly veiled references to one's political opponents. Yet this settlement pattern seems to be more a result than a cause of factionalism, for in recent years partisans have steadily migrated to areas of the village occupied by their allies.

Despite the rancorous divisions in their midst, Hopkins residents tend to agree about the origins of local political strife. Older residents attribute local factionalism to the introduction of elected village councils in the late 1940s, which supplanted the more consensual and nonpartisan *alcalde* system of local governance. Prior to the introduction of the seven-member village council system employed in British colonies, the *alcalde* system served as a form of indirect rule in Maya and Garifuna villages throughout Belize (Dobson 1973: 293 ff.). Like his counterparts in other Garifuna settlements, the Hopkins *alcalde* was responsible for mediating local disputes, imposing minor criminal penalties, and representing the village before colonial authorities. Although *alcaldes* were selected by Garifuna communities in a process of public discussion, their election was usually a consensus decision that affirmed community support for a respected, impartial elder. In contrast, village councils are elected biennially following prolonged, often acrimonious campaigning. While village council elections in Belize are nominally nonpartisan, national political parties have long attempted to consolidate their bases of rural support by seeking control of village councils. Candidates for village council seats rarely identify themselves by party, but villagers conventionally refer to them as PUPs and UDPs.

The country's two major political parties originated in the early 1950s, shortly after the introduction of the village council system in

Silk Grass farmer with grapefruit to be shipped to the processing factory.

rural areas. The appeal of the political parties was originally ideological, entailing opposing positions on national independence and the
presence of the British in Belize (Shoman 1987). Following the attain-
ment of internal self-government in 1963, however, the parties have
gradually converged ideologically. Since winning effective control of
the state from the British, Belizean political parties have also gained
material resources that can be dispensed to vital sectors of the rural
electorate. Patronage has become the primary vote-getting resource at
the disposal of politicians, but loyalties are also inflamed through inflammatory personal attacks on opponents. Even a partisan activist in
Hopkins' political arena commented bitterly on the legacy of party politics for village social relations: "Some years aback we was all brothers
and sisters here. Now you want fu kill your best bally [friend] for what
the politicians them promise you. They break they promise, but we
have to live with the poison they spread."

Older residents describe the village as politically quiescent until the
1960s, while readily acknowledging its contentious atmosphere today.
Evidence that would corroborate their claim that party politics has
heightened village conflict has been reported elsewhere in Belize. Maya

communities in particular have experienced intensified partisanship following the shift from *alcalde* to elected village council systems (Howard 1980: 125). This does not imply that intergroup conflicts were entirely absent prior to village council forms of government, but factionalism was often aggravated and redefined along party lines after village councils were introduced (Howard 1977: 102). Villagers' accounts of the past also receive indirect support from the earliest ethnographic data collected in Hopkins (Taylor 1951). Writing of the village in the late 1940s, Taylor (ibid.: 123) reported little political strife and found that aspiring politicians from outside the community received scant support from its residents. Taylor also noted that the prosecution of interpersonal conflicts through sorcery (*obeah*) was falling into disuse, although belief in its efficacy was still widespread at the time (ibid.: 136).

A form of harmful magic widely reported in the Caribbean, *obeah* involves consulting a bush doctor, whose sorcery is thought to cause misfortune to an adversary. If the intended victim can acquire the services of a more powerful practitioner, he or she may be able to counter the effects of the bush doctor's harmful magic. Taylor's observation on the incidence of *obeah* is of some significance, for it is often thought to be employed between political adversaries today. In 1986 many residents immediately attributed the rather macabre accidental deaths of two politically active villagers to sorcery. One of these men was struck by lightning in his dory only a few yards from shore, within full view of several dozen villagers. Following the accident, witnesses discussed his death in murmured speculation, one confiding enigmatically that "as you sow, so shall you reap." Even the man's relatives were persuaded that his death was in some way perpetrated by his political adversaries.

By the 1960s, the partisanship inherent in electoral politics was being aggravated by selective employment of villagers in public works projects. One such project was Aided Self-Help, a works program introduced in 1963 ostensibly to reinforce village cooperation. Promoters of the program asserted that traditional labor-sharing institutions, such as the *fajina* collective work groups found in Garifuna and Maya communities, would be strengthened if nominal payment were provided to volunteers. Far from reinforcing village *fajina*, however, Aided Self-Help eventually undermined traditional cooperative practices. While politically active supporters of the ruling party were well paid for their labor contributions to the program, others received no payment or merely a token sum. By the time Aided Self-Help was abandoned in the mid-1970s, it had so polarized Hopkins residents that traditional work parties could no longer be assembled. To the present day, most residents refuse to participate in such groups from the belief that organizers receive surreptitious payments from political parties. When asked what caused the decline of village work groups, the now-elderly man who served as Hopkins' last *alcalde* observed, "It was politics that humbugged *fajina*. When I was *alcalde* we never thought about politics. Now you can't get a UDP and a PUP to work together, or even talk together." The payment of party activists also contributed to the prevalent suspicion that major material acquisitions are rewards for political support. Villagers often shush, or gossip, that their politically ambitious neighbors installed zinc roofs or constructed cement houses with the help of nonlocal party officials.

Although factionalism occurs under the guise of party politics, party ideology is a veneer for conflicts over the real or perceived benefits that parties dispense. With the exception of a few prominent activists, most rank-and-file members of each faction cannot programmatically distinguish between the national parties that they support. Even for the relative few who are well versed in the rhetoric of the national parties, political programs are of decidedly secondary importance in determining political affiliation. The relative insignificance of party ideology for most villagers, including the political leaders who regularly invoke it, is indicated by recent changes in the leadership of factions in Hopkins.

In 1984, the leader of the UDP faction, a charismatic man with substantial appeal among village youth, was reportedly offered special consideration for a low-interest loan in exchange for campaign efforts on behalf of the PUP district representative. The leader changed his affiliation "instantly," in the words of several informants, and altered his public statements to accord with the national PUP platform. Although the leader's former supporters were outraged by his betrayal, PUP followers welcomed him into their ranks as an able and dynamic campaigner.

Prior to this individual's conversion, his primary opponent had been an ardent PUP supporter who managed a few tourist cottages with earnings obtained in the United States. When the national government came under UDP control in 1984, she found herself in the uncomfortable position of requesting houselots from a government now headed by her former opponents. She reportedly responded to developments on the national level by becoming a generous UDP contributor. Her change of heart was so persuasive that she was soon assigned the lots she had requested and even awarded an informal cabinet post for her experience in promoting tourism. As a result of such inducements, the two most influential political leaders in the community essentially switched places.

Aside from this dramatic reversal of political leadership, the composition of factional groups was otherwise stable in the late 1980s. When tangible benefits are mobilized by one faction, party lines harden considerably and the members of the successful faction are unlikely to forgive the past offenses of their opponents. At such times the emotions that accompany political struggles within the village run so high that most participants would not attempt to join the opposing faction and probably would not be accepted by it if they tried. Changes in affiliation are more feasible if brokered through powerful party officials at the district or national level. Residents doubted the sincerity of Hopkins' two factional leaders upon their political conversions in 1984. Within the factions that these individuals joined, however, few opposed their realignment since the leaders changed parties to obtain benefits from outside the village rather than access to the faction's local resources.

The primary focus of factional conflict is control of the village council, which allows it to determine requests for central government resources and the allocation of funds. A faction leader's disbursement of government funds, however minor, augments his prestige and may attract additional benefits from nonlocal party officials. More important, if a faction mobilizes support for the ruling national party it can be assured of more substantial patronage rewards. These may take the form of infrastructural support, such as feeder road construction on farms; favors, such as expediting a land application; or control of local hiring for a public works project. These forms of patronage are potentially major benefits for the government's supporters at the local level. As a consequence, village council seats in factionalized communities are contested amid bitter and sometimes violent campaigning when local elections are called every two years.

The Hopkins local elections in March 1986 were no exception to this pattern. Prior to the election, members of the PUP bloc held a four to three majority on the council but were repeatedly stymied by the parliamentary maneuvers of the UDP leader. Council meetings had been polarized by debate over the activities of a Peace Corps volunteer that the majority bloc wished to eject from the village. While many village residents in both factions disliked the American for her imperious (some would say racist) demeanor, a fundamentally political reason underlay the move to expel her. The council chairman, who headed the PUP bloc, charged that the volunteer's projects primarily benefited the minority faction. UDP councillors made no effort to deny these allegations, asserting that their opponents were the first to seek and monopolize various forms of aid from foreign agencies and volunteers. The UDP members claimed that the PUP bloc was attempting to "victimize" them by expelling "their" volunteer, while overlooking the support that a second Peace Corps member provided to a PUP-affiliated women's group. The inability of the parties to resolve the question of Peace Corps involvement in the village not only deadlocked council business but created a volatile level of confrontation between supporters of each bloc.

These frustrations were brought to the fore at a council meeting in which the date of upcoming local elections was announced. During the meeting a dozen or so youths approached the community center to call for the defeat of the PUP majority. The protestors began heckling PUP councillors with the chant of "No more plastic smiles," a reference to the renegade PUP leader who had once been their ally. Although most of the PUP councillors attempted to ignore the taunts, one member was unable to restrain himself. Visibly enraged, he lunged at the protest leader and bellowed, "You are mentally sick!" The councillor was restrained by several of his comrades and the youths withdrew in time to prevent an altercation, but the meeting ended in a shouting match between the blocs and their supporters. Tensions continued to mount during the four weeks preceding the election as each side conducted nighttime rallies filled with inflammatory rhetoric and innuendo.

The issues in the campaign were complex and contradictory, yet villagers ultimately responded to the PUP bloc's promise to electrify the village if granted control of the council. Responsibility for rural electrification ordinarily lies with the national government, which repeatedly told the Hopkins council that it lacked the funds to repair a local generator that had broken down years earlier. The PUP candidates argued that the village was being punished by a hostile UDP national government and proposed that the village council initiate its own electrification program. PUP leaders claimed that in the absence of government support they alone could bring electricity to the village due to their close relationship to the fishermen's cooperative, which operated two diesel generators with surplus capacity. The UDP candidates, on the other hand, were portrayed as enemies of the cooperative and impediments to village progress. Since the PUP candidates were all members of village cooperatives, and few co-op members were UDP supporters, the occasionally extravagant claims of the majority bloc seemed plausible to most villagers. Promising to share the benefits of "their" cooperative with the village, all seven PUP candidates won the election by wide margins.

The differences in local elections in Hopkins and Silk Grass are illustrative of the contrasting political climates in the communities. Four policemen were assigned to Hopkins before and during the election to prevent an anticipated outbreak of violence. While votes were tallied, the policemen were repeatedly called on to separate political opponents who traded insults and blows. As the final ballots were counted to indicate a PUP sweep of all seven council seats, the defeated candidates and their supporters were initially incredulous, then openly defiant. Some threatened ominously that they would exact revenge in one way or another long before the next elections in two years.

In contrast to the confrontational atmosphere in Hopkins, in Silk Grass election day went almost unnoticed except by the government official stationed there to tally votes. A total of 216 villagers, or nearly 80 percent of all eligible residents, cast ballots in Hopkins. Several individuals working elsewhere in the country even returned to the village just in order to vote. In Silk Grass, however, only fourteen votes were cast, a turnout so meager that the Ministry of Local Government nullified the results and rescheduled the elections for later that month. The low level of local political activity is suggested by the fact that no members of the Silk Grass village council could recall any visits by campaigning politicians in the previous two years. Indeed, when interviewed many residents were unable to identify the present village chairman, and all denied that the national political parties had local representatives.

FACTIONS AND THE STATE

Extant analyses of local-level politics are less than adequate in accounting for virulent factionalism such as that found in Hopkins. Transactional theorists have argued that factionalism is a ubiquitous, albeit often overlooked, feature of all rural communities (Barth 1966; Boissevain 1974). Some contend that factionalism was simply ignored in the past by anthropologists who attributed significance only to corporate entities such as kin groups or classes (Boissevain 1968: 542). Political economists have argued that factionalism diminishes class consciousness among the poor by promoting personalistic loyalties across class lines (cf. Silverman and Salisbury 1977; Gilmore 1977; Handleman 1975). Many political economists have erred, however, in asserting that factionalism exists for that reason. This argument neglects the fact that those who promote party loyalties rarely act with unified class interests themselves. The leaders of political parties engage in factional conflict over political strategy, while elite classes are usually characterized by heterogeneous and conflicting economic interests. Since factions divide ruling as well as subordinate classes they cannot be understood simply as a means of maintaining ideological hegemony. Finally, neither transactionalism nor existing political economic approaches account for the varying incidence of factionalism in different communities, such as the virulence of party loyalties in Hopkins and their virtual absence in neighboring Silk Grass.

To explain the origins and consequences of factionalism, analyses of local-level politics need to examine how the state's rulers and their competitors promote intense political loyalty in certain communities. This entails an understanding of the state as a complex decision-making entity, rather than a monolithic institution (cf. Bates 1983: 143). Anthropological theorists often debate the disparate views that the state either coercively enforces the interests of a dominant class (Fried 1967; Carneiro 1970) or governs by providing benefits for its constituents (Service 1975). What these conflicting assessments overlook is that ruling groups commonly maintain power with both coercive means and the tools of legitimacy. When dealing with a variegated citizenry, ruling groups have historically had to rely upon differing combinations of coercion and inducement to maintain control of the state (Johnson and Earle 1987: 268–270). Throughout much of Latin America, where regimes employ state power to maintain highly inequitable social orders, policy has been tenuously balanced between the exigencies of repression and reform (de Janvry 1981: 237–256). Where rural inequities are much less pronounced and highly competitive political parties are able to operate, as in Belize, ruling groups face other obstacles to obtaining the loyalty of local constituents. Elucidating the determinants of state policy under conditions both of repression and reform is critical if the effect of national institutions at the local level is to be understood.

Even the policies of highly repressive Latin American states are constrained to some extent by competition, or the possibility that citizens will challenge the state's rulers if they are adversely affected by existing policies (Zamosc 1989: 102 ff.). Such constraints are not necessarily of an electoral nature, for the prospect of insurrection has been a primary motive of ruling groups in enacting reformist policies that maintain overall patterns of capital accumulation (de Janvry 1981: 202–223). If electoral alternatives to a regime exist, constituents who threaten to support those alternatives will enjoy greater bargaining power with the regime than those lacking such alternatives. While powerholders and their competitors primarily challenge each other for the loyalty of powerful elites, they also require more than tacit support from nonelite groups if they are to control the state. Only against those wholly excluded from the political process, or those whose support has already been conceded to the opposition, is the regime able to impose unambiguously punitive policies, using its monopoly of force if need be.

Competitive constraints on state policy making are most evident in electoral forms of government (Breton 1974), particularly those in which political parties are not clearly distinguished by ideology or class membership. In such political systems, candidates compete with each other in promising resources and services to valued but contested segments of the electorate. When choosing where to allocate resources, political parties also neglect voters whose loyalty may be taken for granted or those whose support has already been secured by an opponent. The differing levels of political activity in Hopkins and Silk Grass may be understood in this sense, for the communities present substantially different potential rewards to elected officials and their opponents. With its population three times that of Silk Grass, Hopkins provides a critical source of votes to politicians attempting to win the National Assembly seat from rural Stann Creek district. As the largest and most prominent Garifuna village in the country, it also exercises much influence over other Garifuna communities, which have historically voted as a bloc in national elections. Given its electoral significance, Hopkins' high political value to national parties insures that the village will be a battleground of contention, the votes of its residents sought through propaganda and patronage. In contrast, Silk Grass, once the beneficiary of government largess intended to produce a show-piece of rural development, has been virtually ignored by both the government and its opponents since its residents began to leave in the late 1960s.

The virulence of factionalism in Hopkins reflects features of political competition noted elsewhere by Hirschmann (1970). Under conditions of duopoly, in which two parties compete for the allegiance of all voters, a party may decide to move toward the ideological center. This ideological shift occurs because the party need not fear losing support at its end of the political spectrum and can gain support by making inroads into its opponent's constituency (ibid.: 67). Under such conditions of convergence toward the center, political ideologies become nearly interchangeable. The loyalty of rank-and-file supporters then becomes most critical to the party, even if strong loyalties appear to be irrational. Given the exit option available to constituents, who may leave one party for another that is ideologically equivalent and materially more attractive, emotive or personalistic loyalty may become the only factors preventing large-scale defections (ibid.: 81). Political parties in such systems often acquire factionlike tendencies, as members coalesce around charismatic leaders and support their party from group loyalty rather than ideological convictions.

This pattern applies to the village level as well, for patronage benefits are often the lesser of the political means used to win the loyalty of Hopkins voters. The personal invective hurled at opponents during local campaigning invokes past injustices suffered at their hands. This method of recruitment invariably heightens the partisan's sense of attachment to his or her party, even if it is programmatically indistinguishable from that of his or her opponents.

The differing degrees of involvement by politicians and parties in Hopkins and Silk Grass have resulted in highly distinct political cultures in the villages. While the rhetoric of political confrontation is the most apparent local manifestation of factionalism, less conspicuous are its structural consequences for rural communities. The factionalism engendered by external political actors now critically determines the economic strategies of Hopkins residents. Contrary to earlier analyses that dismiss factionalism as ephemeral or inconsequential conflict (see chapter 1), in Hopkins factions form the basis of a developing class structure where none existed previously.

FACTIONALISM AND COOPERATIVES

Despite the divisiveness that has accompanied village council elections in recent years, the actual rewards dispensed for political support have been transitory for most party followers. The grandiose promises of favors and material benefits by which leaders acquire a political following rarely materialize in their entirety. Rather, political support is won through a skillful allotment of small-scale or short-term benefits to the faithful, such as assignment to temporary work projects, combined with promises of more lasting rewards to come. While the members of one party or another temporarily gain from these strategies, depending on the composition of the village council's majority, the rewards of patronage are not of the magnitude that they could be directed into new forms of production. The significance of such patronage lies rather in its encouragement of factions as a primary base of local social action. As such, factions stand poised to mobilize and distribute other resources among their members, including resources not allocated by political parties themselves.

Since the late 1970s such resources have entered Belizean communities in the form of development aid, much of it directed toward rural cooperatives and credit unions. With encouragement from governmental and private agencies that help prepare applications for foreign grants, co-ops throughout Belize have increasingly financed their activities with money made available by foreign aid donors. Much of this aid has been made available by agencies that promote community development through self-help efforts and appropriate technology. Between 1971 and 1981, one such grassroots development agency in the United States provided U.S. $784,291 for twenty-eight cooperative and community-based projects in Belize (Palacio 1984), and funding from Commonwealth sources for similar projects has considerably exceeded this amount. Such funding is intended to supplement members' share capital so that co-ops can acquire the infrastructure or equipment necessary to become self-sufficient and economically viable. For many rural poor, however, cooperative formation has become a survival strategy aimed less at developing new forms of production than acquiring relatively large sums of foreign aid otherwise unavailable to individuals. According to the Belizean government department that registers cooperatives, co-op membership throughout the country grew rapidly in response to aid agencies' funding activities. In 1982, twenty-one Hopkins residents formed an agricultural cooperative with the intention of qualifying for such grants. A year later, a fishermen's cooperative and then a women's cooperative were established in order to obtain funds for local development projects.

Much as poor villagers have learned that membership in a cooperative permits access to foreign grants, the officers and members of co-ops have cultivated impression management strategies that are useful with representatives of potential funding agencies. In Hopkins, members of the farmers' and fishermen's cooperatives had known for over a month of the impending visit of a program manager from the Canadian agency that administered grants to both societies. The chairmen asked co-op members to be present during the Canadian's visit in order to sustain the impression of a large, interested membership. On the appointed day, a majority of members turned out, far exceeding the average attendance at membership meetings. Notwithstanding this extraordinary level of attendance, the chairman apologized for the "few" fishermen present, noting that most were "out to sea."

After touring the fishermen's cooperative, the visitor asked to view a farm to evaluate the citrus project initiated by the farmers' cooperative. The farmers had anticipated this request and had spent some time discussing which farm would be shown to the visitor. They chose the farm of a man who, far from being an active co-op member, had repeatedly clashed politically with its leaders. As the man enjoyed a regular salary from his position as the principal of Silk Grass School and had earlier planted citrus and hired labor to maintain the farm, his trees were much closer to maturity than those of the co-op members. The farmers knew they would be able to show off the farm since the teacher would be at school on the day of the visit. After his tour of the citrus orchard, the program manager returned to Canada highly impressed with the progress of the cooperative's development project. He apparently failed to notice, however, that a three-year-old program had produced a farm with five-year-old trees on it.

As conduits for nonlocal resources of substantial size, cooperatives have become major arenas for factional competition in Hopkins. Members of the Hopkins farmers' cooperative acknowledge that a major motivation in establishing the co-op was to qualify for funds that donor agencies allot for rural development. Cooperative members, whose own incomes did not permit the adoption of citrus, viewed such funds as possible sources of agricultural investment. The original members of

Members of the Hopkins Women's Cooperative in front of tourist lodges.

the cooperative were a core group of active PUP supporters, although a few politically noncommitted individuals were admitted in the planning phases. The district cooperative officer, himself a prominent player in the village's factional politics, resided in the village and provided assistance when the cooperative developed its grant proposal. Within a year, the cooperative had applied for funds from development agencies in the United States and Canada, receiving U.S. $49,000 for its members to use as credit in the establishment of citrus on their farms. The funds were issued as loans to members, enabling them to purchase trees and inputs which would be repaid from their crop sales once their trees began to bear fruit.

Having secured a grant, the cooperative members guarded it zealously. Other villagers became interested in the co-op members' plans to adopt citrus on their farms and some submitted membership applications to the farmers' cooperative. Without exception these have been turned down. Given the requirements of its members and finite size of its grant, the cooperative justifies its rejection of new applicants as an effort to prevent the dilution of existing members' benefits. Nonetheless, within the factionalized village setting, UDP supporters are quick

to claim that they have been refused membership for their party affiliation. Political polarization has been heightened with the perception
that members of the PUP bloc have hoarded the benefits of development grants for themselves.

For its part, the PUP faction has done little to dispel the impression
that it has controlled access to grants in a politically biased manner. In
a cooperative meeting in which membership applications were being
evaluated, a local PUP leader denounced several applicants for their
participation in an "anticooperative faction that was active in the
[1986] village council elections." Arguing that the applicants had tried
to join the cooperative not to contribute to the organization but to
"infiltrate and destroy it," the leader persuaded the managing committee to indefinitely table the applications. Those so excluded from the
cooperative are limited in their ability to win development grants due
to the fact that they lack a leader with expertise in grant proposal writing. More problematically, members of the UDP faction are unable to
form a rival organization since national statutes recognize only one
farming cooperative in any locality, a policy ironically intended to prevent the dissolution of cooperatives through factionalism.

Restrictions on membership for political reasons suggest one of the
chief paradoxes of cooperative promotion in relatively egalitarian communities. According to the Department of Cooperatives and Credit
Unions, cooperatives have been promoted to increase food production
and stem urban migration by encouraging new economic opportunities
in rural areas. Pragmatists in the national government also acknowledge the political functions of rural development, for elsewhere in
Central America insurrection has followed closely on the heels of rural
dispossession and poverty. The idea that cooperatives should be a
vehicle of development among the rural poor has been vigorously
pursued as well by some agencies in the metropolitan nations. For
institutions with a mandate to promote development among the Latin
American and Caribbean poor, assistance to cooperatives has been seen
as a way of increasing income levels and averting the "politically desta-
bilizing" consequences of rural poverty (cf. Seibel and Massing 1974;
Tendler, Healy, and O'Laughlin 1982).

The grassroots model of development promoted by such agencies
assumes that associations such as cooperatives and credit unions promote equitable rural development by virtue of their democratic bylaws.
Theoretically, if a cooperative is formed in a relatively egalitarian com-

Members of the Hopkins Farmers' Cooperative work together in clearing new farms.

munity and retains open membership policies, the benefits of participation should be evenly distributed throughout the community. Some
observers have recognized the existence of prior group loyalties within
such communities, but few have addressed how such loyalties affect
membership policies to skew the distribution of benefits. The attention
of policymakers has instead been directed toward cooperation within
rather than between corporate groups. This view is expressed in a
study of Belizean cooperatives for a United States development agency
active in the country: "Serious infighting may weaken a project although it is controlled by a corporate group. Unfortunately, this is
one of the major weaknesses of groups in Belize—the inability to utilize the corporate structure to strengthen their organizations" (Palacio
1984: 12).

Strong group loyalties based on membership in kin groups or factions may also impede a fair distribution of development benefits
within the larger community. When corporate groups form cooperatives, invidious distinctions across kin or political lines often limit
membership and benefits to that group alone. Evidence from other
regions, such as Africa (Vincent 1976) and India (Gough 1978), sug-

gests a close relationship between politics and cooperative membership in highly factionalized communities. Should factional loyalties govern the allocation of cooperative benefits, households may become differentiated on the basis of production as well as politics. As in Hopkins, the consequence is that prior loyalties are transformed over time into class divisions. The grassroots development model thus errs in assuming that only incipient economic distinctions determine whether a process of economic change will be equitable. Stratification may arise on the basis of any criteria that distinguish local groups, if those distinctions also become the criteria for distributing resources.

By converting their development grant to individual credits, members of the Hopkins Farmers' Cooperative have entered a sphere of production otherwise closed to them by their limited incomes. By 1989, Hopkins co-op members had each planted up to five acres of orange trees, and all had either produced their first commercial crop or were about to do so. Although co-op members are a minority of village farmers, they account for almost all locally cultivated citrus, while nonmembers are confined to traditional livelihoods that yield far lower returns. With the advent of commercial citrus production in the village, pronounced wealth divisions are developing between cooperative members and those remaining outside the association.

COOPERATIVES AND VILLAGE CLASS STRUCTURE

All the cooperatives in Hopkins have obtained external funding for their projects, but not all such resources have the capacity to alter the village economy and class structure to the extent of the farmers' cooperative. The Hopkins Women's Cooperative was organized in 1983 by seventeen PUP supporters who were seeking alternative sources of income for village women. Like its counterparts, the women's co-op became quickly embroiled in local factional conflict. Among the income-generating projects it planned was the construction of two small tourist lodges at one end of the village. To obtain land for its Sandy Beach Lodge, members of the cooperative had to overcome formidable opposition by the leader of the UDP faction mentioned earlier. As the operator of the village's only tourist facilities, the UDP leader feared the prospect of competition and filed a competing claim for the lots desired by the cooperative. While the resulting land conflict delayed the cooperative's project considerably, the national land office eventually ruled in its favor. Since 1987 the cooperative has done a steady business catering to the small number of tourists who venture into the village. While the earnings that members realize from the cooperative have been minor thus far, they may afford them a degree of financial independence within their households.

Far more grant money has been awarded to the Hopkins Fishermen's Cooperative than to the farmers' and women's cooperatives combined. Members of the village's PUP faction, which also organized the cooperative, hoped to duplicate the successes of fishing cooperatives elsewhere in the country. The cooperative was planned as a self-sufficient processing and marketing outlet for village fishermen that would sell them fuel, ice, and hardware at competitive prices. In addition to increasing fishermen's incomes by improving their access to export markets for fresh seafood, the cooperative was also intended to generate employment for at least six villagers in its processing facility. The district cooperative officer, who had both envisioned these plans and prepared the grant application to finance them, anticipated that the co-op would benefit nonmembers as well because fishermen would spend much of their increased earnings within the village.

Under the best of circumstances, such plans would require extensive material support, but in a village without electricity or piped water, the entire physical plant and infrastructure had to be imported at great cost. The initial estimates of construction costs provided in the grant proposal turned out to be unrealistically low, and as a result that portion of the grant intended for operating capital was exhausted before the co-op even purchased any fish from its members. The cooperative had to assume a substantial commercial loan simply to pay the import duty on its icemaking machine and would surely have incurred greater debts had members of the local co-ops not completed the physical plant with volunteer labor.

The Hopkins Fishermen's Cooperative was inaugurated during a colorful ceremony in April 1986. The inauguration was both a solemn and festive occasion, marked by the hopeful oratory of government dignitaries, a blessing by the district priest, a Garifuna dance exhibition, and ample servings of rice and beans. Notwithstanding the elaborate celebrations, an air of pessimism hung over the festivities. The cooperative lacked any money to begin operation and could scarcely cover the cost of its own inauguration. By this time, it had become apparent to the cooperative's managers that the society's operating expenses far exceeded their earlier projections. The cooperative spent over Bze $200 per day in fuel simply to generate electricity, to which would be added the costs of maintenance, staff salaries, transportation of its product, and payments to members. Within a week of the inauguration, the district cooperative officer informed the fishermen that their society would require an additional loan for working capital amounting to Bze $225,000 at a commercial bank's 23 percent interest. Despite the magnitude of the debt, the cooperative officer assured the members that it could be quickly repaid if the co-op sold thirty thousand pounds of scale fish per week and one thousand pounds each of lobster and conch per week during their seasons. Less from persuasion than lack of alternatives, the society's membership voted to secure the loan.

The cooperative officer's calculations embodied a number of fatal assumptions. He had estimated that thirty of the society's forty-three members would catch, on average, two hundred pounds of fish per day over a five-day week. In reality, only nine members owned motor-powered dories, and with their partners the number of commercially active members did not exceed twenty. Under consistently good conditions, a motor-equipped fisherman might expect fifty- to seventy-five-pound catches each day, but ordinarily would spend no more than three to four days per week fishing. The estimates for lobster harvests were even more implausible, since just two members consistently fished for lobster and averaged only ten pounds each per day. The actual weekly yields of the active fishermen thus rarely exceeded 10 percent of the cooperative officer's estimates. From the outset, instead of accruing profits for working capital and loan repayments, the fishermen's cooperative began losing Bze $2,000 to $3,000 per month. By December 1986, the bank foreclosed on its unpaid debts and began seizing its equipment, including the generator with which the PUP-controlled village council had earlier promised to electrify the community.

For all its funding, then, the fishing cooperative has had virtually no effect on village incomes since its creation. The collapse of the fishermen's cooperative and comparatively favorable prospects for the farmers' co-op may appear paradoxical in a village that traditionally derived more of its livelihood from the sea than from agriculture. The fishermen's cooperative failed because most village fishermen were unable to generate the volume of production required to meet the co-op's expenses. While the cooperative's organizers allotted their grant to a capital-intensive facility, the productive capacity of its members remained unchanged from a time when most men fished only for home use. Only a small minority of the cooperative's members were adequately equipped, the remainder having joined in the futile hope of securing loans for fishing equipment. In the absence of technical assistance to aspiring commercial fishermen or membership policies that alienated fewer potential producers, the cooperative was doomed by an ambitious and inappropriate physical plant.

The farmers' cooperative, in contrast, adopted an emphasis from its earliest stages on production rather than marketing. Instead of devoting its grant to capital equipment that generates high overhead expenses, the cooperative has sought technical changes on members' farms to promote a shift from subsistence to commercial agriculture. This strategy has already proven far more effective in improving co-op members' incomes and is leading to corresponding changes in village social structure as a class of citrus producers emerges in Hopkins.

The successes of the farmers' cooperative have not gone unnoticed by its opponents. Because of the perception that co-op members are discriminating against their political opponents as well as the obvious economic advantages that cooperative members now enjoy, the divisiveness of local factionalism has deepened since the cooperative's formation. In the late 1980s, the cooperative and its economic advances became the major focus of political conflict in the village. UDP loyalists routinely describe cooperative members as "selfish" men who reveal their true nature by excluding others from the benefits of participation. PUP supporters accuse their opponents of attempting to subvert the cooperative by inviting retaliation on the part of powerful national officeholders. Thus, political conflicts in Hopkins continue to be defined ideologically in the idiom of factionalism rather than class. Yet if the experience of the class-stratified village of Silk Grass is any guide, lasting and irreversible economic disparities are supplanting what until recently were purely political divisions.

CHAPTER 6

HEGEMONY AND RESISTANCE:

UNITY AND DIVISION AMONG

STANN CREEK CITRUS PRODUCERS

Survival strategies of the rural poor at the local level involve the creation of factions and cooperatives, but villagers also act on their economic interests as members of regional class-based organizations. The Citrus Growers' Association (CGA) claims the membership of all Silk Grass and Hopkins citrus farmers, and the fourteen Hopkins men who periodically work on the Dangriga waterfront belong to the United General Workers' Union (UGWU). Since the mid-1970s, these groups have successfully confronted the citrus-processing companies over prices and wages paid to farmers and waterfront workers. Through strikes and other mass movements, each has won substantial increases in its earnings and challenged the once unquestioned prerogatives of processing companies and rural elites.

The incomes of citrus growers and union members have since become heavily contingent on political factors, such as the internal unity of producers vis à vis capital and the state's intervention in conflicts between them. Conflicts between capital and producers are also conditioned by world market factors, which determine the profitability of citrus exports and the magnitude of benefits that may be wrested from processors. It is not coincidental that militancy among both groups, and correspondingly greater earnings for their members, developed in a period of high world prices.

This chapter analyzes how such apparently successful movements of citrus producers developed in the last two decades from a long period of rural quiescence. It examines the strategies and formation of producers' groups as they became emergent classes in the confrontation with local capital. In defying their past subordination to the region's citrus companies, wage workers and citrus growers have had recourse to a potent symbolic arsenal, as well as the more direct and conventional tactics of strikes and boycotts. Both groups have defined their positions in terms of values that few would dare to dispute. Symbolic means enable the poor to hold elites accountable for their behavior, for even the most powerful cannot openly disregard the virtues of "fairness" and "justice for the small man" regularly invoked by workers and citrus growers. From collective action, political alliances, and such symbolic measures, producers extracted significant economic concessions from capital. Yet, as will be seen in the following pages, citrus growers and workers have also become divided among themselves by ethnicity and class. While a genuine shift of power and privilege has taken place in the citrus industry, a new hegemony of elite control has also been established on the growing divisions within producers' ranks.

ETHNICITY AND THE CITRUS WORK FORCE

For the UGWU, confrontations with the citrus processors were in part inspired by the CGA's earlier success in obtaining higher prices for farmers. Until the mid-1970s, waterfront work was considered only marginally more desirable than seasonal harvest labor on the company estates in the Stann Creek valley. A member of the Hopkins waterfront gang who began work in 1961 reported that his initial pay rate was only Bze $1.10 per day. The union had represented waterfront workers since the mid-1960s, but wage rates remained low until Mishek Mawema, a politically active Dangriga schoolteacher, was elected branch secretary a decade later. Under Mawema's leadership, the union agitated for higher wages on the waterfront by enacting a series of work slowdowns that significantly increased the shipment costs for processors. Due to the perishable nature of frozen concentrate and the high costs of shipping, processors are particularly vulnerable to losses from delays when concentrate is loaded onto ships at port. Even a one-day delay in shipment may cost the companies the profit of the entire cargo. While the work would not be considered skilled labor, the rate of on-loading and pay rates closely depend on the internal cooperation of the work gang. Each waterfront gang is a highly cohesive unit whose members must work closely with one another. This means that processors cannot easily replace experienced waterfront workers with untrained workers during a strike.

Like the CGA, the union has had some major successes in promoting the interests of its members in recent decades. By enacting work slowdowns at shipment, where processors can least afford lost production, the union has negotiated dramatic wage increases and severance benefits for waterfront workers. In 1986, waterfront workers reported pay rates of between Bze $200 and $300 per twelve-hour rotation, the highest wages earned by any hourly employees in Belize. Although waterfront workers can expect at most four work rotations per year, earnings from these four days of labor allow them to handsomely supplement their other income sources. Understandably, waterfront work has become the most coveted source of employment in Stann Creek district, as attested by long waiting lists of applicants to fill the positions of retiring dockworkers. Because there are only six gangs, each comprised of twelve to fourteen men, these wage increases have benefited only a small percentage of the region's wage-earning population.

As the UGWU was instituting costly slowdowns to obtain higher pay for waterfront gangs, the processors found other developments in the union to be even more ominous. In 1977 the union's increasingly assertive leadership announced that its struggles on behalf of waterfront workers were a prelude to better pay and working conditions for all industry workers. The union pledged to win pay increases for seasonal harvest laborers, whose numbers greatly exceed those of waterfront workers. Even a modest wage increase for the thousands of harvest laborers employed on the corporate estates would significantly reduce the profits of processors. General wage increases were seen as particularly threatening in the wake of the processors' disastrous 1976 standoff with the CGA, after which they were no longer able to set producer prices. Under the prevailing conditions of CGA militancy and producer price competition, the directors of both citrus processors thought it imperative to neutralize the union before harvest workers were radicalized to the same extent as waterfront workers.

Because waterfront workers were the first citrus employees to be unionized and tend to have more stable, long-term employment than migratory harvest laborers, they have historically dominated the union's leadership. The companies soon learned that they could diffuse the union's militancy by yielding concessions to the tiny minority of workers employed in waterfront gangs while denying them to the much more numerous harvest employees. Despite its stated policy of addressing harvest workers' wages, after the union negotiated favorable contracts for waterfront workers in the late 1970s it was not able to obtain comparable benefits for harvest laborers. In recent years, the union leadership has tacitly collaborated with the processing companies by excluding the issue of harvesters' wages from contract negotiations. Seasonal workers continue to earn the same wage levels as in 1982, averaging Bze $.38 per ninety pounds of harvested fruit, or about Bze $75 to $100 per fifty-hour week.

Wage divisions within the labor force coincide with ethnic differences, for the union is increasingly divided between an African-Belizean leadership earning high wages and a low-paid, predominately Spanish-speaking general membership. The relatively few positions in waterfront work are all held by Garifuna residents of Dangriga or Hopkins. Since the 1970s, however, most of the harvest work force has consisted of migrants from Guatemala, El Salvador, and Honduras. The citrus industry makes its most intensive use of labor during the harvest season between October and May. During this time, local labor supplies are insufficient for the amount of fruit in need of harvesting, causing both processors to recruit foreign workers for the job. Processors contend that these hiring practices are necessary because Belizeans are unwilling to work at prevailing wage rates for harvest labor. This assertion is not, however, borne out by survey data collected in Hopkins and Silk Grass, where seasonal harvest labor is the most common source of wages for male residents. A more telling factor in processors' preference for foreign labor is that non-English-speaking workers, many of them refugees, are likely to be far more docile than Belizeans. While refugees fear deportation for infractions of work rules, Belizean workers are more likely to be aware of their rights and face no such dire consequences if fired. Further, Hispanic migrants often have no nonlocal source of livelihood, while most Belizeans maintain farms or other income sources in town or nearby villages.

Other occupational factors diminish the degree of interaction and perceived common interest among Belizean and Hispanic workers, even when members of both ethnic groups hold similar positions. While many African-Belizean harvest workers reside at home and travel daily to work, foreign workers occupy spartan migrant camps near the processing factories and estates at Pomona (CCB), Alta Vista

(BFP), and Middlesex (CCB). With substantial differences of language, culture, wages, and working conditions separating them from Hispanic workers, Belizean citrus industry employees often harbor deep-seated prejudices about Spanish-speaking "aliens." Anti-Hispanic sentiments in Belize originated early in the colonial era, when white settlers, trading companies, and colonial civil servants promoted a close affinity for West Indian and British institutions (Palacio 1990: 11). Despite post-colonial attempts to foster a pluralistic national identity, anti-Hispanic attitudes have been heightened in recent years by dramatic changes in the country's demography.

Since the late 1970s, an unknown number of refugees from civil strife and economic hardship in El Salvador and Guatemala have settled in rural areas of western and southern Belize. Some argue that as many as sixty thousand immigrants entered the country without documentation between 1980 and 1989, although most estimates are considerably lower (cf. Stone 1990: 102). While the government has granted temporary asylum to many refugees, some political leaders and sectors of the media have depicted the new arrivals as criminally inclined and threatening to Belizeans' livelihoods. These portrayals exacerbate African-Belizeans' concerns about the changing ethnic composition of the country, which is tenuously balanced between the Hispanic orientation of much of its population and the country's official Anglophone and Caribbean identity. The country's ethnic balance has radically shifted with the estimated 15 to 20 percent growth in Belize's Spanish-speaking population since 1980, much of which is accounted for by refugee influx (*Spearhead* 1987). Increasingly, occupational distinctions in citrus industry employment coincide with such invidious ethnic divisions. Under such conditions, the union's ability to win continued concessions from the processors has been greatly diminished, while its vulnerability to outside manipulation has been heightened. Such trends became dramatically apparent in 1986, as the UGWU held elections to fill union executive positions.

At the union's annual convention in May 1986, two slates of candidates vied for the four positions on the union's executive board. Only the candidates endorsed by the outgoing leaders were technically eligible for election; their rivals, a group of dissidents who claimed that their union membership had been unjustly revoked, were effectively barred from running. Many harvest workers charged that the past executive board had been bought off by the processors to ignore their concerns. Spanish-speaking workers, who heavily outnumbered Garifuna and Creole members in the convention, overwhelmingly supported the dissident slate. In contrast, the four nominees of the outgoing board were all Garifuna dock workers from Dangriga who easily claimed the support of the other waterfront workers. For their part, the waterfront workers claimed that the four dissidents, all of whom were affiliated with the local branch of the UDP, had been paid by the governing party to sow discord within the union.

When the outgoing leaders announced that the four opposition candidates had no rights of nomination or voting, pandemonium broke out between supporters of the rival slates. Representatives of each group struggled for control of the speaker's microphone and the blackboard to be used for nominations. Several waterfront workers climbed to the stage and began to chant, "We no want no aliens!" while supporters of the dissidents shouted their candidates' names in nomination. In a final attempt to restore order, one union leader played a tape of the national anthem at deafening volume. While the participants stood at silent attention during the tape, as soon as the last note was played the struggle began where it had left off. Unable to reclaim the microphone from a group of immigrant workers, the executive members adjourned the convention and led their followers out of the hall. Amid cries of "¡Qué siga!" (Let it go on!), the dissident candidates clambered to the front and declared themselves in control of the convention. By this time, however, the police had entered at the request of the leadership and were ushering the remaining members out of the union hall.

The union's leadership waited until late June to reconvene the meeting, knowing that by this time much of the immigrant work force would have left for the off-season. To insure that the remaining harvest workers did not again impede their plan for an uncontested election, they notified delegates on the company estates that the union could not defray their travel costs to the convention. Despite the meager representation of harvest workers, enough Dangriga-based supporters of the barred candidates attended the second convention to reassert the opposition's objections to union nominating procedures. Shouting matches between supporters of each slate again disrupted the balloting, causing the executive to prematurely adjourn the convention for a second time. Two months later the elections were conducted by mailed ballot, although the opposition candidates claimed that ballots were only sent to the waterfront gangs.

The waterfront workers suppressed the opposition's challenge to their control of the union, but they did so at great cost. The union emerged from the elections polarized by ethnic conflict and discontent over wage differentials. By voicing the interests of underrepresented harvest workers the dissidents brought into sharp relief the divisions within the district's work force. These divisions, originally based on the higher wages and prestige of waterfront work, acquired an ethnic component as the perceived inferiority of harvest labor became associated with "Spanish" immigrants. Although an exclusively Garifuna union leadership abetted these ethnic and occupational divisions, they have been exacerbated by the processors' willingness to negotiate with waterfront gangs and intransigence in dealing with seasonal workers.

The establishment of a high-income sector within the citrus labor force has resulted in a "segmented labor market" (Gordon, Edwards, and Reich 1982), in which large disparities in wages, benefits, and working conditions have been created between waterfront and harvest sectors of the citrus industry. As in other industrial and agricultural settings (Fligstein and Fernandez 1988; Nash 1985), class segmentation is a powerful mechanism of labor control, for it renders workers as a whole more malleable from their employers' point of view. By diminishing sources of common identity among all industry workers, the processors have been able to contain wage increases to a small fraction of the work force while reversing some of the benefits they had earlier conceded. Within a year of the contested election, harvest workers seceded from the union and sought separate representation through a rival union. Since then, a greatly weakened UGWU has been unable to defend many of the severance and benefit conditions it had won for waterfront workers in earlier contracts with the citrus companies.

While finding expression in workers' ethnic concerns, political divisions among citrus workers ultimately result from the processors' hiring and negotiating strategies. By insuring that ethnic divisions within the work force increasingly coincide with those of income, working conditions, and prestige, the processors greatly circumscribed the union's influence. In the absence of greater unity among citrus workers, it is doubtful that the benefits won by waterfront gangs will be attained as well by the harvesters who make up the majority of the region's working class. Thus the real gains of the waterfront workers belie an impotence of much greater magnitude for citrus workers as a whole.

ALLIANCES AND DIVISIONS AMONG GROWERS

The Citrus Growers' Association has been notably more successful than the union in recent years at maintaining internal unity when confronting processor interests. This unity is not the consequence of undifferentiated interests among its membership but stems from the processors' failure to exploit the considerable differences that do exist. Indeed, income and landholding disparities among the district's growers are even more pronounced than the wage differences within the citrus industry work force. The large majority of the district's citrus producers are small-scale farmers, the median landholding in citrus being just 6.65 acres. While 335 of the country's 361 commercial citrus producers cultivate farms of less than fifty acres, growers holding more than fifty acres apiece control 76 percent of the district's private land under citrus (see table 8). Less than 40 percent of the fruit processed in Belize in 1986 was grown on company estates or farms belonging to company directors. Processors are thus heavily reliant on deliveries from the independent farm sector, although they have increased their estate holdings since the late 1970s to try to lessen this dependence.

Under the terms of the country's 1967 Citrus Ordinance, which is designed to govern relations between citrus growers and processors, all farmers who annually sell more than twenty contract boxes of fruit (ninety pounds of oranges or eighty pounds of grapefruit) for processing become members of the Citrus Growers' Association. While the CGA originated as a research and extension service, in recent years it has moved beyond its advisory role to represent citrus growers before the government and processing companies. CGA objectives and meeting agendas are largely established by the association's seven-member managing committee. Positions on the committee are filled by annual election among the general membership, but most members of the CGA are automatically excluded from committee positions by restrictive bylaws. Five of the seven committee seats are reserved for growers with ten or more acres who annually sell at least one thousand boxes of fruit to the processors.

Because of these restrictions, the managing committee is strikingly nonrepresentative of the association's general membership. In 1986, the two smallest-scale directors on the CGA board cultivated fourteen and forty-two acres of citrus, respectively. The remaining five committee members held over seventy acres each, and several owned well

Table 8. Distribution of Land Planted in Citrus: Stann Creek District, 1985

Size of Holdings (Acres)	Number of Growers	Percent of All Growers	Total Acres	Percent of All Acres
Less than 5	150	44	459	4
5–<10	92	27	710	6
10–<20	55	15	810	7
20–<30	18	5	519	4
30–<40	5	1	179	1
40–<50	5	1	243	2
50 or more	26	7	9,626	76
Total				
Growers	361	100	12,546	100
Processors	—	—	3,959	—

Source: CGA (1985).

over one hundred acres of citrus. According to CGA membership records, these five largest producers on the managing committee are representative of the top 7 percent of all citrus growers in terms of farm size (CGA 1985). In contrast, 71 percent of all CGA members cultivate ten acres of land or less, and 44 percent hold less than five acres. Even the smallest-scale farmer on the managing committee, who is often identified as the "small man's" representative, owns substantially more land than most Stann Creek citrus farmers. While all independent growers have some common interests before the processing companies, the CGA is internally divided by such disparities in landholdings.

The pricing practices of at least one of the companies have united many citrus growers against it despite the divisions between small- and large-scale farmers. The Citrus Company of Belize (CCB) has incurred considerable anger among growers for the discrepancy between the company's claim to represent growers' interests and what many consider to be deceptive pricing policies. In the late 1970s, when the company was on the verge of bankruptcy, it appealed to the government for help in returning to solvency. The government co-signed a loan for the company totaling Bze $1.6 million, assuming liability for half this amount in the event that the company went bankrupt. In exchange the government obtained representation on CCB's board of directors until it returned to profitability and a pledge that it would remain a public stockholding company with growers represented on its board. Assisted by a ten-year tax holiday, CCB returned to profitability within two years and began to promote itself to Stann Creek district farmers as a "grower-owned and -operated" facility. This claim is nominally true, since almost half the company's twenty-nine shareholders are Belizean farmers, the remainder being Trinidadian investors. Among the company's Belizean shareholders are most of the district's largest landowners. Although small farmers initially welcomed the company's claim to represent the interests of growers, they were soon disillusioned to learn that they were not the growers that CCB's board of directors had in mind.

Despite its rebirth as a "grower's factory," the Citrus Company of Belize has offered consistently lower prices to citrus producers than its foreign-owned rival, Belize Food Products (BFP). Unlike BFP, in the past the company estates of CCB and the farms of its large-scale shareholders supplied the majority of its production. Being less dependent on deliveries from the small farm sector, CCB could afford to offer lower prices to unaffiliated farmers. As foreign markets for Belizean concentrate expanded in the 1980s, however, both processors had to turn to the independent farm sector to increase their production. In what the company described as an effort to purchase more citrus from independent farmers, CCB announced that it would pay "as much as any other processor" for citrus deliveries in the 1984 crop season. Payments for citrus are ordinarily made twice during the year, with growers paid for their fruit at the time of delivery and then paid a bonus after the end of the processing season. In 1984, the first payment by CCB did indeed match that of BFP. The company then announced that the first payment would be the final one for the season and that it had met its obligations to growers. As it had in previous years, however, Belize Food Products went beyond this to make a final payment to farmers, which raised its total crop payments to almost twice CCB's final level.

Other than the few CCB shareholders in their ranks who could look forward to company dividends, most CGA members were infuriated by CCB's refusal to match final payments. At the CGA's request, the case was brought before the government's Citrus Control Board for adjudication. When the board ruled against the company, CCB appealed to the minister of commerce and industry, who upheld the ruling. Having exhausted its appeals, CCB announced in a memorandum over a year after the dispute began that it would make a second payment to growers to bring its final price to parity with BFP. While stating its intent to provide supplementary payments, however, CCB remained resolute in its claim to have already fulfilled its commitment to growers. The second payment, its directors stated, was a goodwill effort solely "to keep peace and harmony" within the industry. CCB further alienated small-scale citrus farmers when it later announced its intention to reorganize as a private company, limiting stock ownership and participation to the few wealthy farmers who comprise its board of directors.

At a CGA meeting in April 1986, members decried the company's refusal to admit that it had broken its commitments. When a CCB announcement was read that growers would be required to sign waivers of any further claim against the company before receiving their "goodwill" bonus, growers howled in protest. Most felt that CCB's condition was a humiliating rebuke to farmers for their litigation against the company. A skillful and provocative speaker, the association's chairman drew sustained applause when he answered CCB's statement: "This is no goodwill payment. This is no charity. This is a payment that they have to make, because now they know they cannot play with us!" More militant farmers termed the waiver statements an "insult" and demanded that the CGA initiate a growers' strike against the company until it provided second payments plus interest. The feeling that CCB betrayed the interests of citrus growers continued to color farmers' perceptions of the company long after the second payments were issued. After the April meeting, a Silk Grass farmer complained of the company's use of the idiomatic Creole expression "Da Fu We" (This is for us), which is stencilled in large letters on its processing plant. Although it had prominently (and, to some, cynically) portrayed itself as Belizean grower-owned, the grower argued that CCB had actually betrayed the small men who supplied it with fruit: "Cho! Da no fu we at all. The big money men pretend they for de little man but they lone advantage we whenever they can."

Farmers' indignation at the Citrus Company of Belize has unified the ranks of the CGA despite the divergent interests of its membership. Differences between directors and general membership of the CGA were skillfully concealed during the association's meetings on CCB pricing practices. The association's directors phrased their denunciations of CCB in terms of the company's betrayal of the small man, inflaming the anger of most CGA members against the processor. Despite their vast landholdings, the directors emerged from the confrontation with CCB as champions of the small farmer. Having identified themselves as the small man's advocate and CCB as his antagonist, the CGA directors diverted farmers' concerns away from the substantial differences that exist between themselves and the membership at large.

While the divisions between small- and large-scale growers do not emerge in CGA confrontations with processors, they clearly affect the association's internal policies. Small farmers are heavily reliant on the CGA for farm services, especially for bushhogging their farms several times per year. By most accounts, small farmers consider the CGA's provision of farm services grossly inadequate. The association owns and rents a tractor for clearing its members' farms at Bze $30 per hour, a rate that is up to 20 percent higher than that charged by private tractor owners. Small growers complain that one tractor is insufficient for the needs of three hundred CGA members and that it is almost never available due to rental by other farmers or periodic breakdowns. Farmers also note that the CGA tractor is too large for bushhogging between tree rows and invariably causes damage to tree trunks and low branches. Small-scale growers periodically raise the issue of equipment rental and other services in membership meetings, but their pleas are typically deflected by the large-scale growers who comprise the managing committee. All the CGA's directors clear their farms with private equipment.

At a meeting in the summer of 1986, many small growers were disgruntled but hardly surprised when the managing committee tabled their request for the purchase of a small tractor better suited to bushhogging members' farms. Despite one smallholder's argument that a used tractor would quickly pay for itself through rentals, a director noted that the CGA's budget for acquiring farm machinery had been depleted. Nonetheless, he praised the farmer's initiative and promised that the issue would be taken up at a later meeting. The farmer and his supporters were astonished to learn only minutes later that the managing committee had decided to import a new passenger van from the United States. The vehicle, directors assured the membership, would allow the CGA to remain in closer contact with rural areas and to better extend services to the small grower. Responding that farm machinery should be a higher priority for the association than a plaything for its directors, some small-scale farmers called for a vote on the issue but found that the funds had already been appropriated in executive session. Within several months it was widely known throughout the district that some small-scale farmers were clandestinely organizing a regional cooperative to provide the services that the CGA neglected. Like the farmers in Hopkins, the cooperative's organizers foresaw the prospect of funding by foreign grassroots agencies, and once registered they planned to submit a grant proposal for, among other things, the tractor they had unsuccessfully requested from the CGA.

The cooperative's organizers originally met in secret partly because they remained uncertain about their eventual relationship with the Citrus Growers' Association. In addition to providing technical services and equipment to small farmers throughout the district, the cooperative planned to market members' fruit in bulk and thereby negotiate a higher crop price than that obtained by the CGA. By combining these service and marketing functions, co-op members would be left with little reason to remain within the CGA other than the Belize Citrus Ordinance, which requires that all citrus farmers pay CGA dues on fruit sold to the processors. Several organizers favored challenging the ordinance in court so that co-op members would not have to pay dues for CGA services they did not consume. The co-op was thus seen by its members and opponents alike as a secessionist movement that would eventually rival the CGA. The CGA's directors viewed this possibility with some alarm and vowed to keep small farmers within the organization, by litigation if necessary.

Rather than suppressing the cooperative directly through a legal challenge, large growers found it more advantageous to co-opt it. Following the cooperative's registration in 1987, the organization's membership and charter underwent a rapid transformation. The membership of the cooperative has been increasingly drawn from the ranks of medium- and large-scale farmers, while the militant small farmers who organized the cooperative were excluded from leadership positions. With arable and accessible land becoming scarce and expensive in Stann Creek district, the two thousand acres allotted by the government to the cooperative have enticed many farmers into the association. Small farmers in the cooperative have grown anxious about the eventual distribution of land among its members, for the cooperative's managing committee intends to allot parcels in accordance with the number of shares held by members. For large-scale growers who would otherwise pay premium prices for accessible land, the allocation plan provides an inexpensive means of expanding landholdings. For their part, small farmers fear they will be overlooked in the allocations or consigned to meager if not marginal parcels. With the cooperative's agenda turned toward land acquisition, there are no longer any references made to the organization as a breakaway movement promoting small farmers' interests. To the relief of the elites whose control of the CGA seemed in some jeopardy at the end of 1986, the threat of small farmers deserting the association has been effectively quelled.

The fate of the citrus growers' cooperative is indicative of the obstacles that small-scale farmers confront when challenging the power of those better organized than themselves. In a manner reminiscent of Marx's observations on the peasantry of France (Marx 1977c [1851]: 317), small farmers in Belize are divided in numerous ways that impede their recognition of class interests or inhibit their ability to act on them. Further, the divisions that exist between individual farmers—of dispersed settlement, occupation, ethnicity, and politics—are rarely present to the same degree among the processing companies and the large growers that they confront. The powerful not only count greater political and economic resources in the arsenal of class warfare but are free of the crippling disadvantages with which small farmers must contend.

Among the more than three hundred small-scale farmers belonging to the Citrus Growers' Association, uncounted livelihoods besides citrus farming are actually represented. According to CGA surveys, less than 30 percent of all farmers holding fewer than ten acres of citrus derive their earnings from farming alone. In addition to contributing about 25 percent of the nation's citrus production, small farmers work in day labor for wages or are employed professionally in town; they keep shops in the villages or run rural transport services; they hire seasonal labor or are hired themselves. Within this diverse group there is little of the uniformity of occupational interest or class position that characterizes the handful of growers having fifty acres or more. The small farmer's seeming diversity of interest is abetted by his dispersal in the countryside. Small farmers are scattered widely throughout the district and lack either the proximity or transportation by which large farmers remain in frequent contact. Ethnic boundaries also play a role in maintaining these divisions. The largest farmers on the CGA's managing committee are all light-skinned, and most of them are foreign-born. Small farmers, however, are Creoles, Garifuna, mestizos, Mopan Maya, and Kekchi, divided among themselves by language and often persisting stereotypes concerning one another.

Finally, politics must be added to the mechanisms by which large-scale growers maintain their hegemony over the small. Differences of party affiliation exist among large-scale producers, yet they are less likely to assume the venemous proportions that they do among village residents. The reason for this is that small-scale farmers, like rural residents in general, have been more intensively targeted by political parties for their electoral support. Unlike the avocational interest that the wealthy exhibit in party politics, factionalism for the poor is an earnest struggle for the resources that permit survival. One result of the patronage that characterizes political life in communities like Hopkins is that the rural poor often develop a "client" consciousness (Johnson 1989) rather than one of class. In recent decades rural residents have been encouraged to seek individual benefits from elites and political parties, instead of working collectively toward the same ends. The intervention of such elites largely accounts for the sudden and unprecedented mobilization of small farmers in the mid-1970s after a prolonged period of quiescence.

From the combined political and economic strength of small-scale farmers in 1975 the relations between processors and growers were fundamentally redefined. Yet theirs was not a political movement that emerged from the initiative and consciousness of the small growers themselves. It was rather a group of large-scale farmers—today's elites—who provided the information and organizational skills required to mobilize small farmers, a mobilization that coincidentally served their own interests. As in other agrarian political movements (Wolf 1969; Eckstein 1989), the rural poor find that the benefits of their political sacrifices have been appropriated by others. The success of this movement rested ultimately on the small farmer's power of numbers, yet the essential tragedy of the small farmer is that he cannot wield that power purely in his own interest. When he attempts to, as when organizing a cooperative to satisfy needs ignored by large-scale farmers, he finds himself suddenly without allies and poorly armed to resist the inroads of elites.

RESISTANCE AND ACCOMMODATION
AMONG THE RURAL POOR

Survival strategies of the rural poor assume a startling array of forms. In the strategizing of factional leaders and followers, the "impression management" of cooperative members, and the militant demands of abused workers and small farmers, rural residents struggle in numerous ways to win control of their political and economic destinies. To the observer of political movements among the poor and dispossessed, the interests and contradictions that characterize these actions seem to defy generalization. What motivates the political behavior of the rural poor, and in whose interest do they act? Is the course of their political action one in which they overcome daunting forces marshalled against them by powerful elites and a capricious world market? Or does it take the form of a Greek tragedy whose conclusion is foregone and in which they merely enact a script written by other failed movements of the past? Finally, and for some, most critically, do they behave in terms of a "scientific" understanding of their class interests, or are they duped into ineffectual activity by hegemonic tools at the disposal of the powerful?

These questions, typical of those raised of agrarian political movements in the past (Moore 1966; Wolf 1969; Scott 1985), drastically oversimplify the nature of political action among the rural poor. In the militancy of their unions and producers' associations, the poor clearly recognize their interests and act upon them, albeit in ways that may be ultimately self-defeating or contrary to their intended goals. Class-based political action is merely one element in the repertoire of techniques by which they assert their interests. In other circumstances, as with the waterfront workers' unwillingness to uphold the interests of non-Belizean workers, the altruism of class consciousness gives way to collaboration and the pursuit of self-interest. The only generalization permitted of such disparate strategies is that agency is often the overdetermined outcome of economic, ethnic, and individual factors. Only on rare occasions does the convergence of these factors assume a class character, while regional and world history suggests that they typically do not. As in the citrus work force, where wage differentials and hiring practices exacerbate ethnic tensions, the ultimate dominance of rural elites usually remains undisputed.

However decisive in appearance, the outcome of political action is rarely unequivocal. Even an ostensible defeat, as in the domination of the citrus growers' cooperative by large farmers, provides the poor with victories on a small scale. Like elites everywhere, large-scale farmers in Belize find themselves unable to act politically without publicly rationalizing their action. To do so they have recourse to an extensive universe of symbols, the most potent of which is their stated compassion for the plight of the small farmer. However cynical or insincere the employment of such values in justifying their public behavior, the wealthy concede ground on the terrain of class struggle when they do so. In the eyes of the poor, such pronouncements provide them with the moral right to appraise the behavior of elites and to insure that their deeds conform to the powerful values that they have invoked. These symbols constitute, in Scott's (1985) words, the "weapons of the weak," enabling the poor to turn every act of cynicism on the part of the rich into one of treachery. If they are to avert overt class conflict, the powerful who both need and must contend with the poor recognize that by invoking shared values they have rendered their own behavior somewhat negotiable.

Acting as organized groups or as self-seeking individuals, and in ways both conscious and contingent, the rural poor shape to varying degrees the political economy in which they act. Far from being ephemeral conflict operating independently of local social structure, factionalism in Hopkins has become the primary means by which outside resources are locally distributed. The subsistence changes that resulted from factional strategies have altered community class structure as first disparities of income, then those of class, developed between citrus producers and traditional agriculturalists. Informal groups such as factions are thus the antecedents of new social structure, for tomorrow's class divisions find nascent expression in the political divisions of the present. Notwithstanding the benefits that some have gained from them, factional strategies also carry heavy penalties for communities at large and especially for their poorer members. Feeding upon personalistic ideologies and community polarization, factionalism preempts other forms of group identity, whether they be of a class nature or traditional forms of cooperative effort.

On the regional level, the experiences of the waterfront workers and Citrus Growers' Association demonstrate the extent to which subordinated social groups can ameliorate their dependence. Despite the significant material concessions that their movements have extracted from the processing companies, citrus producers and waterfront workers remain subordinated to them in fundamental ways. The UGWU has attained high wages for waterfront workers, but its gains have been achieved at least partly because the processors recognized that a divided union was in their best interests. Similarly, the CGA's apparent unity in the face of the processors barely masks a sharp divergence of interests between its now-elite directors and the small growers who make up the bulk of its members. Having once supported the association's directors as allies against the processors, small-scale farmers now find that the actions taken in their name primarily benefit a new elite.

In such actions agency and structure reveal their dialectical interconnections. By merely rationalizing their acts as beneficial to the small man, the wealthy provide the poor with the symbolic means to challenge their domination. The resulting political strategies adopted by the rural poor are not merely occasionally successful at wresting benefits from the powerful; they also transform the rural political economy. As citrus producers throughout Stann Creek district negotiated higher wages and prices in recent years they themselves changed the complexion of the rural economy by making waterfront work and citrus production far more attractive livelihoods than in the past. For their part, Hopkins residents have responded creatively to these incentives by mobilizing the resources required of citrus production. Yet the rural poor throughout Stann Creek district have also strengthened existing structures of dependence as more and more rural households are incorporated into a world market over which they have little control. If recent history is any guide, it may be expected that the poor will invent new forms of political action that seek to define the effects of that world market in the years to come.

CHAPTER 7

"KEEP ON FIGHTING IT":

STRUCTURE AND AGENCY

IN FIVE LIVES

When speaking about their lives, villagers often refer to turning points in the history of their communities. Many of these critical events originated in distant metropolitan markets, policies implemented by the state, or the vagaries of nature. At the village level, such developments may seem arbitrary in origin, if not bewildering. Notwithstanding the remoteness of the world markets that consume their products and labor, village residents reveal in their narratives an extensive working knowledge of how the external environment affects their lives. Far from being the "cultural dopes or mere 'bearers of a mode of production'" portrayed in anthropological analyses that discount people's reasons for their own action (Giddens 1979: 71), villagers readily employ this knowledge to their own ends.

The working life histories of Hopkins and Silk Grass residents illustrate how the political economic forces analyzed in preceding chapters have been experienced locally. Some individuals respond to these forces by resisting them, while others attempt to accommodate change. All, however, seek some autonomy and choice in a rapidly shifting economic environment. Structure is both realized and recreated in the lives of these individuals. In responding to the constraints and incentives of a changing economy villagers create precedents that others may follow. As their once novel choices are routinized over time, new behavioral rules and opportunities come into existence for the members of rural communities. In this process, which Giddens refers to as "structuration" (1986: 16), the decisions and strategies of individuals become the raw material of new social structures.

Among Hopkins farmers, the working life history of Martin Ramírez (age fifty-four) exemplifies a pattern common to many Garifuna men. As is true of most Hopkins men of his generation, mobility during youth was followed by an increased commitment to farming toward middle age. Yet for Ramírez, the opportunities presented by the farmers' cooperative signal a departure from the limited subsistence choices of the past.

"I don't really belongs to Hopkins, you know, since I was born in Seine Bight, where me father was a fisherman. When I was nine years old my ma died as she give birth to me only sister. Me daddy couldn't work and take care of both of we, so he sent we to live with me aunt in Hopkins. That was a hard woman, let me tell you! She kept me out of school just to work on she farm, even when she never gone to bush herself. If I come back before midday she'd lash me; sometime she'd lash me for no reason at all. I run away from she house after a few years, even before I finish school. My first job was for Belize Estate and Produce, which built up Mango Creek as a mill town. They start me working in the office—you know, cleaning and doing errands and such—when I was thirteen years old. That was in 1946. A lot of men done come home from the war then or from Panama side, so jobs was scarce for true and they pay bad. You known how much they pay in those days for ten hours' work at the mill? Cho! Seventy-five cents! But everything more cheaper then, too. A pound of flour was five cents and I could buy a new shirt for fifty [cents].

"So I continues at that job for a few years. They made me head office boy, and then I worked nights as watchman and I cleaned up the office after the men gone home. In all my life the only luck I ever had was in that job. I remember one night that a heavy storm come up. Most nights the boss lock up the door to the room with the cash box before he gone home, but this night he forget to lock it. Before I could close all the windows against the rain, a heavy squall blowed that door wide open! Without a second thought I gone into the room and open the cash box and, man, I never seen so much money before or since. But the fear catch me so I left the room to be sure nobody approach; I even look outside in the rain and dark to be sure the way is clear. Then I gone back into that room and fill me trousers with dollars until they couldn't hold no more. Lone five and ten dollar bills! Well, I find me a lee baking powder tin, put the money inna de tin, and then later before I knock off for the night I get a spade and bury it in the bush.

"The next morning I was afraid that the boss would see the door unlocked, but he put the key in and open it just as he always done. Eventually they count the money missing but they never did blame me since I have no key for the room. Two weeks later I pretend catch fever and tell the boss I want to go home to rest off. That night I dig up me tin and catch passage to Seine Bight and then go through to Hopkins by dory. Boy, I never live so good as when I reach me aunt house. I eat up, drink up with me friends and still the tin almost filled with money. After some time me aunt start to vex me again, so I hides the tin inna she house and gone back to Mango Creek. Man, that's the last I seen of the money. When I pass Christmas back in Hopkins, Ha! tin and money gone! The old lady said somebody thief it, but I know that somebody was she. Well, as the Creoles say, when thief thief from thief, God laugh.

". . . Now most youths my age then never work steady; they work what we call 'jack and bolt,' especially because the work then was all seasonal. But also the youths them like to work a few months and then rest off at they mother's house until time for work again. In my case, I never had no real home—not with that old lady—so I was working full time, right through. I stay at Mango Creek over ten years, until 1961 when [Hurricane] Hattie strike. By that time I was foreman and making good wages. But Hattie finish the sawmill quick time and I lost me job.

". . . Things was hard for a while. I gone to Stann Creek to look for work, but there's none that side, least not right off. There was nothing left of Hopkins, maybe one-one [a few] house and some people killed too. In Stann Creek the whole town was bruk up, and they call up the army to stop looting. In those days, the government give each man 75 cents a day for food, but the food always scarce. Often I miss my ration even when I queue up hours before. Later then there was a lot of work in rebuilding the town, and that's how I learn me lee carpentry. But that work finish as soon as the town done rebuilding, so less than a year after the storm I'm looking for a next job.

"Later I begin to reap citrus at Pomona. When reaping done that year I gone back to Hopkins and begin to cut farm and do some fishing. Well, I work at Pomona some five or six years, but the work hard and in those days they pay bad. That was before the union come in and the Citrus Company they advantage the workers because we never have no say about conditions and such. Sometimes after reaping season I scarce bring home money after I pay me bill at the commissary. I begin to think that I'm not a young man no more; I got a woman and children to support and can't waste no more time with this foolishness. Since then I no job out again; I cut new farms each year and do carpentry to earn me cash. But you'll always be fighting it under this milpa system and you got nothing for your work but some lee rice or corn. So I begins to think a few years aback of planting a citrus walk. Then when I'm old I can hire me bally [friend] to tend to the farm and always have some lee cash coming in.

"What hold me back so long was the finance, you see. You know, citrus no easy; you pay out a lot before you begin to see profit. That's why I join up with the co-op. If God spare life, and if I keep fighting it a few more years, I'll have me citrus and can pay back the credits they done give me. Maybe then I can begin to rest easy."

Most of Ramírez's narrative is taken up with what he describes as a fleeting escape from poverty in his youth, the opportunity to raid an untended coffer. The actual dimensions of his theft (indeed, whether the incident occurred at all) are perhaps less significant than the perceptions revealed by the narrative. The tale of his short-lived wealth is a metaphor for the widely held view that well-being is fortuitous, unpredictable, and ultimately elusive. In a similar sense, the arbitrary behavior of his aunt was responsible for the loss of his windfall. In this regard, Ramírez's story resembles the "treasure tales" not infrequently documented in "peasant" narratives elsewhere (e.g., Foster 1988: 145 ff.).

After a series of temporary jobs buffeted by the vagaries of nature and the world economy, Ramírez returns home, like many men, to full-time farming in middle age. Unlike the preceding generation, however, he forsakes traditional crops for a more lucrative alternative. Having adopted citrus farming through the Hopkins cooperative, Ramírez describes the future in essentially optimistic terms. His confidence that he will at last gain a measure of material well-being through his own efforts stands in marked contrast to an earlier period of his life when material security was elusive.

Members of the oldest living generation in the village appear more resigned to the paths their lives have taken, perhaps because the opportunities offered by cooperatives and permanent migration are of only recent origin. The narrative of one such Hopkins resident, Victor Martínez (age seventy-eight), is notable for its time depth and the variety of his work experiences, which also parallel the changing fortunes of Belize in the world economy.

"I was born in Newtown in the year 1908. In those times Newtown was much smaller than Hopkins now—there was less than a hundred people in the village and you could only reach there by sea. Even Stann Creek town was only a little bigger than Hopkins today, and that was the biggest place we knew. My father worked for Mr. Santino, who was an Englishman that shipped coconut from Stann Creek to Belize [City]. Every month a boat left with coconuts for Belize, where they made copra. During the first war the business grew up because we was shipping coconuts to England to make war materials, gunpowder and such [Britain used coconut shells in the manufacture of World War I gas masks].

"When I was seven, the Englishman post himself to Belize and take my father with him to work in the shipping office. So I was raised up in Belize while my daddy worked there. After the war the coconut-shipping business closed down and so we moved back to Newtown, where my daddy kept a plantation [i.e., any farm, usually not a commercial estate]. I left school and worked with him at the farm and then, since I want to help myself, I begin looking for work.

"My first work was cutting mahogany over in Gallon Jug [a forest camp near the Guatemalan border], where I jobbed out every year until 1927. In those days, mahogany cutting was a seasonal business; you have about nine months of work each year and then go home in September or October. Each year I contract for an advance before Christmas and then after Christmas I'm on my way to the mahogany works. Most of them camps was out west and far remote from any kind of town or village. So there you was, out in the bush with your gang and away from your people most of the year. That was a very hard life then, even for a young man. It was hard not just because you miss home for so long but because the pay was never sufficient for your provisions. Then the next year you sign up again since you owe the company money for your groceries from the last time.

"I met my first woman in Stann Creek one year and we done had our first daughter right off. But then one time back from a year at the camp I hear of better jobs down in Honduras. Even though I owe some money to Belize Estate, I borrow some passage money and we gone to Honduras in 1927. Down that side I worked for the United Fruit Company as a driver and they taught me to do some mechanical kinds of work. You see in those days the Fruit Company was stationed in all the republics and hired mostly the Spanish, but they employed many Belizeans too for the better jobs because we could talk English.

"My job paid good and we was mostly satisfied with the conditions there. When I gone to Honduras I planned to stay a year or two, but we stayed over that side eleven years. Finally I knew we was there too long and I wanted to go home. In the days before we left, the revolution [i.e., military reprisals against the Garifuna mentioned in chapter 3] begun in Honduras and many people was being killed, especially the Carib people there. By the time we got on the ship my wife was down with fever, and she died almost as we reach Belize. We done had four children by then, and so I sent them to live with my sisters in Stann Creek. In 1938 when I reach Belize there was no work to be found here at all, on account we was no longer shipping mahogany. So I gone back to Newtown to cut farm and just rest off.

"In 1940 they started the next war and the English asked for volunteers from British Honduras to join the fight. So I joined up with the North Caribbean Units and we shipped out from Belize for Trinidad. Because of the German submarines we stayed over in Port of Spain two months until the passage was safe and then we crossed over to England. We station some time in London and worked for the Home Defence and then they sent us to different parts of the country. At first I worked in a forest camp up in Scotland, and then they sent me back to London to work in the hospital dispensary. I never seen nothing like England in all my life. There was so much people, cars, trains, and other advancements. And they done treat us good, too. Before we left in '44 there was a fine ceremony for all of us from the North Caribbean Units. The duke of Edinburgh was there and he thanked us for our efforts and promised us land and a pension when we was sent home. But later on our own government never said nothing about our money, and then they forgot all about what we done in the war.

"When we left England the war never finished yet. The Germans put a torpedo in our ship and we just reached Iceland before it gone down. They put us on another ship and we gone on to New York, then by train to New Orleans, and then by sea again to Belize.

"In Belize after the war times was very hard on account of all the men who come back from the war. I stayed in Stann Creek in those times and met my second woman. I couldn't find no work and so we went back to Hopkins and I did some farming and fishing. My second woman died then, and by now my other children are gone to Belize [City] or the States . . . I stayed just as you see me now and didn't job out again until 1979, when I worked for two seasons for Lamott on Glover's Reef [a tourist resort operated by a European]. But Lamott is no good; he never paid me or nobody else for our work, and so I stopped work for him. Since that time I been here resting off with my daughter and her family. I want to go fishing out at the cayes again but I'm just too tired for that now.

". . . So now you know my story and the story of our ways of life here. I only regret that I never gone to the States as a young man to advance myself there. There's so much things that happened in my life here that was like a mystery to me; you work one day and the next you can't, one year there's sufficient money and the next is mauger [lean]. There's those that say it's God's will our lives are hard, but when I seen the advancements of places like England, I know it's *not* His will for men to live like we did here. I know that but I can't say why it's so."

In recounting the "mystery" of alternating steady earnings and hard times, Martínez is in fact acutely aware of the factors involved in these fluctuations. Having been taken from Newtown when he was less than ten years old, Martínez's working life was one of ever farther excursions from his village in pursuit of a livelihood. In succeeding years, as he began "to help himself," or to become independent of his family, he joined a mahogany gang in what was then the only source of wage labor commonly available. As forestry work lost its appeal, his response was to return neither to the limited subsistence base of his home village nor to the servitude of the mahogany gangs. Instead Martínez seized opportunities for migration of a longer distance, culminating in volunteer service during the Second World War.

His exposure to the "advancements" of Britain and the United States fueled an intense desire to permanently migrate, in which he was frustrated for reasons of age and income. For those of a later generation, knowledge of the amenities and opportunities of the developed countries is gained at a much earlier age. Since the early 1970s, younger adults in large numbers have employed this knowledge in seeking alternatives to the narrow range of livelihoods available in Belize.

The account of Jim Castillo (age forty-three) suggests both the difficulties and opportunities awaiting Belizeans who migrate to the United States. Born and raised in Hopkins, Castillo briefly visited the village in 1986 for the first time since moving to Chicago fifteen years before. His narrative, recounted in the idioms of American speech, reveals the facility with which members of his generation move between radically different cultures.

"I was born in Hopkins in 1943, not long after the '41 hurricane that caused my family to move from Newtown. My dad had a coconut farm near Newtown which was also destroyed and when he came to Hopkins he started to replant it at the north end of the village. Coconuts have always brought a good price if you sell them in town, so our family was a little better off than most villagers. At least we had a stable income.

". . . Naturally when I was a boy I had to help out on the farm, but my parents really stressed the schooling. They didn't want me to work if it took time out of my studies. After I graduated from standard six in Hopkins I went to high school in Dangriga and boarded with my mother's family there. It's still a big sacrifice for most families in the village to send their kids to high school, and when I was a boy it was almost unheard of. But somehow many of we Garinagu [Garifuna people] have managed to get a secondary education, and that's why so many—well, most in fact—of the country's teachers are Garifuna. Unfortunately, attending high school then didn't qualify you for much but teaching, and that's not exactly a high-paying job in Belize. But at least it's steady work. So like many of my schoolmates I wound up teaching in primary schools. I worked in Dangriga, Cayo, and some of the villages out-district. The problem with teaching is not just the low pay; it's the fact that you can be transferred at the whim of your school manager. So it's hard to put down roots in any one place. Maybe that's why teaching appeals to many of our young men, since they like to move around a lot.

"While I was working as a teacher, I always came back to Hopkins to stay with my folks during my summer vacations, and then I resumed my post in September. On one of those vacations I met my wife, Anna, and we were married later that same year. Believe me, living on a teacher's salary when you're single is one thing, but it's really hard when you're supporting a family like I was. Like a lot of Belizeans then— and there are even more now—I was infected with the States fever. I thought emigration was the only way to get ahead and that everything in Belize could only lead to a dead end. My wife and I talked it over and we agreed that I should go first while she and the girls stayed behind in Hopkins. Then I could send for them later on, after I was established. At first, I planned to go to Los Angeles, but I had a contact—the brother of a friend of mine—who lived in Chicago, and so I decided to go there. It was our original plan to be up there just a few years, but as you can see, things worked out differently.

"When I arrived in Chicago—the year was 1971—there were hardly any Belizeans living there, and nobody else from Hopkins. My contact helped me get a place to live and even arranged it so there was a Social Security card waiting for me when I got there. Finding a job was a lot harder than I expected, though, and the first one was a real letdown. I settled for washing dishes in a restaurant. Even when I was working forty-eight hours a week I could barely save anything toward my family's airfare after I paid my share of the rent and groceries. Yeah, economically the first few years were really rough, and being apart from my family didn't help things any. I thought that a high school diploma would bring me a better job than most immigrants, but it was three years before I found something that wasn't low-paying drudge work. I finally found a clerical job in the accounting department of a Chicago firm and I was able to send for Anna and the kids in late 1974. Then Anna went to work while I took night classes at electronics school for a year. After graduating I got a job as a serviceman for Zenith, which paid quite well.

"Since then, we've had another daughter and Anna has gone back to being a full-time housewife. After my first six years at Zenith, we saved enough for the down payment on a home. In some ways, we've really been lucky. I guess you could say that we've attained the American dream, or maybe the Belizean dream in America. Unfortunately, for most of my fellow Belizeans in the States, especially the ones who've just arrived, things aren't so rosy. I've seen a lot of people come to the United States from Hopkins in the last few years, sweat some minimum-wage shit work, and then go back no better off than when they came. Jobs are really hard to find in Chicago these days . . . and I know of some cases where our people have gone on to L.A. after trying to find work in Chicago for a year or more.

"I think every Belizean who reaches the United States sooner or later senses the same kind of disappointment that I did fifteen years ago. We go there with a certain picture of America in our minds and expect golden opportunities to just drop from heaven, but it just ain't so. For one thing, we all have to come to terms with racism in America, which is something we almost never think about before we get there. The fact that in Chicago in the 1980s you still can't live or even shop in certain areas just because you're black comes as a big shock to every new migrant. And it really hurts us, too—makes us feel . . . betrayed—because deep down Belizeans feel a lot of attachment to Americans and American culture. You only have to listen to the music on Radio Belize to know that. As Garinagu in Belize many of us have experienced put-downs from time to time by Creoles, but that's nothing compared to the situation in the States. There racism puts all blacks in the same class and one effect of it—maybe the only good thing to come of it—is that Garifuna and Creoles see their common interests better in the United States than in Belize.

". . . In the United States those of us who are from Hopkins do our best to keep the traditions alive. Some [new] immigrants are surprised to find that people from Hopkins still speak Garifuna in our homes in the States. I'm proud to say that my daughter born in the United States can understand Garifuna even though she's never set foot on Belizean soil. Because we keep up contact with one another, live near each other, and help out new arrivals from Belize, I don't think Garifuna culture is changing as much as some of the old people fear. It's just moving to another place. And then it's true that many of the people from Hopkins who go to the States don't go permanently. We all hope to return some day and I would bet that half of us do. This is my first trip back to Belize in fifteen years and the changes that I've seen this week in Hopkins are really remarkable. When I left it last this was a very isolated place. There was no road, no vehicles, and very few people ever left the village for long. At that time most of the people lived in what we called bush houses; there were only a few houses of lumber and zinc and none made of cement. Now I count almost thirty cement houses here and I can tell you this—just about every one of them was paid for by money earned in the United States, mostly in Chicago.

". . . It won't be too long before I'm able to retire and when I do we're planning to return here. After so many years in the States, it will take a lot of adjustment to come back to village life. But to come back here, to build a comfortable house and live in security is what we've been after all these years. You know, we didn't go to the States with the dream of becoming Americans, though we did put roots down there.

We went there hoping to find a better life for ourselves in Belize, even if it took us fifteen or twenty-five years to do it."

Both Castillo and Victor Martínez before him viewed migration as a means to get ahead, although Castillo's was the first generation to act on this belief in a systematic way. His life history also reflects the changing fortunes of Belizeans who have migrated to the United States in pursuit of improved employment opportunities. After a period of low-paying work and disillusionment with racism in the United States, Castillo attained a relatively middle-class standard of living in the late 1970s. Most Belizean migrants in the 1980s were not as successful due to contracting job opportunities.

Early migrants such as Castillo paved the way for later arrivals through arranging documentation, places to live, and employment references. The importance of such contacts is indicated by the fact that most Hopkins migrants are employed in only a few workplaces and occupations in the United States. Dozens of Hopkins men and women, for example, have worked on the custodial and service staff of one of Chicago's museums. The preference that Hopkins migrants express for Chicago over other destinations is entirely due to the advantages offered by an established migrant community, of which Castillo was a founding member. In an increasingly adverse economic situation, even the advantages of social support may not prove as fruitful as migration to another locale. From the decision of some migrants to leave Chicago in the early 1980s there have developed embryonic communities of Hopkins migrants in Los Angeles and New York that attracted more members by the end of the decade.

For many villagers, stories such as Castillo's are first a major incentive to migrate and later a cruel counterpoint to their own experiences in the United States. Most migrants since 1981 have remitted little of their sparse earnings or returned to Belize with few savings. Among the founders of the Hopkins Farmers' Cooperative are several men who were deported after entering the United States illegally. Others returned embittered by frustrating years of low-paying work. These and many other men deepened their involvement in cash-crop production as a result of new opportunities in the region's citrus economy and their lack of prior investments or commitment to other forms of production. Such individuals cite as their role models the relatively successful citrus farmers of the neighboring village of Silk Grass.

Farmer Dembigh Williams (age sixty) is representative of a number of Silk Grass residents who have benefited from the local expansion of citrus farming in recent years. As Williams himself states, the orange trees that he began planting in 1969 as a source of retirement income have provided an unexpected windfall since the early 1980s.

"My name is Dembigh Williams and I was born in Sittee River in 1926. My people goes way back in Sittee so I no know when the first Williams reach dey. My pop was mostly a banana farmer, but he worked some too at the sawmill at Sittee. In them days, this pine ridge area from Silk Grass Creek to South Stann Creek was all heavy forest, and the sawmill was working overtime milling pine lumber. Back then we Williams lived in the part of Sittee they call Freetown, which is the most closest to the sea.

"My daddy sold his bananas to United Fruit when the company dey de station in the Stann Creek part of the country. Around the time I was born the banana farmers them hit hard times because of the Panama disease, but my pa no have no trouble with that. But what humbug him for good was when the [United] Fruit Company left Belize so he couldn't sell his bananas but locally no more. So as long as I knowed him my daddy was a poor farmer and mostly sawed wood to maintain we. Later, when I was a boy, he plant out a lee coconut walk and sell some of the nuts, but mostly he work at the mill. You see, the reason he never could rely on much permanent crops in Sittee, such as coconut or citrus, was that we only hire the land each year from the Kramer Estates. Without no title in he hand, lone fool-fool develop farm that no fu he.

". . . There was four of we boys in me daddy's house that lived to be men, and all of we worked on the farm and sawed wood when we was old enough to work. When I was eighteen I get a wish to leave home and find something different. But cho! in those days, lone sawmill work was all there was. Well, I job out at a few mills but I gone back to Sittee after two years. Those were the war years, you know, so dey was a lot of work and the pay dey good then. Then just as sudden as it begun war finished and they begin to throw men out of work. Well, I kept me job but de pay de drop to a dollar a day and so eventually I walks off and begin to cut farm full time.

"I no job out again until 1951, when the citrus start coming good at Pomona. What I like about that job is they pay contract, so de more you work de more dey pay. I work out four seasons reaping and then dey get me work in the factory. Inside the work easier and de pay more better. But that work still seasonal you know, so every April I gone back a Sittee to look after de plantation dey. My brothers gone off one-one in the '50s so that left fu me me daddy coconut walk. By those times I think I had three manzanas [six acres] in coconut, which brought some lee pretty cash, let me tell you. But then I need every copper I could get since the *pikni* [children] start to come; you know the family de grow and the small children them never work yet. And like most boys I got some children outside [of marriage] too, so them I maintain as I can.

". . . The trouble come in '61 with Hattie of course. Man, I'll never forget how the squall blow that night. When the breeze start to pick up, all of we move off to me sister house in Middle Bank [farther inland]. As we reach dey the wind already knocking down trees all around us—not just plantain but coconut and mango, too. When I seen that I know our plantation finished. Well, that storm done take most of Sittee with it. My family and me sister family move once more that night when the squall take de zinc [roof] offa she house. We spend the night with a next four families in a lee house in High Sand, about three mile to the back of [inland from] we house. After the storm pass the next morning we seen the river raise up so that the village was like in a lagoon, only nobody could go no place since all the dories done wash away or bruk up in de night. We spend a next night in that house with those people—no food and no way to move on. On the evening of the second day some soldiers come past in a skiff looking for victims and we call out to they. I tell the officer make we sail by Free Town area where our house be and he me say, 'Man, dey nothing left dey now.' But I press him and so we circle past. But what the man de say was true. Our house no de dey, not one tree or even one lee house post. And me and me wife and *pikni* with only the clothes on we backs. So I asks, 'What we de do now?' They take we to a refugee center in Stann Creek and there we station for some months while I work for public works in common labor for reconstruction.

"Then I hears about the Silk Grass project for people that lost they homes in the storm. They promised new houses, light, and land and I thought that sound good for true. By the start of the next year we was already here and so was many people from Sittee and Hopkins, but most from Sittee. This was a raw place in those days, boy. Dey was no shade yet because dey was no trees, so sun hot. And then water always been a big problem here too. Later they done cross us when they want we to pay for the houses and light. So some people was gone already by '65 or '66, and we still losing some today. Most of them gone to the States. But that no vex me because that means more land for the rest that stays.

". . . Even after I cut farm at Silk Grass I work out full time at May-flower [a nearby sawmill], doing mill work like before. Some of the farmers them get the idea to plant citrus in those days and even though citrus prices was bad I decide to join in. I begin to think that I can't always work out and a man got to consider the future, no true? I buy me first budded trees in 1965 for 2 shillings [50 cents] each and start to plant out one acre. The more I plant the more work there is, but I still working out five days a week so time become a problem. I can't afford to walk off the job but as I work out so much my plantation begin suffering. So I talk to the foreman and explain my situations and asks if I can work three days a week so's to attend my citrus. At first he said no, you be here full time or no time. But then I tell him it will be no time then since my future more important than that job. I's playing poker, see, because I know I'm his best mill hand and he can't afford to let me go. And so after awhile he agreed to my plan and from that time I spend three days on the job and the next four on the farm.

". . . In those days we scarcely use fertilizer or gramoxone [paraquat] or such for lack of finance. It was all hand work and the first crops we reap was small and no pay hardly at all. But the price rise steady in the '70s till we could afford fertilizer and so on and with that our yields and profits rise up, too. By 1979 I done quit my job at Forestry and had over five acres of mature citrus, and bearing good, too. As the orange price continues up after that I get some more land and now I just finish plant out my fourth bloc [forty acres].

". . . To be frank with you, I always been a hard worker, both on the job and on the farm. I like to think that's why I done so good in the last years, but I know that's not all. Now some of these boys them they start to plant citrus only when the price gone up so they just reap they first lee crop this year. They hope to catch up but they done missed the boat because the price already on its way down again. And now they got big debts to pay and the price next year won't even cover their interest and the cost of their fertilizer and such [in late 1986, widespread rumors predicted an imminent collapse of citrus prices, but such fears never materialized]. Now I don't blame them—that's just my point. Most of they are hard-working and I could be just like they, but because I start citrus early on I seen my share of benefits, mostly this year and last. Now I worry for the future, too, but I done plant out my citrus so my main costs are past me. I'll make it through all right, but I don't know about some of these boys. Call it my good luck that I'm not where they are now."

Farmers throughout Stann Creek district have long relied on citrus for a modest retirement income. When Williams planted his first citrus trees with this in mind, he could not have foreseen the favorable turn of producer prices that occurred in the late 1970s. On the other hand, he would not have been able to fully capture the benefits of high producer prices had he not skillfully negotiated the transition from wage labor to citrus production. Full-time wage laborers find great difficulty in adopting citrus farming not just for its high start-up costs but because of scheduling conflicts and insufficient household labor to allot to farming. At a time that he was still dependent on wages earned at the sawmill, Williams succeeded in reducing his involvement in wage work and increasing his commitment to citrus. This he did through behavior that was openly strategic; in his words, "playing poker" with the mill foreman by bluffing about his intention to quit.

On this strategy depended much of the subsequent success of Williams' citrus farm and the substantial farm earnings that he attained in the mid-1980s. By 1989 Williams had forty-one acres of citrus under cultivation and was earning Bze $32,000 in net income from his farm. Unlike Dembigh Williams, other villagers have seen little improvement in their economic well-being, despite years of hard work on area farms. Such individuals constitute a growing majority left behind in the wake of others' advances.

Like a small and steadily diminishing number of Mopan Maya residents, Vicente Chol (age sixty-three) came to Silk Grass from the village of San Antonio in the Toledo district. In his account, Chol draws an unfavorable comparison between life in the predominately Creole settlement of Silk Grass with the Indian village in which he was raised.

"I was raised in San Antonio, Toledo district, but my own people don't belong to there. My parents came from Pueblo Viejo, near the Guatemalan border. When I was a young boy, my pa moved us to San Antonio because it was on the main [road], so there was more opportunities to earn a living there. In some of those villages in the bush you could scarce sell anything because there's no market and no way to reach town, but my country people [i.e., other members of one's own

ethnic group] in San Antonio always brought their produce or pigs to
P.G. [Punta Gorda] to earn their lee cash. That was all good land in
Toledo district—all black cohune ridge soil so you could grow anything you wanted, except permanent crops. The government in those
days decreed all the land around Toledo villages as Maya reserve, which
meant you could cut new farms each year for a five-dollar rent but they
never would give you title to that land. People who no been to Toledo
say the Indians them never want to civilize the land with permanent
crops, but that's not so. Until just a few years aback, this reserve system
prevented us from planting citrus or cocoa, so we had no choice but to
use the milpa system.

"I was the oldest boy in my family and when I was seventeen I took
over to head the family because my pa done died. Our living in those
days was from selling hogs in P.G. because the people in town them ate
pork but they never produced it theyselves. In 1942, when I was nine-
teen, the government sent out word that work was there in Panama for
as much Belizeans as want it. They offered us pay of a shilling U.S.
[U.S. $.25] for an hour of common labor, which was big money in
those days. At that time in San Antonio, one egg cost just one cent, five
eggs for five cents. How much is an egg now? Thirty-five cents! Well,
since the pay was so good and my next brother was old enough to take
charge [of the family farm], I begin to think maybe I'll take a lee walk
[journey] to Panama. So I get my passport and leave from Belize in
April 1942. We never had to pay for passage to go and come since they
deduct it from our first paychecks. But the work was never what I
hoped it to be. I worked ten hours to a night shift, discharging big
trucks and loading a warehouse. That was very heavy work for true,
and many men was falling ill and dying from fever and overwork. Then
I never like the food there neither, and it was very costly. It was all
Chinee-type food, and the rice tarry [sticky], just like lab [porridge].
I begun to miss home and me lee corn tortilla and beans, so soon
I'm back in San Antonio with scarce anything saved from my year in
Panama.

"By this time I met my wife here and we built a house of our own
near my family's. I gone back to farming, selling pigs and rice at P.G.,
but sometimes I worked out, too. In the 1960s they were exporting
bananas from Alabama [a settlement in southern Stann Creek district]
and the managers hired about fifty of us from San Antonio to work
their plantation. This was full-time, year-round work, so I left San An-

Maya residents of Silk Grass.

tonio and we lived right there at Alabama about three years. For some time we made shipments regular, and since there was some good land to the back, the workers there could cut their own farms in their spare time. The pay was never good, but with the crops from my own farm there we made it somehow. Well, in 1970 the Sigatoka disease hit Alabama hard and all eight hundred acres of bananas was condemned. The company closed up and we workers was laid off. Most of them returned to San Antonio. But some stayed on to go back to farming full-time for themselves. And that's how Alabama became the village of Maya Mopan.

"As for me, my family by that time was of a size that I needed some work since farming never paid enough to support all of them. That was when I moved up to Silk Grass since I heard that houses and land was available here and jobs not too far away at the Citrus Company and Forestry [Department]. I got a ten-acre bloc by location ticket [a discontinued form of land tenure assignment] and bought this lee house. Each year I cut a farm on my bloc and then after I reaped my corn and rice I moved over to Pomona to work for the Citrus Company. I reaped oranges that way for five seasons, then I find a job as a common laborer at Mayflower. That was much better than Pomona, since Mayflower's closer and I come back every evening. When I worked Pomona side I could never plant beans on my farm since the citrus reaping kept me away at *mata hambre* time [literally "kill hunger," this refers to crops planted in December after rice and corn are harvested]. But when I worked at Mayflower I could tend the farm right through if I was never too tired when I reach home. In 1983 the government laid off all common labor at Forestry—with no pensions and no gratuity—so since then I've done lone farming. I begin then to plant some citrus on my bloc and I have five acres planted out, but the trees no bear as yet.

". . . I'm constant fighting for a living now, because the land I have at Silk Grass Creek is no good. It's low and it floods too much, so really it's best to plant rice there. But rice is too much work at my age and most of our food is this blessed corn, which is hard to grow on flood land. Whenever my country people cut farm they always look for slopey land that drains off the rain, so they can grow plenty corn. Here you have to cut five acres to grow as much corn as two acres at San Antonio. I'm going broke here having to buy most of our food, and you can't get a man to help you here unless you hire him. In our Maya and Kekchi villages we don't need a single copper to live, neither to buy food or to hire a man. We Indians grow all we eat and we help out each other on our farms, but never in Silk Grass. The people here don't know how to cooperate, they only know the value of money but not the value of helping your neighbors. Now, our different nations of people here pull together all right, but if you need a man's help you better be able to pay for it. That's why most of my country people who come here in the past are gone now to Maya Centre or Red Bank.

"Next year I plan to knock down this house and move it to Maya Centre myself. I know there's good land for corn there, and many of my own San Antonio people are settled there. I been here too long fighting by myself and paying for things that's free in other places. I know when I reach Maya Centre that I'll reach home at last."

Chol's narrative illustrates the changing composition of Silk Grass's population and the erosion of local subsistence production as its residents turn to citrus farming. Like other Maya residents who left Silk Grass for exclusively Indian villages, his is among the few voices raised in opposition to the community's involvement in export production. Noting the lack of cooperation and difficulties in satisfying his subsistence needs in Silk Grass, Chol repudiates the increasing monetariza-

tion of village social relations. In contrast, most of his Creole and Garifuna counterparts, as well as some Maya, have furthered these trends
by entering the labor market or abandoning staple crop production for
citrus.

Chol's ability to resist these trends is enhanced by the continued
existence of Maya enclaves not fully penetrated by wage and commodity relations. Compared to surrounding communities, such areas
are "regions of refuge" (Aguirre-Beltran 1979) from the dislocations
accompanying village production for export markets. Yet even in comparatively remote Maya areas of southern Belize, indigenous commodity producers are embracing the innovations of citrus and cocoa
production. Chol's flight from wage relations may be short-lived as
communal institutions in villages throughout the region are undermined by an expanding export commodity market.

Common themes emerge from the working life histories of these
village residents. In spite of their diverse experiences, villagers are
acutely conscious of the nonlocal factors that shape their livelihoods
and communities. For many villagers, awareness of these factors results
from extensive experience outside their communities in a variety of
occupations. Three of the five men lived for periods of time outside
Belize, yet the breadth of their work and travel experience is not atypi-
cal of village residents. While the consciousness of these men is the
product of social relations in which they take part, their behavior does
not simply reproduce those relations in unchanged form. Like Vicente
Chol, some individuals enact roles that remain within the limits of
existing social relations and resist the onset of change. Others, like
Dembigh Williams, exhibit a willingness to take risks and experiment
with new behaviors to expand the array of opportunities available to
them. Such experiments are viewed by others and, if judged worth-
while and feasible, they are adopted on a wider scale and routinized as
new normative practices. From their understanding of existing structures, individuals explore new possibilities that may provide the raw
material for altered sets of rules and relationships.

This process of structuration is most evident at critical junctures in
the working lives of several village residents. In some cases, innovative
choices made by just one or two individuals established precedents
which diffused rapidly through the wider community. The specific patterns of migration and remittances that join Hopkins households with
the world economy are ultimately attributable to the past actions of

one such person. Jim Castillo's migration to Chicago resulted from highly contingent circumstances, yet in residing there he established the nucleus of an expatriate community in which later migrants found jobs, housing, and social support. Castillo's decision not only set a precedent for migration as a household survival strategy but also tied the outcome of that strategy to the economic fortunes of a single locale in the United States. Migration has thus had different implications for Hopkins residents (both those who leave and those who receive remittances) than for migrants from Dangriga, most of whom settled in Los Angeles. Similarly, the decisions of Silk Grass farmers who planted citrus in the 1960s, such as Dembigh Williams, culminated more than a decade later in a stratified village social order. As land was consolidated in the hands of citrus-farming residents, the possibility of citrus production was foreclosed for other villagers. In their relationship to later changes in village class structure, it is possible to see in these cases that the innovative behaviors of some altered the range of choices later available to all villagers.

Factional politics, the mobilization of citrus producers, and the citrus workers' movements described earlier illustrate agency in its contingent and intentional dimensions. In capturing a larger share of world market prices through political means citrus growers achieved their goals of improved incomes and consumption levels. Among other contingent effects, their successes also increased the disparities between themselves and other agriculturalists, readily observable in such communities as Silk Grass. Having obtained higher prices for citrus, the region's farmers have created new possibilities for domestic economies and new avenues for investment. These precedents encouraged Hopkins farmers to adopt citrus, a decision resulting in the emergence of classes in their once relatively egalitarian community. The range of household productive activities and the social structures that correspond to them are not passive reflections of the world market but result from such antecedent and innovative forms of agency.

Domestic economies and social relations in both Silk Grass and Hopkins have experienced substantial changes since the early 1970s, when the communities were last documented ethnographically. Villagers' dependence on external income grew during this period, as did class disparities between citrus producers and traditional agriculturalists or wage laborers. Some observers may describe these changes as the result of an all-embracing world economy or technological changes "introduced" into village settings. These assessments, characteristic of some anthropological approaches to social change, neglect the fact that change does not occur at the analytical and abstract level of structure. Rather, the new social relations in rural Stann Creek district are a form of adaptation, resulting from the strategies of agents who strive to realize their objectives, satisfy their needs, and make sense of a rapidly changing world (cf. Bennett 1976: 847). These strategies in turn ultimately originate in individuals' decisions and the consciousness that governs them. The narratives presented here illustrate how such decisions, both of an innovative and conservative nature, arise as individuals respond to a changing political economy. Their responses may be attempts to break free of existing constraints or efforts to reproduce existing roles and expectations. As change took place in the political economy of rural Stann Creek district, the innovations of some were consciously adopted by others. These strategies account for the fact that the members of these communities had thoroughly refashioned, rather than merely reproduced, the village social and economic structures of twenty years before.

CHAPTER 8

BETWEEN AGENCY AND DEPENDENCE:

LESSONS FROM A

CHANGING WORLD SYSTEM

I n the summer of 1989, I returned to rural Stann Creek district to renew acquaintances and follow up on my earlier predictions. During my absence the expansion of citrus farming had noticeably accelerated throughout southern Belize. This was apparent even before my arrival in Dangriga, as the bus on which I traveled began its winding descent from the Maya Mountains to the coastal plain. In places where primary forest had been virtually untouched since prehistory there stood newly established citrus farms. Bulldozers and chainsaws were incessantly at work along the road, leveling ancient tropical forest with indifferent ease. Rows of recently planted orange seedlings clung to steep foothill slopes, while feeder roads opened once-untraveled areas to cultivation. Closer to town, hundreds of acres of forest had been cleared to accommodate the expanding citrus holdings of one of Stann Creek's nouveau riche growers.

The most apparent feature of citrus expansion in southern Belize in recent years has been its growing inequality. Although Belize has often been considered an exception to the patterns of land tenure prevailing in commercial agriculture elsewhere in Central America, such is no longer the case. Current conditions in much of Stann Creek district suggest latifundia in the making. By the end of the 1980s a handful of families had quietly assumed control of the majority of the district's land under citrus and banana cultivation. Such land acquisitions have been made at an astonishing rate through access to state institutions and credit sources denied small farmers. A past director of the CGA, for example, expanded his holdings under citrus from thirty-five acres in 1978 to over three thousand ten years later. Meanwhile, smaller-scale citrus farmers in communities such as Silk Grass struggle with little success for additional land to expand their own holdings. In a region where arable land is increasingly scarce, the ability to acquire land for expansion has become dependent not only on finances but also on political influence with the state bodies that allocate public lands for private use. Whether such disparate treatment by the state, and the consequent marginalization of the rural poor and small farmer, will engender the same degree of class consciousness and overt confrontation encountered elsewhere in Central America remains to be determined. In this context, perhaps the comment of a Guatemalan banana worker in southern Stann Creek is most telling: "Lo hemos visto en otra parte. Y el latifundismo se realiza aquí también" (We've seen it happening elsewhere. And latifundia are being created here, too).

In hamlets and villages along the Southern Highway, the frenetic pace of land clearing and planting attested to that region's deepening involvement in the citrus economy as well. In Hopkins, the attention of villagers in 1989 was temporarily diverted from these economic changes, despite the troubling disparities that had resulted from them. As it planned the first national elections in five years, the government poured resources into Hopkins with conspicuous generosity. In large part this was because the ruling party's candidate vied with the village's PUP leader for the district seat in the National Assembly, an office considered critical to the governing party's ability to survive a close election. As speculation grew over the date of the impending elections, long-delayed plans for electrification were hastened to completion and Public Works trucks unloaded building materials for village residents on an almost daily basis. Noting the government's lavish attempts to win their loyalty, many Hopkins residents quietly congratulated themselves on their indispensability to the "big men" of national politics.

The use of patronage during the 1989 elections provides an apt metaphor for the political and economic struggles of the rural poor in Stann Creek district. However much the powerful attempt to manipulate the poor in their interests, manipulation clearly extends in both directions. Villagers are conscious of their necessity to the powerful and employ that fact to extract concessions from them. While savoring the benefits of such strategizing (as measured in meals at campaign rallies, assignments to works projects, or village electrification), the rural poor do not tally all the costs of bidding for the favors of politicians and elites. The pervasive factionalism that polarizes kin and neighbors alike in Hopkins is one such penalty, as is the inequitable distribution of resources intended for village development.

In contrast to the powerless masses that populate many scholarly and popular accounts of Third World societies, rural Belizeans struggle in numerous ways to control a shifting and uncertain economic environment. Such efforts occur first in the realm of production, where in response to the limitations of traditional livelihoods many villagers seek more profitable alternatives. However welcome export agriculture may be in the short term, it also entails immediate costs that exceed the returns of staple crops and wage work. Here villagers' struggles enter the political sphere, for factional conflicts determine how external resources are distributed and mobilized into subsistence change. Finally, as commodity producers for the world market, rural residents also confront capital over the share of world market prices they receive for their products and labor. At all levels, the acts of individuals and groups continuously alter the array of choices they confront by creating new alternatives and foreclosing others.

Villagers' efforts to secure a livelihood and assert their interests within a changing political economy suggest several lessons for ethnographers of the world system. Perhaps the most apparent of these pertains to the relationship between humans, their cultural practices, and the environment. Theories derived from ecology (Netting 1977; Harris 1980) maintain that social relations are ultimately determined by technological adaptation, population density and growth rates, and other aspects of the human-environment relationship. Given similar demographic and techno-environmental profiles, ecological models would predict the evolution of similar social relations (Harris 1980: 55 ff.). In Belize, productive technology, settlement patterns, and soil and resource endowments clearly constrain the range of options available to rural producers. Yet the differing livelihoods and social relations actually exhibited by Creoles, Garifuna, Maya, and mestizos within similar constraints indicate that village economies are culturally as well as ecologically organized. In satisfying their material needs, people act according to their understanding of the natural and social worlds, a con-

Hopkins farmer and newly bearing orange trees, 1989.

sciousness which is derived from experience as well as their culture and history (cf. Ellen 1982; Bargatzky 1984). The human-environment relationship is mediated by technology, social relations of production, and even symbolic representations, all of which are the products of each group's unique culture history.

The subsistence changes occurring throughout Stann Creek district are inseparable from political economic determinants that render some forms of livelihood more attractive to villagers than others. Yet it is in conscious activity and its unintended consequences that such factors as world commodity prices are experienced on the local level. The configuration of the region's political economy is largely the outcome of such agency. Were it not for the militancy of the Citrus Growers' Association, the factional politics of Hopkins farmers, or even the strategizing of individuals such as Dembigh Williams, village and domestic economies in southern Belize would differ radically from their depiction here. The actions of even the apparently powerless, then, are both instrumental and structurally significant. To reduce behavior to the functional requirements of economic utility, group adaptation, or political economy is to deny the rural poor the very agency demonstrated in the preceding chapters.

The role of agency in a changing rural economy is best illustrated in Hopkins, where some residents have brought about major changes in subsistence through the rewards of patronage and factionalism. Villagers' adoption of citrus production may yield higher cash incomes in the short term but in the long run will leave them more dependent than before on nonlocal food sources, expensive farm inputs, and volatile market fluctuations. Insofar as factional struggles diffuse class consciousness and corresponding forms of political action, these survival strategies also perpetuate elite control over smallholders and wage laborers. However much it contributes to substantial gains among some villagers, factionalism is a flawed adaptation. It limits the ability of the rural poor *as a class* to change the fundamental conditions of their lives. Rural Belizeans exhibit recognizably human characteristics when responding to economic change: They may fail to anticipate the future, make mistaken predictions, and occasionally emerge worse off than before. However faulty and uncertain, their efforts to control their economic destinies also distinguish them from the unidimensional and passive figures residing in other accounts of economic change.

The second lesson of this study pertains to the consequences of agency among the rural poor. Prevailing views within political anthropology (Alavi 1973; Frankel and von Vorys 1972) would dismiss a good deal of local political activity as irrelevant infighting orchestrated by powerful outsiders. Such views neglect the lasting effects of patronage and village factionalism, which are neither extrinsic to class relations nor neutral in their impact on social structure. Hopkins factions have acquired class features by mobilizing resources that can be channeled into commercial agriculture. Contrary to classical Marxist approaches to social differentiation, village stratification has not arisen from random advantages within the sphere of production, nor has it dissolved earlier affiliations. Hopkins households are differentiating along the lines of prior social relations from the economic and political strategies of local farmers. In this process, factionalism has been intensified by the exclusionary policies of the farmers' cooperative, rather than being supplanted by class consciousness. The use of factional politics to bring about changes in production illustrates how social structural change emerges from conscious activity. This case suggests that the shift to rural capitalism cannot be understood through inevitable tendencies of the world market or the "laws of motion" of peripheral capitalism. It is instead a historically specific and often contingent process.

Villagers' efforts to interpret and influence the external political economy also suggest a third lesson of the study. Despite the constraints of their dependence, the rural poor of Stann Creek district are not without leverage over the nonlocal determinants of their livelihoods. Obviously, many factors that govern their well-being are beyond their control. Belizeans cannot determine the cost of tractors and petrochemicals, the world price of citrus concentrate, or tariff preferences. In a variety of ways, however, they have influenced how these factors are expressed locally. The success of the waterfront workers and Citrus Growers' Association in securing higher earnings for their members has had a significant impact on villagers' livelihoods. These producers benefited from citrus price trends not due to improved world market conditions but because they confronted processors over their share of income from that market as prices rose in the 1970s and 1980s. Through such organized efforts, rural Belizeans demonstrate that they are not the stationary targets of metropolitan-based economic forces. In struggling with the elites that mediate between them and the world market, the rural poor have been surprisingly successful at defining market forces to their advantage.

In contrast to some studies of the incorporation of the Third World poor into commodity relations (Bradby 1982; Scott 1985), Belizean villagers, with a few exceptions, do not resist the transition from subsistence agriculture to commercial production. Rural residents readily acknowledge the immediate input costs of this transition but rarely the social costs of stratification, market volatility, or reduced food self-sufficiency. Despite the latter consequences of incorporation into the world system, most agricultural households adopt citrus if possible because of the dearth, poor returns, or riskiness of local income-earning alternatives.

From the enticements of citrus production, and even greater allure of United States migration, it is not at all apparent that rural residents perceive ongoing economic changes away from traditional livelihoods in an unfavorable light. To suggest, then, that the poor invariably resist market incorporation is to neglect the many forms of agency by which people not only accommodate change but actively embrace it. Perhaps unwittingly, analyses of resistance to commodity relations reinforce an entrenched stereotype that the rural poor are conservative adherents of unchanging tradition. A further implication is that their efforts, however concerted, are ultimately futile given the inevitability of capitalist expansion. In contrast, the image of the poor that emerges here is that they creatively strive to control their economic destinies by whatever means available to them. Given appropriate resources or at the least the hope of attaining them, they are as likely to be the exponents of rural capitalism as its foes.

For most rural Belizeans, the world system has seemed to create more opportunities than disincentives for involvement. Notwithstanding the often severe consequences of that involvement (effects which may go unrecognized during periods of market expansion), the transition to rural capitalism in this case has scarcely been met by resistance in the realm of production. Resistance is rather confined to a limited political sphere where many rural producers vociferously assert their interests before those of capital. Yet even in the political realm, some select a strategy of accommodation, hoping perhaps that collaboration with local elites and foreign capital will yield greater benefits than asserting the interests of their class. The task, then, confronting analyses of the incorporation process is to determine what conditions engender resistance or accommodation and under what circumstances individuals forsake an identification with their class for self-interested dealings with elites. As is suggested in this work, class-based resistance is merely one of a number of strategies adopted by individuals in the face of economic change.

The final, critical lesson of this study applies to institutions attempting to implement development projects in communities such as Hopkins and Silk Grass. As a nation of little industrialization, attenuated local markets, primitive infrastructure, and heavy reliance on unpredictable world commodity markets, Belize is almost a textbook case in underdevelopment. These lessons apply then to other societies as well. The impact of foreign assistance in Hopkins has undeniably been a sort of development, if that process is defined as technical changes in production leading to increased agricultural incomes. The promotion of sustainable, purportedly nonideological organizations aimed at increasing rural production levels and incomes has become a priority of the grassroots model of development in Latin America and the Caribbean (Bray 1991). Even institutions such as the World Bank, which once exclusively favored large-scale and heavily capitalized development projects, now recognize that traditional development efforts usually bypass the rural poor (Kottak 1985: 326 ff.). While assistance to large-scale commercial agriculture at most offers the poor some seasonal employment, local decentralized organizations such as cooperatives are increasingly seen as conduits of direct development assistance to impoverished communities. Less benignly, the grassroots model also embraces the implicit political objective of earlier rural development policies: that of diminishing the appeal of populist or revolutionary political movements in rural areas (cf. de Janvry 1981: 252).

A primary stated goal of the grassroots model is its technological and economic feasibility for poor communities. Depending on the degree to which this emphasis is observed in planning, grassroots development efforts may avert some of the more pronounced social dislocations arising from development programs, such as the Green Revolution, that favor already wealthy farmers. As the demise of the Hopkins Fishermen's Cooperative illustrates, even grassroots projects are not immune from poor planning. Nor does strict adherence to criteria of technological and economic appropriateness insure that projects will have equitable consequences. Considering the "pervasive factionalism" long documented even in egalitarian communities (Siegel and Beals 1960), development policymakers should realize that funds injected into rural communities may be monopolized by one group to the exclusion of others. Given the divisions within Hopkins and the absence of cash-earning alternatives to citrus, stratification is an unavoidable consequence of the agricultural changes described in this book. Entirely aside from the stratification, dependence, and uncertainty that attend citrus production, however, a more fundamental question remains whether this form of development best meets the needs of the majority of the rural population.

The composite of household incomes presented in table 2 (chapter 3) indicates that, on average, agriculture constitutes a far smaller portion of Hopkins incomes than other sources. Indeed, in only a very small number of Hopkins households (12 percent of the total) did agricultural earnings in 1986 exceed those of wage labor or fishing. As in other rural communities in the Americas (Painter 1984; Deere and de Janvry 1979), agriculture for most Hopkins households is a subsidiary economic activity that permits survival on earnings from other productive activities. Despite its highly positive effects on the income of cooperative members, agricultural development may not improve the living standards of as many villagers as would policies addressing the other income sources that make up rural livelihoods. Foremost among these, of course, are the wages earned on corporate citrus and banana estates.

As discussed earlier, one of the bases of disarticulated accumulation has been an overall suppression of wage rates in peripheral economies. This study has documented a variety of ways in which disarticulated accumulation is enacted in Belize. Cheap food policies, the maintenance of household subsistence production as a subsidy to capital, and political weakening of workers' organizations all contribute to a lowering of average wages by diminishing the consumption needs and capacities of workers. An examination of villagers' livelihoods suggests that living standards of the rural poor would be more dramatically improved by increasing their wage earnings rather than their agricultural incomes. Such policies would obviously imply the dismantling of the institutional bases of disarticulated accumulation. Development that does not merely subsidize capital accumulation with low wages requires the expansion of internal markets by elevating consumption standards among the producing classes of the country.

Development as it has actually occurred in Stann Creek district exhibits none of these features. Dramatic growth has taken place within export agriculture, while staple crop production languishes due to the constraints on its profitability. Like the other nations of the Caribbean Common Market (CARICOM), Belize has committed itself to diversifying exports away from agricultural commodities, such as sugar, that experienced sharp declines in world prices in the early 1980s (Deere et al. 1990: 46). Such plans represent a reversion in development policy making away from import substitution toward the earlier model of comparative advantage, whereby Third World nations specialize in the export of commodities that cannot be produced in the industrialized nations. The industries to be established under such policies—citrus production, garment manufacturing, and tourism, for example—are nontraditional for Belize. Yet they remain export-oriented sectors with few linkages to the local economy or local demand. Emblematic of this process is the motor of development in Stann Creek district, where 96 percent of all citrus production is exported for metropolitan consumption.

Far from lessening the structure of disarticulated accumulation, today's diversified development strategies strengthen an existing system of production based upon low wages. Foremost among the resources that Belize provides at comparative advantage is its low-cost labor relative to developed regions in the world economy. Liberal investment codes now lure foreign capital to establish export-oriented manufacturing sectors. By 1986, Belize had established two industrial parks that were in effect free-trade zones where foreign investors could import raw materials and export finished commodities free of duty. Under the most liberal terms in the Anglophone Caribbean, investors in Belize were granted ten- to fifteen-year tax holidays and unlimited rights to profit repatriation (Deere et al. 1990: 145). But perhaps the most attractive incentive for prospective investors in Belize is the prevailing wage of 85 cents per hour in export-processing industries, which ranks within the lowest quartile of wage rates among CARICOM nations (ibid.: 149).

Export diversification has alleviated some of the balance of payments deficits Belize encountered in the early 1980s, when world sugar prices fell dramatically (Government of Belize 1991: 5). As a long-term strategy of development, however, it does little to reduce the country's vulnerability to fluctuating world demand for its products. What is produced in Belize remains subject to consumer demand in metropolitan countries, which is likely to change with as much volatility in the future as it has in the past. Export-driven development also insures that the needs of the rural and urban poor will remain unmet, for under disarticulated accumulation they are denied the earnings necessary to acquire adequate housing, food, clothing, and sanitation. Unable to generate demand for such basic needs, the limited consumption capacity of the poor virtually guarantees that they will not be produced.

An alternative form of development may be envisioned, one which resolves today's contradictions of economic growth and accompanying poverty. Some dependency and world systems theorists have advocated "delinking" from the world economy as the only viable strategy of equitable growth in the Third World (Frank 1969; Weisskopf 1978; Amin 1990). Given the limited productive and investment capacities of Belizean industries and the state, such policies if implemented in full would imply a level of austerity intolerable to all but the poorest of rural residents. Yet one need not endorse utopian or agrarian ideals of autarky to recognize the need for greater economic self-reliance in countries such as Belize. The fundamental element of any alternative model of equitable development would be sectoral articulation, a linkage between incomes and productivity increases throughout the economy. As new investment occurs wages must be permitted to rise in tandem, allowing consumption capacity to increase accordingly. Coupled with state investment priorities for domestic social needs, such policies would not only improve the living standards of the poor but also encourage countries such as Belize to produce more of what they consume. The essential outlines of development must not follow the austerity prescriptions of comparative advantage but rather emulate the political and economic features that afforded the now-developed countries a degree of equitable growth in the postwar period.

Such essential changes could occur only at the behest of the state and would inevitably incur formidable resistance from those that benefit from a low-wage economy. Required changes in state policy ultimately have to emerge from the demands of producing classes as expressed electorally and in their confrontations with capital and elites. Political mobilization of this sort is not improbable considering the proven ability of rural producers to organize themselves and express their interests, as well as the democratic attributes of Belizean society. It is here that the nonideological attributes of grassroots development become crippling liabilities on the road to equitable growth. While grassroots organizations have permitted some rural households in Belize to prosper from the world citrus market, development with equity will have to await changes that are far more comprehensive than the adoption of new crops and agricultural technologies. Such changes are inherently political, for they affect how the benefits of economic growth are socially distributed. If they are able to assemble the array of forces required of development that articulates growth and consumption, Belizeans will have won their final victory over the world system.

METHODOLOGY

The field research on which this monograph is based took place during a period of continuous residence in the village of Hopkins between December 1985 and December 1986 and a return visit to the communities during the summers of 1989 and 1990. During my residence in Hopkins I also made biweekly visits to Silk Grass. The methods of data collection consisted of participant observation, semistructured and unstructured interviews, the collection of working life histories, and a household economic survey administered in the final third of field research. Some participant observation took place as I assisted villagers in agricultural and fishing activities. Experience in local agriculture helped corroborate estimates of labor inputs obtained from interviews with farmers. Overall, there was a high degree of correspondence between calculations of productive inputs derived from participant observation and informants' estimates. Consequently, I feel confident in reporting informants' estimates for those activities that I was not able to directly observe or measure.

Observing interaction in daily and formal settings, such as meetings of village councils, cooperatives, and producers' associations, provided data on the major factional divisions among villagers and within groups. These data were illuminated by open-ended discussions with participants and key informants after the events I had witnessed. My records of these events are in all cases composites of their own accounts. However vigorously participants and partisans disagreed with each other on the merits of their positions, I am confident that they themselves would narrate these events in similar (albeit more colorful) terms.

The collection of working life histories was not part of my planned research methodology but emerged as I grew acquainted with various individuals in both villages. The narratives of villagers' lives were easily collected, since I met few adult males in either community who were unwilling to talk about themselves and express their opinions. Working life narratives were assembled as they reflected the significant social forces in each community's history. I am aware that the representativeness of the narratives is greatly limited by the fact that they were collected only from male residents. As a solitary male fieldworker, I had little recourse but to assemble life histories in the manner I did. Notwithstanding their cooperation with the economic survey, women were more reticent in discussing many important details of their lives.

As earlier mentioned, I deferred the administration of a household economic survey until the last stage of fieldwork, when I was well known to all members of the communities and could reliably gauge the accuracy of their responses to structured questionnaires. This delay allowed me to refine my survey from the crude instrument that I brought with me to the field. I also had to devise an adequate procedure for measuring community stratification though survey data. Where households engage in varying mixes of subsistence and cash-earning activities, cash income cannot be adopted as a reliable measure of stratification. It could not, for example, measure the relative wealth differences between a wage-earning household that purchases much of its food and one engaged primarily in subsistence farming. The methods advocated elsewhere to circumvent this difficulty, in which cash values are assigned to subsistence production (cf. Chibnik 1978), appeared problematic for agricultural systems in which production levels of certain staples could not be easily measured. In addition to the difficulty of measuring groundfood and plantain yields, much produce is simply given away in noncash exchanges between Garifuna households.

As an alternative method I quantified household food expenditures from economic surveys and subtracted them from the household's total income. This procedure yielded a measure of disposable income above the household's subsistence needs, which represents real wealth differences between households and the ability of their members to invest in subsistence change. Data on household food expenditure were relatively easily obtained, since many households kept monthly accounts at village shops, and their members could easily estimate weekly expenditures for other purchased staples, such as fish, meat, milk, or eggs. In other cases, I was able to achieve intuitively reasonable estimates of food expenditure by eliciting from informants the composition of their diets for the preceding several days. The resulting data on household food expenditures are compatible with my own observations of household diets, as well as other research on food expenditures in Belize (cf. MacInnes 1983). For the longitudinal comparison of household earnings presented as a Lorenz curve in figure 8 (chapter 4), total rather than disposable income was employed due to the absence of consumption data from Chibnik's 1971 survey.

Having devised a prototype questionnaire, I administered it on an experimental basis to several key informants. Their answers, I felt, would indicate the instrument's adequacy in measuring incomes and expenditures, as well as setting the parameters of reliability for the community as a whole. I was gratified when, after my first administration of the survey, my neighbor praised our interview as a "good discussion." After adjustments to my questionnaire (most of which he himself recommended), I proceeded to spend the next three months conducting a comprehensive economic survey of the villages.

To render my household survey data comparable with earlier research in the area, I designed my sample selection procedure after that of Chibnik (1975). To Chibnik's systematic sampling procedure I added some modifications to survey a broader cross-section of households. I sampled alternate households when counting from one end of each village to the other, deleting only those households whose members had engaged in no cash-earning activities in the preceding year. My resulting sample differs from that of Chibnik in respect to its somewhat larger size (eighty-two rather than fifty households) and its inclusion of households headed by women and those involved in nonagricultural pursuits. I deleted from sampling consideration three economically inactive households, which in all cases consisted of single elderly women who subsisted from foreign remittances. The resulting sample, therefore, is not entirely representative with respect to the age and sex of household heads, nor does it fully reflect the importance of remittances in the village economies. Several other deviations from randomness also occurred in Hopkins, where one individual refused to participate in the survey, and three others with whom I was acquainted asked to be included despite the fact that my sampling procedure had omitted their households. These adjustments of the sample do not, I believe, detract from its representation of the economically active village populations. In both villages, the survey accounts for approximately 60 percent of all income-earning households.

The administration of each household survey required between two and three hours, with each survey completed over two visits. The first visit was devoted to a census of household members, a survey of agricultural activities, and identification of food expenditures. The second visit elicited additional occupational information about household members and identified the sources and levels of household income. The survey was concluded with a short series of questions on participation in local cooperatives. To check for the consistency of informants' responses, several of the quantitative questions regarding food consumption and expenditure were repeated during the second visit. This repetition of this portion of the survey failed to disclose any significant variance in informants' estimates of their expenditures for food. Although some informants took considerably longer than others to identify their income and expenditure levels, none, I feel, provided unrealistic or frivolous answers to the survey.

CITRUS, STRATIFICATION,

AND HOUSEHOLD EXPENSES

Data obtained from eighty-two households in Silk Grass and Hopkins yielded measures of household disposable income, calculated as the aggregate of earnings from various income sources (sales of milpa crops, citrus, wage labor, fishing, artesanal production, remittances, etc.). The following statistical measures test the hypothesis that citrus cultivation is associated with a number of quantifiable socioeconomic characteristics, including village stratification, increased use of farm inputs, and heightened expenditures to meet domestic food require-ments. Because household surveys yielded interval-level data on house-hold composition and labor expenditure, land areas under cultivation in various crops, and expenditures for food, wages, and inputs, the Pearson product-moment correlation was selected as the most appro-priate statistical measure of association (cf. Thomas 1986: 383). This procedure yields a coefficient (r) indicating the strength of association between two variables. The Pearson correlation coefficient ranges be-tween -1 (a perfect negative correlation) to 1 (a perfect positive associa-tion). As coefficients approach 0, a weaker association between variables is indicated. The probability levels of coefficients are also provided. I have set the level of statistical significance (i.e., the point at which correlations are considered nonrandom occurrences) at $p < .05$. A minor controversy remains within the social sciences regarding the use of parametric statistics, such as Pearson's r or t-tests, with data that are measured intervally but that are nonnormally distributed, such as skewed household incomes. The hypotheses tested in this research were evaluated both with parametric measures and the "weaker" non-parametric equivalents (chi-square, Wilcoxon tests, and Spearmann

Table 9. Pearson Correlation Coefficients (r): Silk Grass (n = 25)

	Citrus Income	U.S. Remittances
Disposable income	.71	.41
	p = .0001	p = .04
Per capita disposable income	.67	.49
	p = .0002	p = .01
	Entrepreneurial Income	Milpa Crop Income
Disposable income	.56	.018
	p = .004	n.s. at p = .05
Per capita disposable income	.37	.087
	n.s. at p = .05	n.s. at p = .05
	Coconut Income	Wage Income
Disposable income	−.16	−.055
	n.s. at p = .05	n.s. at p = .05
Per capita disposable income	−.13	−.078
	n.s. at p = .05	n.s. at p = .05

correlations). In no instances did the selection of the test lead to differing conclusions with respect to statistical hypotheses. As it has been experimentally determined that parametric measures yield valid inferences with nonnormal data as long as their assumptions of sample size and level of measurement are satisfied (Thomas 1986: 256), I have chosen to indicate the outcome of statistical tests with the more powerful parametric measures.

In Silk Grass, the relationship between stratification and citrus cultivation is strongly implied by measures of correlation. Of all income sources recorded in household surveys, only United States remittances, profits from entrepreneurial activities (such as ownership of a shop, club, or transport service), and citrus earnings were positively correlated at high significance levels with household disposable income, here taken as a measure of stratification (table 9). The high degrees of correlation between disposable income and the latter two income sources are notable in that most village entrepreneurs are also citrus farmers who have started or expanded their entrepreneurial activities with citrus profits. Similarly, several households with large citrus earnings are also recipients of substantial foreign remittances, which have been invested in citrus expansion. Interestingly, this contrasts with the pattern of remittance expenditure in Hopkins, where most remittance recipients are past their productive years and where no correlation exists between disposable household incomes and remittances from abroad. As seen in table 9, the strong correlation between disposable income and citrus earnings is not a function of household size, for the statistical association persists when disposable income per capita is calculated (household disposable income divided by the number of household members).

Other measures support the hypothesis that citrus cultivation and stratification are related. While the total land area under cultivation by Silk Grass households is positively correlated with disposable income ($r = .41$, $p = .038$), stronger correlations are generated between disposable income and total areas planted in citrus ($r = .55$, $p = .007$) and land areas containing only mature citrus ($r = .47$, $p = .018$). The apparent anomaly of a slightly weaker association of productive citrus lands with disposable income is attributable to one relatively high-income citrus grower who devoted most of his land to the production of immature "budded" trees for sale to other farmers and consequently had few mature trees of his own.

Other measures indicate that citrus cultivation is closely related to class as well as income differentiation in Silk Grass. Local agricultural changes have resulted in a growing concentration of land among citrus farmers and differential participation in wage relations within the village. Citrus-producing households account for 46 percent of the village's households but receive 77 percent of its total disposable income and possess 87 percent of its cultivated land. Citrus income is strongly correlated with the number of workers employed by households ($r = .58$, $p = .002$), farm input expenditures ($r = .8$, $p = .0001$), and wage expenses for hired labor ($r = .69$, $p = .0001$). These correlations suggest that citrus farmers are not only more likely than their milpa farming counterparts to invest in agricultural inputs that increase production levels but also engage in semicapitalist production relations distinct from milpa-based simple commodity production utilizing family labor. The strongly negative correlations between wage income and citrus income ($r = -.59$, $p = .002$) and land area under citrus cultivation ($r = -.66$, $p = .0004$) further imply that village residents are differentiating into wage earners and citrus growers, who seasonally

Table 10. Pearson Correlation Coefficients (r): Silk Grass (n = 25)

	Rice Area	Bean Area
Food expense	−.28	.26
	n.s. at p = .05	n.s. at p = .05
	Corn Area	Plantain Area
Food expense	−.09	−.12
	n.s. at p = .05	n.s. at p = .05
	Groundfood Area	Peanut Area
Food expense	−.19	−.14
	n.s. at p = .05	n.s. at p = .05
	Citrus Area	Citrus Income
Food expense	.10	.15
	n.s. at p = .05	n.s. at p = .05
	Wage Income	
Food expense	.46	
	p = .019	

hire the labor of nonfarming households. Thus, the growing income disparities between citrus producers and other villagers are clearly associated with developing class differences, if class is defined by the relations of production in which the members of households are engaged.

The hypothesis that citrus cultivation is related to heightened household food expenses due to the transfer of farmland from staple crop to citrus production is not directly evident from the Silk Grass subsample (table 10). The relationship between citrus farming and food expenditure is obscured when the entire Silk Grass subsample is considered due to the substantial number of full-time wage laborers in the community and their attendant high food expenses. Although citrus growers purchase more food than staple crop producers, the wage earners who make up almost half the village population spend more on food than any other group. When only the farming population of Silk Grass is considered, however, household food expenses correlate at signifi-

Table 11. Pearson Correlation Coefficients (r): Hopkins (n = 57)

	Rice Area	Bean Area
Food expense	− .04	− .04
	n.s. at p = .05	n.s. at p = .05
	Corn Area	Plantain Area
Food expense	− .11	.08
	n.s. at p = .05	n.s. at p = .05
	Groundfood Area	Peanut Area
Food expense	− .01	− .04
	n.s. at p = .05	n.s. at p = .05
	Citrus Area	Fishing Income
Food expense	− .15	.40
	n.s. at p = .05	p = .0017
	Wage Income	
Food expense	.39	
	p = .0025	

cant levels with the area of land under citrus cultivation ($r = .26$, $p = .01$) and household income from citrus farming ($r = .25$, $p = .01$). As indicated in table 11, Hopkins farmers, being at an earlier point in the transition to commercial citrus production, are not yet as dependent on purchased food as their Silk Grass counterparts. In Hopkins, citrus farmers retained considerable land under staple crops as of the mid-1980s.

In addition to indicating whether a relationship exists between stratification and citrus production, statistical analysis of household data reveals the relative profitability of various production strategies. For the total sample of Silk Grass and Hopkins, the only sources of income positively correlated with disposable income at high levels of probability are citrus farming and entrepreneurial activities ($r = .7$, $p = .0001$ and $r = .53$, $p = .0001$, respectively). When only the Hopkins subsample is considered, earnings from commercial fishing ($r = .6$, $p = .0001$) and wages ($r = .35$, $p = .008$) are also correlated with

Table 12. Pearson Correlation Coefficients (r): Hopkins (n = 57)

	Milpa Income	Fishing Income
Disposable income	−.28	.65
	p = .035	p = .0001
Per capita dispos- able income	−.29	.29
	p = .028	p = .025
	Wage Income	Processing Income
Disposable income	.35	.004
	p = .008	n.s. at p = .05
Per capita dispos- able income	.14	−.02
	n.s. at p = .05	n.s. at p = .05
	Livestock Income	Remittance Income
Disposable income	−.11	.001
	n.s. at p = .05	n.s. at p = .05
Per capita dispos- able income	−.10	.02
	n.s. at p = .05	n.s. at p = .05

disposable income, although associations become much weaker or in-significant when these variables are correlated with disposable income per capita (table 12).

Correlation measures suggest that households selecting economic strategies that generate income above their subsistence needs are also severely limited in their ability to simultaneously engage in other forms of production. Production strategies that minimize input costs as well as food expenses tend also to generate low levels of disposable income, while a number of more costly and profitable (albeit risky) production strategies are mutually exclusive. In Hopkins, where citrus production remains in its incipient stages, a negative association already exists between income derived from fishing and acreage planted in citrus trees $(r = -.29, p = .026)$, as well as the number of days of household farm labor per week $(r = -.48, p = .0001)$. These inverse correlations imply that either limited household labor or resources for investment prevent simultaneous involvement in different cash-maximizing activities. Increased incomes are thus negatively associated, if not in-

Table 13. Pearson Correlation Coefficients (r): Hopkins (n = 57)

	Rice Area	Bean Area
Disposable income	−.33	−.27
	p = .012	p = .04
Per capita disposable income	−.29	−.25
	p = .026	n.s. at p = .05
	Corn Area	Plantain Area
Disposable income	−.24	−.22
	n.s. at p = .05	n.s. at p = .05
Per capita disposable income	−.18	−.25
	n.s. at p = .05	n.s. at p = .05
	Groundfood Area	Peanut Area
Disposable income	−.26	−.31
	p = .05	p = .01
Per capita disposable income	−.23	−.25
	n.s. at p = .05	n.s. at p = .05

compatible with, a diversified livelihood that might avert some of the risks of specialized commodity production for the world market.

Conversely, a production strategy that can be conceived of as safety-oriented in its direct provision of all or most of a household's food needs and articulation with local rather than world markets can be shown to have adverse consequences for the generation of cash income (table 13). In Hopkins, measures related to the production of milpa crops (whether for the market or household) are negatively associated with disposable income, particularly with respect to the acreage planted in staple or nonpermanent crops (e.g., rice, beans, groundfood, and peanuts). The negative correlations presented in table 13 suggest that households requiring additional cash income would be able most effectively to obtain it through export agriculture, wages, fishing, or other activities. These associations also corroborate arguments made in preceding pages on the unprofitability of staple crop production in Belize due to unfavorable marketing arrangements and state control of staple crop prices. The negative correlation of staple crop production and disposable income would also confirm the difficulties that many milpa farmers confront in undertaking changes from subsistence agriculture to more commercial-oriented activities, since milpa crop incomes are rarely sufficient by themselves to generate the levels of investment required of citrus farming or commercial fishing.

BIBLIOGRAPHY

Aguirre-Beltran, G.
  1979   *Regions of Refuge.* Washington: Society for Applied Anthropology.
Alavi, H.
  1973   "Peasant Classes and Primordial Loyalties." *Journal of Peasant Studies* 1: 23–62.
Aldana, E., and P. Lee
  1982   "The Rice Industry." In R. H. Neal and E. A. Awe, eds., *Proceedings.* Fourth Annual National Agricultural Research and Development Symposium. Belmopan: Ministry of Natural Resources.
Amin, S.
  1976   *Unequal Development.* New York: Modern Reader.
  1990   *Delinking: Towards a Polycentric World.* London: ZED.
Asad, T.
  1972   "Market Model, Class Structure and Consent: A Reconsideration of Swat Political Organisation." *Man* n.s. 7: 74–94.
Ashcraft, N.
  1973   *Colonialism and Underdevelopment: Processes of Political Economic Change in British Honduras.* New York: Teachers College Press.
Ashdown, P.
  1978   "Antonio Soberanis and the Disturbances in Belize, 1934–37." *Caribbean Quarterly* 24: 61–74.
Bailey, F. G.
  1969   *Stratagems and Spoils: A Social Anthropology of Politics.* Oxford: Blackwell.
Baran, P.
  1957   *The Political Economy of Growth.* New York: Prometheus.
Bargatzky, T.
  1984   "Culture, Environment, and the Ills of Adaptationism." *Current Anthropology* 25: 399–415.
Barlett, P.
  1982   *Agricultural Choice and Change: Decision-Making in a Costa Rican Community.* New Brunswick, N.J.: Rutgers University Press.
Barnett, C.
  1985   "The Impact of the Mexican Peso Devaluation on Belize—1982." *Belcast: Journal of Belizean Affairs* 2: 29–36.

Barth, F.
   1959   *Political Leadership among Swat Pathans*. London: Athlone Press.
   1966   *Models of Social Organization*. Occasional Paper no. 23. London:
          Royal Anthropological Institute.
Bates, R.
   1983   *Essays on the Political Economy of Rural Africa*. London: Cambridge
          University Press.
Beckford, G.
   1972   *Persistent Poverty: Underdevelopment in Plantation Economies of the
          Third World*. New York: Oxford University Press.
Belize Chamber of Commerce and Industry
   1985   *Newsletter* 2 (November): 10.
Beneria, L., and G. Sen
   1981   "Accumulation, Reproduction, and Women's Role in Economic
          Development: Boserup Revisited." *Signs* 7: 279–298.
Bennett, J.
   1976   "Anticipation, Adaptation, and the Concept of Culture in Anthro-
          pology." *Science* 192: 847–853.
Bernstein, R. H., and R. W. Herdt
   1977   "Towards an Understanding of Milpa Agriculture: The Belize
          Case." *Journal of Developing Areas* 11: 373–392.
Boissevain, J.
   1968   "The Place of Non-Groups in the Social Sciences." *Man* 3:
          542–556.
   1974   *Friends of Friends: Networks, Manipulators and Coalitions*. Oxford:
          Blackwell.
   1977   "Of Men and Marbles: Notes toward a Reconsideration of Faction-
          alism." In M. Silverman and R. F. Salisbury, eds., *A House Divided?:
          Anthropological Studies of Factionalism*. Memorial University of
          Newfoundland.
Bolland, O. N.
   1986   *Belize: A New Nation in Central America*. Boulder: Westview Press.
   1988   *Colonialism and Resistance in Belize: Essays in Historical Sociology*.
          Belize City: Cubola.
Bolland, O. N., and A. Shoman
   1977   *Land in Belize: 1765–1871*. Mona, Jamaica: University of the West
          Indies.
Bradby, B.
   1975   "The Destruction of Natural Economy." *Economy and Society* 2:
          127–161.
   1982   "Resistance to Capitalism in the Peruvian Andes." In D. Lehmann,

ed., *Ecology and Exchange in the Andes*. Cambridge: Cambridge University Press.

Bray, D.
  1991   "'Defiance' and the Search for Sustainable Small Farmer Organizations: A Paraguayan Case Study and a Research Agenda." *Human Organization* 50: 125–135.

Brenner, R.
  1977   "The Origins of Capitalist Development: A Critique of Neo-Smithian Marxism." *New Left Review* 104: 25–92.

Breton, A.
  1974   *The Economic Theory of Representative Government*. Chicago: Aldine.

Bujra, J.
  1973   "The Dynamics of Political Action: A New Look at Factionalism." *American Anthropologist* 75: 132–152.

Burdon, J.
  1931   *Archives of British Honduras, Being Extracts and Précis from Records, with Maps*. London: Sifton, Praed, and Company.

Cancian, F.
  1987   "Proletarianization in Zinacantan, 1960 to 1983." In M. Maclachlan, ed., *Household Economies and Their Transformations*. Lanham, Md.: University Press of America.

Cardoso, F. H., and E. Faletto
  1979   *Dependency and Development in Latin America*. Berkeley: University of California Press.

Carneiro, R.
  1970   "A Theory of the Origin of the State." *Science* 169: 733–738.

Central Bank of Belize
  1983   *Second Annual Report and Accounts*. Belize City.
  1984   *Third Annual Report and Accounts*. Belize City.
  1985   *Quarterly Review*. Vol. 9. Belize City.

CGA (Citrus Growers' Association of Belize)
  1985   *Annual Report*. Dangriga.
  1989   *Annual Report*. Dangriga.
  1990   *Annual Report*. Dangriga.

Chaffee, S.
  1986   "Belize Release Me, Let Me Go: The Impact of U.S. Mass Media on Emigration in Belize." *Belizean Studies* 14: 1–30.

Chambers, R.
  1983   *Rural Development: Putting the Last First*. London: Verso.

Chayanov, A. V.
  1966   (1925) *The Theory of Peasant Economy*. D. Thorner, B. Kerblay, and R. Smith, eds. Homewood, Ill.: American Economic Association.

Chevalier, J.
    1983   "There's Nothing Simple about Simple Commodity Production."
            Journal of Peasant Studies 10: 153–186.
Chibnik, M.
    1975   "Economic Strategies of Small Farmers in Stann Creek District,
            British Honduras." Ph.D. dissertation. Department of Anthropol-
            ogy, Columbia University.
    1978   "The Value of Subsistence Production." *Journal of Anthropological
            Research* 34: 561–576.
    1980   "Working Out or Working In: The Choice between Wage Labor
            and Cash Cropping in Rural Belize." *American Ethnologist* 7: 86–105.
Clammer, J.
    1978   *The New Economic Anthropology.* New York: St. Martin's.
Conzemius, E.
    1928   "Ethnographical Notes on the Black Carib (Garif)." *American An-
            thropologist* 30: 183–205.
Cook, S.
    1982   *Zapotec Stoneworkers: The Dynamics of Simple Commodity Production
            in Modern Mexico.* Lanham, Md.: University Press of America.
Cotler, J.
    1970   "Traditional Haciendas and Communities in a Context of Political
            Mobilization in Peru." In R. Stavenhagen, ed., *Agrarian Problems
            and Peasant Movements in Latin America.* Garden City, N.Y.:
            Anchor.
Davidson, W.
    1976   "Black Carib (Garifuna) Habitats in Central America." In M. Helms
            and F. Loveland, eds., *Frontier Adaptations in Lower Central
            America.* Philadelphia: Institute for the Study of Human Issues.
Davis, S.
    1975   *Victims of the Miracle: Development and the Indians of Brazil.*
            New York: Cambridge University Press.
Deere, C. D., and A. de Janvry
    1979   "A Conceptual Framework for the Empirical Analysis of Peasants."
            American Journal of Agricultural Economics 69: 601–611.
Deere, C. D., P. Antrobus, L. Bolles, E. Melendez, P. Phillips, M. Rivera, and
    H. Safa
    1990   *In the Shadows of the Sun: Caribbean Development Alternatives and
            U.S. Policy.* Boulder: Westview.
de Janvry, A.
    1981   *The Agrarian Question and Reformism in Latin America.* Baltimore:
            Johns Hopkins University Press.

DeWalt, B.
  1979   *Modernization in a Mexican Ejido: A Study in Economic Adaptation.*
          New York: Cambridge University Press.
Dobson, N.
  1973   *A History of Belize.* London: Longman.
Durrenberger, E. P. (ed.)
  1984   *Chayanov, Peasants and Economic Anthropology.* Orlando, Fla.:
          Academic Press.
Eckstein, S.
  1989   "Power and Popular Protest in Latin America." In S. Eckstein,
          ed., *Power and Popular Protest: Latin American Social Movements.*
          Berkeley: University of California Press.
Economist
  1985   *Quarterly Economic Review.* London.
Edelman, M.
  1987   "From Costa Rican Pasture to North American Hamburger." In
          M. Harris and E. Ross, eds., *Food and Evolution: Toward a Theory of
          Human Food Habits.* Philadelphia: Temple University Press.
Ellen, R.
  1982   *Environment, Subsistence and System: The Ecology of Small-Scale
          Social Formations.* Cambridge: Cambridge University Press.
Fligstein, N., and R. Fernandez
  1988   "Worker Power, Firm Power, and the Structure of Labor Markets."
          Sociological Quarterly 29: 5–28.
Forman, S.
  1975   *The Brazilian Peasantry.* New York: Columbia University Press.
Foster, G.
  1988   *Tzintzuntzan: Mexican Peasants in a Changing World.* Prospect
          Heights, Ill.: Waveland Press.
Frank, A. G.
  1967   "Sociology of Underdevelopment and the Underdevelopment of
          Sociology." *Catalyst* 3: 20–73.
  1969   *Capitalism and Underdevelopment in Latin America.* New York:
          Monthly Review Press.
Frankel, F., and K. von Vorys
  1972   *The Political Challenge of the Green Revolution: Shifting Patterns of
          Peasant Participation in India and Pakistan.* Princeton, N.J.: Prince-
          ton University Press.
Fried, M.
  1967   *The Evolution of Political Society.* New York: Random House.

Friedmann, H.
  1980 "Household Production and the National Economy: Concepts for the Analysis of Agrarian Formations." *Journal of Peasant Studies* 7: 158–184.
Furley, P. A.
  1972 "The Small-Scale Citrus Grower in British Honduras." In P. A. Furley, ed., *University of Edinburgh Expedition to Central America.* Vol. 1, Edinburgh: Department of Geography, University of Edinburgh.
Genovese, E.
  1974 *Roll, Jordan, Roll: The World the Slaves Made.* New York: Pantheon.
Giddens, A.
  1979 *Central Problems in Social Theory: Action, Structure and Contradiction in Social Analysis.* Berkeley: University of California Press.
  1986 *The Constitution of Society: Outline of a Theory of Structuration.* Berkeley: University of California Press.
Gilmore, D.
  1977 "Patronage and Class Conflict in Southern Spain." *Man* 12: 446–458.
Gonzalez, N. S.
  1969 *Black Carib Household Structure: A Study of Migration and Modernization.* Seattle: University of Washington Press.
  1988 *Sojourners of the Caribbean: Ethnogenesis and Ethnohistory of the Garifuna.* Urbana: University of Illinois Press.
Goodman, D., and M. Redclift
  1982 *From Peasant to Proletarian: Capitalist Development and Agrarian Transitions.* New York: St. Martin's.
Gordon, D., R. Edwards, and M. Reich
  1982 *Segmented Work, Divided Workers: The Historical Transformation of Labor in the United States.* New York: Cambridge University Press.
Gough, K.
  1978 "Agrarian Relations in Southeast India, 1750–1976." *Review* (New Delhi) 2: 25–53.
Government of Belize (British Honduras)
  1966 *Report of the Tripartite Economic Survey of British Honduras.* Belize City.
  1970–1980 *Economic Surveys.* Belmopan: Central Planning Unit.
  1971 "Report of the Price Control Advisory Committee." Unpublished report. Belize City.
  1971–1985 *Trade Reports.* Belmopan: Central Statistical Office.
  1971–1988 *Annual Reports.* Belmopan: Department (Ministry) of Agriculture.

1974   *Population Census 1970*. Belmopan: Central Planning Unit.
1982   *Agricultural Development Plan*. Belmopan: Ministry of Natural Resources.
1983a   *Population Census 1980*. Belmopan: Central Statistical Unit.
1983b   *National Fisheries Development Plan 1983–1988*. Belmopan: Ministry of Commerce and Industry, Fisheries and Cooperatives.
1984   *Annual Report and Summary of Statistics*. Belmopan: Ministry of Natural Resources.
1985   *Five Year Macro Economic Plan for Belize, 1985–1989*. Belmopan: Ministry of Foreign Affairs and Economic Development.
1986a   *Belize: Consumer Price Index*. Belmopan: Ministry of Economic Development.
1986b   *Belize in Figures*. Belmopan: Ministry of Economic Development.
1991   "Budget '91—More Benefits." *Belize Today*. Belmopan: Belize Information Service.

Gramsci, A.
1971   (1929–1935) *Selections from the Prison Notebooks*. New York: International.

Grant, C. H.
1976   *The Making of Modern Belize: Politics, Society and British Colonialism in Central America*. Cambridge: Cambridge University Press.

Greenhalgh, S.
1985   "Is Inequality Demographically Induced?: The Family Cycle and the Distribution of Income in Taiwan." *American Anthropologist* 87: 571–594.

Gregory, J.
1984   *The Mopan: Culture and Ethnicity in a Changing Belizean Community*. Monographs in Anthropology no. 7. Columbia: University of Missouri.

Griffin, K.
1968   *Underdevelopment in Spanish America*. London: George Allen and Unwin.
1975   *The Political Economy of Agrarian Change: An Essay on the Green Revolution*. London: Macmillan.

Gross, D., and B. Underwood
1971   "Technological Change and Caloric Costs: Sisal Agriculture in Northeastern Brazil." *American Anthropologist* 73: 725–740.

Gudeman, S.
1978   *The Demise of a Rural Economy: From Subsistence to Capitalism in a Latin American Village*. Boston: Routledge and Kegan Paul.

Hall, J.
1983   "The Place of Climatic Hazards in Food Scarcity: A Case Study of

Belize." In K. Hewitt, ed., *Interpretations of Calamity, from the Viewpoint of Human Ecology*. Boston: Allen and Unwin.

Hammond, N.
    1982   *Ancient Mayan Civilization*. New Brunswick, N.J.: Rutgers University Press.

Handleman, H.
    1975   *Struggle in the Andes: Peasant Political Mobilization in Peru*. Austin: University of Texas Press.

Harris, M.
    1977   *Cannibals and Kings: The Origins of Cultures*. New York: Random House.
    1980   *Cultural Materialism: The Struggle for a Science of Culture*. New York: Vintage.

Harrison, M.
    1977   "The Peasant Mode of Production in the Work of A. V. Chayanov." *Journal of Peasant Studies* 4: 323–336.

Hartshorn, G., et al.
    1984   *Belize: A Country Environmental Profile*. Belize City: Robert Nicolait and Associates.

Helms, M.
    1981   "Black Carib Domestic Organization in Historical Perspective: Traditional Origins of Contemporary Patterns." *Ethnology* 20: 77–86.

Higgins, B. H.
    1968   *Economic Development: Problems, Principles and Policies*. New York: Norton.

Hirschmann, A.
    1970   *Exit, Voice, and Loyalty: Responses to Decline in Firms, Organizations and States*. Cambridge, Mass.: Harvard University Press.

History of Belize
    1983   Belize City: Cubola Publications.

Howard, M.
    1977   *Political Change in a Mayan Village in Southern Belize*. Greeley, Colo.: Museum of Anthropology, University of Northern Colorado.
    1980   "Ethnicity and Economic Integration in Southern Belize." *Ethnicity* 7: 119–136.

Johnson, A. W.
    1971a   "Security and Risk-Taking among Poor Peasants: A Brazilian Case." In G. Dalton, ed., *Studies in Economic Anthropology*. Washington, D.C.: American Anthropological Association.
    1971b   *Sharecroppers of the Sertão: Economics and Dependence on a Brazilian Plantation*. Stanford: Stanford University Press.
    1989   "Class Consciousness and the Market Economy: Two Decades of

Economic Change on a Brazilian Fazenda." Paper presented at the Southwestern Anthropological Association, Riverside, Calif.

Johnson, A., and T. Earle
  1987 *The Evolution of Human Societies.* Stanford: Stanford University Press.

Johnson, H. G.
  1967 *Economic Policies toward Less Developed Countries.* Washington, D.C.: Brookings Institution.

Jones, G.
  1971 *The Politics of Agricultural Development in Northern British Honduras.* Winston-Salem, N.C.: Wake Forest University Developing Nations Monograph no. 4.
  1987 "Maya-Spanish Relations in Sixteenth Century Belize." In L. Krohn et al., eds., *Readings in Belizean History.* Belize City: Belizean Studies.

Kapferer, B.
  1976 "Introduction: Transactional Models Reconsidered." In B. Kapferer, ed., *Transaction and Meaning.* ASA Essays in Social Anthropology. Philadelphia: Institute for the Study of Human Issues.

Kay, G.
  1975 *Development and Underdevelopment: A Marxist Analysis.* New York: St. Martin's.

Kerblay, B.
  1971 "Chayanov and the Theory of Peasantry as a Specific Type of Economy." In T. Shanin, ed., *Peasants and Peasant Societies.* Baltimore: Penguin Books.

Kerns, V.
  1983 *Women and the Ancestors: Black Carib Kinship and Ritual.* Urbana: University of Illinois Press.

Kottak, C.
  1985 "When People Don't Come First: Some Sociological Lessons from Completed Projects." In M. Cernea, ed., *Putting People First: Sociological Variables in Rural Development.* New York: Oxford University Press.

Kroshus Medina, L.
  1987 "Belize Citrus Politics: Dialectic of Strategy and Structure." M.A. Paper. Department of Anthropology, University of California, Los Angeles.

Laclau, E.
  1971 "Feudalism and Capitalism in Latin America." *New Left Review* 67: 19–38.

Lambert, J., and J. Arnason
  1982   *Traditional Milpa Agriculture in Belize*. Ottawa: Institute for International Development and Cooperation, University of Ottawa.
Lappé, F. M., and J. Collins
  1979   *Food First: Beyond the Myth of Scarcity*. New York: Ballantine.
Latin American Regional Report (Caribbean)
  1986   "Belize: Debt and Exchange Policies Pay Off." January 17: 3.
Lenin, V.
  1964   (1899) *The Development of Capitalism in Russia*. Moscow: Progress Publishers.
  1975   (1917) *Imperialism, the Highest Stage of Capitalism*. Peking: Foreign Languages Press.
Lewis, G.
  1969   *The Making of the Modern West Indies*. New York: Monthly Review.
Leys, C.
  1977   "Underdevelopment and Dependency: Critical Notes." *Journal of Contemporary Asia* 12: 7–18.
Lipton, M.
  1977   *Why Poor People Stay Poor: A Study of Urban Bias in World Development*. Cambridge, Mass.: Harvard University Press.
Lukacs, G.
  1971   *History and Class Consciousness*. Cambridge: Cambridge University Press.
Luxemburg, R.
  1972   (1913) *The Accumulation of Capital: An Anti-Critique*. New York: Modern Reader.
MacInnes, I. I.
  1983   "The Internal Marketing of Foodstuffs in Belize." In G. M. Robinson and P. A. Furley, eds., *Resources and Development in Belize*. Edinburgh: Department of Geography, University of Edinburgh.
Marx, K.
  1977a (1867) *Capital*. Vol. 1. New York: Vintage.
  1977b (1844) "Economic and Philosophical Manuscripts." In D. McLellan, ed., *Karl Marx: Selected Writings*. Oxford: Oxford University Press.
  1977c (1851) "Eighteenth Brumaire of Louis Bonaparte." In D. McLellan, ed., *Karl Marx: Selected Writings*. Oxford: Oxford University Press.
Massey, D., R. Alarcón, J. Durand, and U. Gonzalez
  1987   *Return to Aztlán: The Social Processes of International Migration from Western Mexico*. Berkeley: University of California Press.

Meillassoux, C.
   1981   *Maidens, Meal and Money: Capitalism and the Domestic Economy.*
           Cambridge: Cambridge University Press.
Mintz, S.
   1977   "The So-Called World System: Local Initiative and Local Re-
           sponse." *Dialectical Anthropology* 2: 253–270.
Moberg, M.
   1988   "Between Agency and Dependence: Belizean Households in a
           Changing World System." Ph.D. dissertation. Department of An-
           thropology, University of California, Los Angeles.
Moore, B.
   1966   *Social Origins of Dictatorship and Democracy.* Boston: Beacon Press.
Morris, D.
   1883   *The Colony of British Honduras: Its Resources and Prospects.* London:
           Edward Standard.
Nash, J.
   1981   "Ethnographic Aspects of the World Capitalist System." *Annual Re-
           view of Anthropology* 10: 393–424.
   1985   "Segmentation of the Work Process in the International Division of
           Labor." In S. Sanderson, ed., *The Americas in the New International
           Division of Labor.* New York: Homes and Meier.
Netting, R. M.
   1977   *Cultural Ecology.* 2d ed. Menlo Park, Calif.: Cummings.
Nicholas, R.
   1977   "Factions: A Comparative Analysis." In S. Schmidt, J. Scott, C.
           Lande, and L. Guasti, eds., *Friends, Followers and Factions.* Berke-
           ley: University of California Press.
Ong, A.
   1987   *Spirits of Resistance and Capitalist Discipline: Factory Women in Ma-
           laysia.* Albany: State University of New York Press.
Orlove, B., and M. Foley
   1989   "Anthropology, Capitalism, and the State: An Introduction." In
           B. Orlove, M. Foley, and T. Love, eds., *State, Capital, and Rural
           Society.* Boulder: Westview.
Paige, J.
   1975   *Agrarian Revolution: Social Movements and Export Agriculture in the
           Underdeveloped World.* New York: Free Press.
Paine, R.
   1974   *Second Thoughts about Barth's Models.* London: Royal Anthropologi-
           cal Institute.

Painter, M.
1984 "Changing Relations of Production and Rural Underdevelopment."
Journal of Anthropological Research 40: 271–292.

Palacio, J.
1981 "Food and Social Relations in a Belizean Garifuna Village." Ph.D.
dissertation. Department of Anthropology, University of California,
Berkeley.
1982 "Post Hurricane Resettlement in Belize." In A. Hansen and A.
Oliver-Smith, eds., *The Problems and Responses of Dislocated People*.
Boulder: Westview.
1984 "Review of IAF Projects in Belize." Unpublished manuscript. Washington: InterAmerican Foundation.
1987 "A Rural/Urban Environment for Central American Immigrants in
Belize." *Caribbean Quarterly* 33: 29–41.
1990 *Socioeconomic Integration of Central American Immigrants in Belize*.
Belize City: SPEAR (Society for the Promotion of Education and
Research).

Palma, G.
1978 "Dependency: A Formal Theory of Underdevelopment or a Methodology of Concrete Situations of Underdevelopment?" *World Development* 6: 881–924.

Pastor, R., ed.
1985 *Migration and Development in the Caribbean: The Unexplored Connection*. Boulder: Westview Press.

Patnaik, U.
1979 "Neo-Populism and Marxism: The Chayanovian View of the
Agrarian Question and Its Fundamental Fallacy." *Journal of Peasant
Studies* 6: 375–420.

Pearse, J.
1980 *Seeds of Plenty, Seeds of Want: Social and Economic Implications of the
Green Revolution*. Oxford: Clarendon.

Petch, T.
1986 "Dependency, Land and Oranges in Belize." *Third World Quarterly*
8: 1002–1019.

Reinhardt, N.
1988 *Our Daily Bread: The Peasant Question and Family Farming in the
Colombian Andes*. Berkeley: University of California Press.

Robinson, G. M.
1983 "Smallholder Agriculture in the Belize Valley." In G. M. Robinson
and P. A. Furley, eds., *Resources and Development in Belize*. Edinburgh: University of Edinburgh.

Rogers, E.
    1969   *Modernization among Peasants: The Impact of Communication*. New
            York: Holt, Rinehart and Winston.
Roseberry, W.
    1976   "Rent, Differentiation, and the Development of Capitalism among
            Peasants." *American Anthropologist* 78: 45–58.
    1989a   "Anthropology, History, and Modes of Production." In B. Orlove
            et al., eds., *State, Capital, and Rural Society*. Boulder: Westview.
    1989b   *Anthropologies and Histories*. New Brunswick, N.J.: Rutgers Uni-
            versity Press.
Sahlins, M.
    1972   *Stone Age Economics*. Chicago: Aldine.
Schneider, W., and M. Schneider
    1988   "Food and Factions: The Local Politics of Sedako Agricultural De-
            velopment." *Human Organization* 47: 58–64.
Schryer, F. J.
    1980   *The Rancheros of Pisaflores: The History of Peasant Bourgeoisie in
            Twentieth Century Mexico*. Toronto: University of Toronto Press.
Schultz, T.
    1968   *Economic Growth and Agriculture*. New York: McGraw-Hill.
Scott, J.
    1976   *The Moral Economy of the Peasant*. New Haven: Yale University
            Press.
    1985   *Weapons of the Weak: Everyday Forms of Peasant Resistance*. New
            Haven: Yale University Press.
Seibel, H., and A. Massing
    1974   *Traditional Organizations and Economic Development*. New York:
            Praeger.
Sella, D.
    1977   "The World System and Its Dangers." *Journal of Peasant Studies* 6:
            29–32.
Service, E.
    1975   *Origins of the State and Civilization*. New York: Norton.
Setzekorn, W. D.
    1975   *Formerly British Honduras: A Profile of the New Nation of Belize*.
            Newark, Calif.: Dumbarton.
Shoman, A.
    1987   *Party Politics in Belize, 1950–1986*. Belize City: Cubola.
Siegel, B., and A. Beals
    1960   "Pervasive Factionalism." *American Anthropologist* 62: 394–417.

Silverman, M.
  1979 "Dependency, Mediation and Class Formation in Rural Guyana."
       American Ethnologist 6: 466–490.
  1980 *Rich People and Rice: Factional Politics in Rural Guyana*. Leiden, Hol-
       land: Brill.
Silverman, M., and R. F. Salisbury
  1977 "Introduction: Factions and the Dialectic." In M. Silverman and
       R. F. Salisbury, eds., *A House Divided?: Anthropological Studies of
       Factionalism*. St. Johns: Memorial University of Newfoundland.
Spearhead
  1987 Belize City: Society for the Promotion of Education and Research
       (April/May).
Stein, W.
  1984 "How Peasants Are Exploited: The Extraction of Unpaid Labor in
       Rural Peru." In B. Isaac, ed., *Research in Economic Anthropology*.
       Greenwich, Conn.: JAL Press.
Stone, M.
  1990 "Backabush: Settlement on the Belmopan Periphery and the Chal-
       lenge to Rural Development in Belize." *SPEAReports* 6. Belize City:
       SPEAR (Society for the Promotion of Education and Research).
Taussig, M.
  1980 *The Devil and Commodity Fetishism in South America*. Chapel Hill:
       University of North Carolina Press.
Taylor, D.
  1951 *The Black Carib of British Honduras*. New York: Viking Fund Publi-
       cations in Anthropology.
Tendler, J., K. Healy, and C. O'Laughlin
  1982 *What to Think about Cooperatives: A Guide from Bolivia*. Washing-
       ton, D.C.: InterAmerican Foundation.
Texier, J.
  1979 "Gramsci, Theoretician of Superstructures." In C. Mouffe, ed.,
       Gramsci and Marxist Theory. London: Routledge and Kegan Paul.
Thomas, D.
  1986 *Refiguring Anthropology: First Principles of Probability and Statistics*.
       Prospect Heights, Ill.: Waveland Press.
Trimberger, K.
  1979 "World Systems Analysis: The Problem of Unequal Development."
       Theory and Society 8: 127–137.
Vincent, J.
  1976 "Rural Competition and the Cooperative Monopoly: A Ugandan
       Case Study." In J. Nash, J. Dandler, and N. S. Hopkins, eds., *Popu-*

lar Participation in Social Change: Cooperatives, Collectives and Nationalized Industry. The Hague: Mouton.

1980   *Teso in Transformation*. Berkeley: University of California Press.
Waddell, D.
1961   *British Honduras: A Historical and Contemporary Survey*. Oxford: Oxford University Press.
Wallerstein, I.
1974   *The Modern World System: Capitalist Agriculture and the Origins of the European World System in the Sixteenth Century*. New York: Academic Press.
Weisskopf, T.
1978   "Imperialism and the Economic Development of the Third World." In R. Edwards, M. Reich, and T. Weisskopf, eds., *The Capitalist System*, 2d ed. Englewood Cliffs, N.J.: Prentice-Hall.
Weldes, J.
1989   "Marxism and Methodological Individualism." *Theory and Society* 18: 353–386.
White, B.
1975   "The Economic Importance of Children in a Javanese Village." In M. Nag, ed., *Population and Social Evolution*. The Hague: Mouton.
Wilk, R.
1984   "Rural Settlement Change in Belize, 1970–1980: The Effects of Roads." *Belizean Studies* 12: 1–9.
1987   "The Kekchi and the Settlement of Toledo District." *Belizean Studies* 15: 33–50.
Wolf, E. R.
1966   *Peasants*. Englewood Cliffs, N.J.: Prentice-Hall.
1969   *Peasant Wars of the Twentieth Century*. New York: Harper and Row.
1982   *Europe and the People without History*. Berkeley: University of California Press.
Wolpe, H.
1980   "Capitalism and Cheap Labour-Power in South Africa: From Segregation to Apartheid." In H. Wolpe, ed., *The Articulation of Modes of Production: Essays from Economy and Society*. London: Routledge and Kegan Paul.
World Bank
1984   *Belize: Economic Report*. Washington, D.C.: World Bank.
Wright, A. C. S., D. H. Romney, R. H. Arbuckle, and V. E. Vial
1959   *Land in British Honduras: Report of the British Honduras Land Use Survey Team*. London: Her Majesty's Stationer's Office.

Young, A.
  1978   "Ethnic Politics in Belize." *Caribbean Review* 7: 38–42.
Zamosc, L.
  1989   "Peasant Struggles of the 1970s in Colombia." In S. Eckstein, ed.,
         Power and Popular Protest: Latin American Social Movements. Berke-
         ley: University of California Press.

INDEX